Sailing Safe in Cyberspace

Sailing Safe in Cyberspace

Cyberspace

Protect Your Identity and Data

Anjali Kaushik

 SAGE www.sagepublications.com
Los Angeles • London • New Delhi • Singapore • Washington DC

First published in 2013 by

SAGE Publications India Pvt Ltd
B1/I-1 Mohan Cooperative Industrial Area
Mathura Road, New Delhi 110 044, India
www.sagepub.in

SAGE Publications Inc
2455 Teller Road
Thousand Oaks, California 91320, USA

SAGE Publications Ltd
1 Oliver's Yard, 55 City Road
London EC1Y 1SP, United Kingdom

SAGE Publications Asia-Pacific Pte Ltd
33 Pekin Street
#02-01 Far East Square
Singapore 048763

Published by Vivek Mehra for SAGE Publications India Pvt Ltd, Phototypeset in 10/15 Times New Roman by RECTO Graphics, Delhi and printed at Saurabh Printers Pvt Ltd.

Library of Congress Cataloging-in-Publication Data
Kaushik, Anjali.
    Sailing safe in cyberspace : protect your identity and data / Anjali
Kaushik.
        pages cm
    Includes bibliographical references.
    1. Computer crimes—Prevention. 2. Computer security—Government policy.
3. Computer crimes—Prevention—Government policy. I. Title.
    HV8079.C65K38   364.16'8—dc23   2013   2013019951

ISBN: 978-81-321-1122-1 (PB)

The SAGE Team: Shambhu Sahu, Shreya Lall and Rajib Chatterjee

Dedicated to
U and UR Data

Thank you for choosing a SAGE product! If you have any comment, observation or feedback, I would like to personally hear from you. Please write to me at <u>contactceo@sagepub.in</u>

—Vivek Mehra, Managing Director and CEO,
SAGE Publications India Pvt Ltd, New Delhi

Bulk Sales
SAGE India offers special discounts for purchase of books in bulk. We also make available special imprints and excerpts from our books on demand.
For orders and enquiries, write to us at

Marketing Department
SAGE Publications India Pvt Ltd
B1/I-1, Mohan Cooperative Industrial Area
Mathura Road, Post Bag 7
New Delhi 110044, India
E-mail us at <u>marketing@sagepub.in</u>

Get to know more about SAGE, be invited to SAGE events, get on our mailing list. Write today to <u>marketing@sagepub.in</u>

This book is also available as an e-book.

CONTENTS

———•◦•———

Section II: Threats and Methods

LIST OF FIGURES

LIST OF ABBREVIATIONS

$	United States Dollar
ACH	Automated Clearing House
API	Application Programming Interface
APT	Advanced Persistent Threat
ATM	Automated Teller Machine
AV	Antivirus
C&C	Command and Control
CD	Compact Disk
CERT	Computer Emergency Response Team
CERT-In	Indian Computer Emergency Response Team
CIA	Central Intelligence Agency
CNCERT/CC	National Computer Network Emergency Response Coordination Center of China
CRS	Congressional Research Service
DDoS	Distributed Denial-of-Service
DNS	Domain Name System
DoD	United States Department of Defense
DoS	Denial-of-Service
DSN	Delivery Status Notification
DVD	Digital Video Disk
EU	European Union
FBI	Federal Bureau of Investigation
FTP	File Transfer Protocol
Gbps	Gigabits per second
GPS	Global Positioning System
HIPAA	Health Insurance Portability and Accountability Act, 1996
HTML	HyperText Markup Language
HTTP	Hypertext Transfer Protocol
ICANN	Internet Corporation for Assigned Names and Numbers
IDS	Intrusion Detection System

IM	Instant Message/Messaging
IMF	International Monetary Fund
IP	Internet Protocol
IPS	Intrusion Prevention Systems
IPR	Intellectual Property Rights
IRC	Internet Relay Chat
ISO	International Organization for Standardization
ISP	Internet Service Provider
IT	Information Technology
KWh	Kilowatt Hour
MB	Megabyte
Mbps	Megabits per second
MEA	Ministry of External Affairs, Government of India
MLM	Multilevel Marketing
MSDE	Microsoft SQL Server Desktop Engine
NASA	National Aeronautics and Space Administration
NDR	Non-Delivery Receipt
NIC	National Informatics Centre
OECD	Organisation for Economic Co-operation and Development
OEM	Original Equipment Manufacturer
OS	Operating System
PC	Personal Computer
PCI DSS	Payment Card Industry Data Security Standard
PDA	Personal Digital Assistant
PDF	Portable Document Format
PIN	Personal Information Number
PKI	Public Key Infrastructure
PLC	Programmable Logic Controller
POS	Point of Sale
RBN	Russian Business Network
SNS	Social Networking Site
SQL	Structured Query Language
SSL	Secure Sockets Layer
TCP	Transmission Control Protocol
TLD	Top-Level Domain
TWh	Terawatt Hour
URL	Uniform Resource Locator
USB	Universal Serial Bus
VPN	Virtual Private Networks
WTO	World Trade Organization

PREFACE

———•◦•———

Let us not look back in anger or forward in fear, but around in awareness.
—James Thurber

The anonymity of cyberspace has indeed rendered all boundaries meaningless. Cybersecurity is not a local issue any more. It is impossible to fight cybercrime or secure one's cyberspace single-handedly. Rather, it takes on a global magnitude that needs to be addressed by all governments across the globe, in unison. Cybersecurity is not a technical subject that can be resolved like any other IT-related problem. It is a 'risk', which can be mitigated only by creating awareness and getting the right combination of technology and careful analysis. Understanding the sheer scale of the problem is important for planning at all levels.

As Internet usage continues to rise throughout the world, the threat of cybercrime also grows. While some of these crimes are relatively harmless and commonplace, others are more serious. The speed, ease, and reach of the Internet cannot be underestimated. These very features are what cybercriminals capitalize on to swindle unsuspecting users of huge resources. A personal computer connected to the Internet without protection may be infected with malicious software within no time.

Threats are intertwined—meaning almost every threat comprises multiple components for attacking, infecting and compromising data. At the same time, newer threats related to cloud computing, mobile telephony, and social networking are just about emerging. Convergence of technology has its pros and cons. On one hand, it allows users to literally browse the web 'on the go' while on the other hand, it widens the playing field for attackers, who are constantly looking to proliferate their ware.

Cybercrime will make people reluctant to enter and trust the electronic world. This will hinder interchange of information between people, businesses, and governments, impacting everything from education to commerce. Therefore, we need to understand cybercrime in greater detail and take adequate protection measures so that the users feel safe online.

LAWS AND REGULATIONS ARE BUILDING UP BUT SO IS CYBERCRIME

Crimes perpetuated through computers are becoming a growing menace for law enforcement officials around the world. Unfortunately, since the Internet crimes typically involve people scattered across many different geographical areas, tracking and punishing the guilty parties is a difficult task. Malicious actors exploit the distributed and global nature of the Internet as well as the complications of law and jurisdiction bound by traditional physical boundaries to diminish the risks of being identified and prosecuted. From the standpoint of organized criminal groups, a part of the fascinating character of the Internet stems from the fact that cyberspace is characterized by less governance and a weak rule of law. For example, a large portion of data trapped by attackers using key loggers was transmitted internationally to countries where laws against cybercrime were nascent, non-existent, or not easily enforceable. Although countries across the globe have recognized the seriousness of cybercrime and many have taken legislative action to help reprimand criminals, not all have legal frameworks that support the prosecution of cybercriminals. The problem however, is even more complicated as information may be compromised in one country by a criminal acting from another country through servers located in a third country.

To meet the challenge posed by new kinds of cybercrimes and criminal profiles, many countries have also reviewed their respective domestic criminal laws so as to prevent computer-related crimes. The governments are also making legislations ensuring that every company from large organizations to mid-sized and small ones have Internet policies and security solutions in place. Looking at the dynamic and fast-changing technologies, new types of threats may come up frequently. However, cyberthreats are moving at such a high speed that law enforcement cannot catch up with it. If the current trend continued, then in three or four years people would start to think twice about transacting on the Web.

THE SECURITY PARADOX

While launching a cyberattack does not cost much, setting up an effective security system entails substantial investments in monetary terms. This inverse relationship works to the advantage of cybercriminals. Organizations today treat security at par with other functions and do not think twice about spending huge sums for it. There is an increasing trend in the demand for information security. However, what is unfortunate is that there is almost no correlation between security spending and security levels. Real progress should see a reduction in IT (security) spending. Although we have much better security tools for managing threats today than we had about a decade ago, the proportion of threats going unattended is on the rise.

The magnitude of the problem is immense. The cost in dollars and the economic value of cybercrime is tremendous and consistently on the rise. At the same time, security is proving to be an expensive proposition. Deploying more and comprehensive security solutions is not the way out since the threats are dynamic in nature. Cybercriminals use newer tools to launch their attacks. For instance, the Trojans are being used more and more. With these Trojans, the cybercriminals can build botnets to steal passwords and confidential data or to conduct Denial-of-Service (DoS) attacks. The evolution of new technologies and social media such as Facebook and Twitter has made personal information easily available and easy to steal or compromise. Cybercrime is spreading rapidly through social networking sites.

AWARENESS BUILDING AND COLLABORATION IS THE KEY

Along with technology solutions, firewalls, anti-virus, etc., awareness building, better management practices, and collaboration are important. It is felt that a lot of people become victims of cybercrime because of a fundamental lack of awareness on this issue. Many organizations and individuals do not have the awareness, resources, skills or expertise to prevent and/or respond effectively to cyberattacks and the associated secondary crimes which flow from those attacks, such as phishing, identity theft, fraud, etc. There is a need to spread awareness on the commonly used modes of cybercrime, such as phishing, identity theft, botnets, Denial of Service/Distributed Denial of

Service and so on. It is important to understand the nature of cybercriminal activity and the risk that ensues, so that protection programs can be suitably planned. Protection has other vital components, such as the profiling of cyber-criminals, awareness building and systematic analysis and study.

Considering the growth in cybercrime, the commitment of governments, businesses and the global community to fight it is not surprising. Collaboration (cross-border, public–private and government–private) is needed to shut down the affected domains, freeze payment accounts that are suspected of fraud, isolate bad networks, etc. Also, it is important that a knowledge repository of best practices on cybersecurity be built and shared across organizations. The organized action against malicious programs is not necessarily keeping pace.

It is known that cybercriminals are getting more organized today than ever before. Therefore, our response to them must also take on new structure and focus. Individuals, organizations, law enforcement, and info-tech solu-tions providers must all join hands to study and meet the evolving challenge posed by cybercrime, specifically in the design of new strategies and solu-tions, which will become necessary in key areas—people, process, policies and technology.

HOW WAS THE IDEA FOR THIS BOOK DEVELOPED?

My association with consulting assignments[1] related to cybersecurity revealed that the awareness on issues related to cybercrime, protection mechanisms, governance structures and management practices are lacking in a lot of organi-zations. We conducted a survey of more than 300 organizations in 2010–11 and found them inadequate in terms of awareness of cyberthreats and security planning. The organizations were also found lacking in governance mecha-nisms related to information security.

For individuals, while the Internet has penetrated the homes, the aware-ness on how to keep safe has not necessarily kept pace. There is a gap in understanding the latest information security issues and practices and unless steps are taken to build awareness, people will become fearful of using the Internet to its full potential.

[1] Dr Anjali Kaushik has been the Chief Investigator on prestigious assignments such as developing the 'Information Security Best Practices Framework for Government Sector in India' for Ministry of Communication and IT (MoCIT) from 2010 to 2012.

The existing work on global cybercrime analysis is fragmented in nature. We have media reports of cybercrime as and when it happens and vendor reports which tend to be biased. This study intends to bridge this gap by undertaking a structured and thorough analysis of cyber incidents worldwide. The work includes in-depth analysis of motivation, types and techniques for more than 50 major cybercrime incidents worldwide over the last 10 years.

Every office user, home user, all individuals and organizations are plagued by issues and concerns related to cybercrime and have been victim in one form or the other. If they have not been victim, they fear it might happen sometime in future. Apart from technology, you need awareness on issues related to cybersecurity planning and practices to be less vulnerable to security issues. This is where this book will help.

The information for this book was collected from academic research, media reports and vendor reports for the last ten years and the basic insights gathered in consulting on cybersecurity-related issues over the years. Though vendor reports have been used in analysing the data on techniques used, an attempt has been made to make the analysis as vendor neutral as possible by referring to multiple sources for each technique.

WHY IS THIS BOOK IMPORTANT?

If we look at the pattern of cybercrimes, we will see that many underlying assumptions about cybercrimes are flawed and unrealistic and fail to explain it. Clearly, substantial and deeper research is required to understand it. This is a research work based on extensive study and comparative analysis of the existing official documents, literature reviews, reports and media content of the last decade. This work analyses the cybercrimes and data breaches globally and draws out major trends and study parameters, such as the tools and methods used in cybercrime, newer threat scenarios, economic implications, sociocultural factors, country specific analysis, legal regime, government, and industry policies. The research also tries to see the position of different countries on issues related to cybersecurity.

An attempt is also made to discuss the *protection mechanisms and 'best practices' in the management of information security* in view of these threats. The book also covers security tips for sailing safe for individual computer users and practical suggestions for organizational users for securing information and information systems. Cybersecurity should be treated with as much importance as any other matter of national policy and governance, such as technology, policy, law, ethics and national security. They should be debated and discussed widely both within and outside the government and at national and international fora, since they cannot be contained merely by extending geographical borders or national laws to the virtual world. Recent events in cyberspace such as the 'GhostNet' attacks on governments and large multinational corporations, thefts of intellectual property and attacks on free speech bring out the significance of this issue and the priority with which it needs to be dealt.

There have been cases in the past when cyberterrorism has been used for ethical and political considerations, as in the Estonian crisis (2007) and in the cyberattacks on Georgia (2008). Individuals, businesses and governments are therefore not wrong when they worry about the security of their systems, networks and IT infrastructure.

This book includes in-depth analysis of more than 50 global cybercrime incidents worldwide and describes how these incidents are a complex interplay of motivations and techniques and discusses their impact. It includes comprehensive analysis of newer threats related to cloud computing, mobile telephony, and social networking with important security tips. It covers worldwide legal initiatives and regulations in information security domain. This work analyses prominent techniques used for cybercrime such as spam, phishing, botnets, malware, SQL injection, etc. It discusses each of these techniques/methods in detail and also covers their major trends. Also covered are the motives behind cybercrime. One of the most crucial elements that can help comprehend why individuals within the computer community do what they do may be motivation. The understanding of the behavioural aspects, motives and profiling of cybercriminals is important for planning security.

This book is an excellent resource on safe computing which gives indepth exposure to the various ways in which the security of information on computers can be compromised, how the cybercrime markets work and what is to be done to ensure safety at individual and organizational level. In brief, this book is an attempt to help all those associated with the cyber world to understand the nature of vulnerabilities and threats and develop appropriate defence mechanisms. It is an earnest effort to provide research, managerial and policy implications associated with cybersecurity and allied areas.

I gratefully acknowledge the role of various assignments, projects, conferences, seminars which built up my awareness on the very important issue of cybersecurity. On a personal note, I want to thank my family members and friends for their unflinching support—I could not have done what I do, without you. Finally, it is hoped that this book will aid better understanding, awareness and analyses of the rapidly transforming landscape of cybercrime and security planning.

SECTION I

MOTIVATION AND TYPES OF CYBERCRIME

Cyberspace emerges as the new domain for operational and strategic dominance alongside military and economic domains.

SECTION I

MOTIVATION AND TYPES OF CYBERCRIME

ONE

INTRODUCTION

———•◦•———

1.1. CYBERCRIME—A GROWING REALITY

New technological developments, such as the Internet and the connectivity they bring are shaping the way business is transacted today. The Internet has attributed to this entire process a sense of independence from 'time' and 'location' as never experienced before. It has enhanced the reach of organizations and individuals, helped define newer business models and redefined the rules of business. The periphery of the enterprise network has expanded well beyond the office and data centres and is now limited only by the geographical dispersion of employees. Times are converging and so is space.

These phenomena are known to have imparted a whole new level to global business, and the benefits have been enormous. However, they have also brought with them a dark side called 'cybercrime'. Cybercrime is now a universal phenomenon. Businesses, governments and individuals have all fallen prey to it. The accelerated use of the Internet has enabled a dramatic rise in criminal activity, which exploits the Internet's interconnectivity for illicit financial gains and other malicious purposes, such as Internet fraud, child exploitation and identity theft. The growth of malware, and the new ways in which information technology (IT) is being used to steal personal data, conduct espionage, harm governmental and business operations or deny user access to information and services, is a potentially serious threat to the virtual economy as well as to the ability to promote e-governance in citizens' services, to individuals' online social activities and to national security.

Criminal activities via the Internet range from fraud, theft, pervasive pornography, paedophile rings and drug trafficking to cyber extortion, hacking, and so on. The severity and effect of cybercrime on business, society and the government is unquantifiable. Cyberattacks are becoming more frequent and effective. Cybercrime today is attracting the scrutiny and attention of authorities for various reasons; the most important of them being one simple fact—money can be transferred through the Internet. This is achieved by making electronic payments, that is, transferring money online, through credit or cash cards, electronic money and so on. There is no internationally accepted method of verifying the integrity and accuracy of the information that flows through the Web. Frauds committed via the Internet pose complicated enforcement and jurisdictional problems to investigative agencies and the judiciary. Despite the myriad problems, it is impossible to think of modern commerce without electronic commerce. Electronic commerce is here to stay and so are the associated online crimes. What is important is to build awareness.

The year 2011 was particularly challenging for the Internet security industry, as several organizations succumbed to targeted data breach attacks that soiled their reputations through the loss of confidential information and in turn caused them to spend huge sums of money for fixing the damage. Owners of two of the biggest targets—RSA1 and Sony PlayStation2—were left with no choice but to publicly disclose facts about the attacks against their infrastructure so their customers could ensure proper mitigation. 2011 was dubbed the 'Year of Data Breaches' by some, marring organizations worldwide owing to huge information and financial losses.

Add to it the fact that IT security spends and the cost of security technology have been increasing. However, the severity, frequency and volume of security incidents continue to increase as well. There is almost no correlation between security spending and level of security. It is appropriate that real progress should witness a reduction in IT spending. But with every passing moment, crimeware, malware, spam-generating capabilities and botnets get cheaper, and cybercrime gets more organized, sophisticated and dynamic. The fight against cybercrime fails to keep the requisite pace.

Enterprises are buried in laws, regulations and compliance efforts. India's Information Technology Act, 2000, United Kingdom's Computer Misuse Act, 1990, Malaysia's Computer Crimes Act, 1997, United States' Electronic Signatures in Global and National Commerce Act, 2000, Health Insurance

Portability and Accountability Act (HIPAA), 1996, and United States' Sarbanes–Oxley Act, 2002, Australia's Electronic Transactions Act, 1999, Mexico's E-Commerce Act, 2000, International Organization for Standardization (ISO) 27001, Payment Card Industry Data Security Standard (PCI DSS) and so on are some of the prominent legal efforts that have been conceived in order to address the problem of growing cyber and allied crimes. But laws and regulations have not yielded constructive results, and legislators continue to plan additional regulations to force organizations to assess, plan and audit the security of their IT systems. There is an urgent need to understand and build awareness on the issue of cybercrime at the levels of the individual, enterprise and nation. Equally important is the attempt at building and sharing strategies on managing this issue so that the benefits of the Internet and connectivity are not lost.

1.2. FACTORS CONTRIBUTING TO THE GROWTH OF CYBER INCIDENTS

1.2.1. The Ubiquity of the Internet

According to Fertik and Thompson (2010: 44), 'The Internet has turned reputation on its head. What was once private is now public. What was once local is now global. What was once fleeting is now permanent. And what was once trustworthy is now unreliable'.

One of the most distinct characteristics of the Internet is how quickly and fluidly it evolves, how technology originally designed for research and collaboration today powers millions of lives, both real and virtual.

The Internet has quickly grown into an essential platform for interaction. Young, educated people form a huge segment of Internet users. As Internet usage continues to rise throughout the world, the threat of cybercrime also grows. While some of these crimes are relatively harmless and commonplace, others are more serious. Researchers have noted that as Internet penetration increased, there were more avenues for cybercrime and this affected most countries. Analysing the trend of cybercrime activities across counties, analysts have suggested 10–15 per cent Internet penetration as the threshold level for the generation of significant hacking activities (Reilly 2007). It is important to note that Internet penetration in many developing countries has reached this level. As noted in 2008 by the Organisation for Economic Co-operation and Development (OECD), protecting against, detecting and responding to malware have become increasingly complex as malware and the underlying criminal activity which it supports are rapidly evolving and taking advantage of the global nature of the Internet. Many organizations and individuals do not have the resources, skills or expertise to prevent and/or respond effectively to malware attacks and the associated secondary crimes which flow from those attacks, such as identity theft, fraud and distributed denial-of-service (DDoS) attacks.

Cybercrime activities trace their origins to the evolution of the Internet and other technological innovations of the modern times. The speed, ease and reach of the Internet cannot be underestimated. These very features are what cybercriminals capitalize on to swindle unsuspecting users of huge resources. A personal computer connected to the Internet without protection may be infected with malicious software in less than a minute. The Internet's rapid diffusion and digitization of economic activities has led to the emergence of a new breed of criminals. The impact of such cybercrime has received consider-able attention in recent years.

Crimes perpetuated through computers are becoming a growing menace for law enforcement officials around the world. Unfortunately, since Internet crimes typically involve people scattered across many different geographical areas, tracking and punishing the guilty parties is a difficult task.

Offering a wide range of online services alone will not be sufficient to reduce customer churn; it must be accompanied by enhanced security features that provide customers with confidence and, in turn, result in winning and safeguarding their long-term trust and loyalty.

1.2.2. Social Media Threats

With the evolution of new technologies and the growing popularity of social media like Facebook and Twitter, the world is actually witnessing an increase in the kinds of threats to information security. As evidenced by the recent attacks on Twitter, Facebook and MySpace, cybercriminals are exploiting the viral nature of Web 2.0. Cybercrime is spreading rapidly through social net-working sites. High-profile websites are becoming highly targeted.

1.2.3. Cloud Computing and Security

With cloud computing becoming increasingly popular, concerns are being voiced about associated security issues that have arisen due to adoption of this new model. Since the characteristics of this innovative deployment model differ drastically from those with traditional architecture, the effectiveness and efficiency of traditional protection mechanisms need to be reconsidered.

1.2.4. Integration with Mobile and Mobile Threats

Today, an increasing number of consumers are using mobile devices and tablets in their daily lives as well as at work. Recent technological developments have enabled seamless integration between traditional desktops and mobile devices. Unfortunately, a majority of the users do not realize that most of the threats such as phishing attacks, which they face online using traditional devices, can also hound their mobile experiences.

1.2.5. Convergence of Threats across Platforms

Convergence of technology has its pros and cons. On the one hand, it allows users to literally browse the Web 'on the go' while on the other hand, it widens the playing field for attackers, who are constantly looking to proliferate their wares.

1.2.6. Globalization and Interdependence

Cybersecurity is not a local issue any more. Rather, it is of a global magnitude and needs to be addressed by all governments across the globe, in unison. It is impossible to fight cybercrime or secure one's cyberspace, single-handedly. Cybersecurity is not a technical matter that can be resolved like any other IT-related problem. It is a 'risk' which can be mitigated only by creating awareness and the right combination of technology and careful analysis. Understanding the sheer scale of the problem is important to planning at all levels.

Cyberattacks should be treated with as much importance as any other matter of national policy and governance, such as technology, policy, law, ethics and national security. They should be debated and discussed widely both within and outside the government and at national and international forums, since they cannot be contained merely by extending geographical borders or national laws to the virtual world. Recent events in cyberspace such as the 'GhostNet' attacks on governments and large multinational corporations, thefts of intellectual property and attacks on free speech bring out the significance of this crime and the priority with which it needs to be dealt. Increasingly, the military and economic strength of a country would depend on how well it manages its cyberspace.

According to the United Nations Human Development Report for 1999, 'Globalization opens many opportunities for crime, and crime is rapidly becoming global, outpacing international cooperation to fight it' (United Nations Development Programme 1999).

In prior literature, researchers have found that the nature of crime has changed significantly within a single generation. Just 20 years ago, crime was organized in a hierarchy of operations. It was 'industrial' in that it contained division of labour and specialization of operations. But a large proportion of cyberattacks are international in scope. According to a report released by the Federal Bureau of Investigation (FBI) in January 2006, the agency tracked cyberattacks targeting the United States from 36 different countries (Regan 2006).

This structure extended internationally, as organized crime mirrored the business world. According to the 2008 OECD (2008b) report, malicious actors exploit the distributed and global nature of the Internet, as well as the complications of law and jurisdiction that are bound by traditional physical boundaries, to diminish the risks of being identified and prosecuted. For example, a large portion of data trapped by attackers using key loggers was transmitted internationally to countries where laws against cybercrime were nascent, nonexistent or not easily enforceable. Although countries across the globe have recognized the seriousness of cybercrime and many have taken legislative action to help reprimand criminals, not all have legal frameworks that support the prosecution of cybercriminals. The problem however is even more complicated as information may be compromised in one country by a criminal acting from another country through servers located in a third country.

Bruce Schneier has remarked:

> History has taught us: never underestimate the amount of money, time, and
> effort someone will expend to thwart a security system. It's always better to

assume the worst. Assume your adversaries are better than they are. Assume science and technology will soon be able to do things they cannot yet. Give yourself a margin for error. Give yourself more security than you need today. When the unexpected happens, you'll be glad you did.

Cybercrime is emerging as an alarming threat to society. It may in fact be one of the most dangerous criminal threats we will ever face. The cybercrime environments of countries across the world are becoming more dangerous and increasingly interconnected. Less-advanced cyberthreat environments are catching up to those prevalent in the developed world more quickly than estimated by most experts.

Michael Fraser, Director of the Communications Law Centre at the University of Technology, Sydney, has observed that if the current trend continues, then, in three or four years people would start to think twice about transacting on the Web. 'The way it's trending now, the Web could be so full of rubbish that people won't trust it', Fraser said, 'that could destroy the potential of the whole knowledge economy, which so many developed economies are counting on for the competitive advantage' (Voigt 2009).

The profile of the typical cybercriminal is changing fast too. In most cases, the emergence of attack toolkits has made cybercrime available to everyone regardless of whether they possess computer skills or not. Over a period of time, cybercrime has evolved as an industry carrying out illegal activities. Political motivations are increasingly becoming critical factors governing the spread of cybercrime across countries. Prior research has noted that cybercrime has also increased due to the existing sociocultural and geopolitical atmosphere worldwide.

There is no universally accepted definition of cybercrime. Cybercrime involves the use of IT for abusive and criminal purposes. It represents a technological shift in the nature of crime and the methods used rather than an altogether new form of criminal behaviour. According to Kshetri (2010), 'Cybercrime is defined as a criminal activity in which computers or computer networks are the principal means of committing an offense or violating laws, rules, or regulations.' Examples of cybercrime include: denial-of-service (DoS) attacks, online fraud, online money laundering, criminal uses of Internet communications, identity fraud, use of computers to further traditional crimes and cyber extortions.

Threats to legitimate users have evolved with the Internet. We have reached a tipping point, where any modern Internet user, from a child at home to network engineers in multinational corporations, must rethink what they consider important when securing their assets. Every new device that employees bring into an organization opens new avenues for threats to infiltrate the network from the inside. Prudent companies have made significant investments in stopping external threats. Many widely distributed attacks are easily identified and stopped before they become a danger to the network. This has caused cybercriminals to look for ways to penetrate a network from the inside, where defences are often less formidable. In many cases, hackers attack the weakest link in the security chain, the user.

The production of crime requires the presence of (a) motivated offenders, (b) suitable targets (individuals or their property) and (c) the absence of effective guardians (Cantor and Land 1985). What this means is that a crime is only possible when a motivated offender interacts with an ineffectively guarded target. The major determinants of crime can be classified into five major categories, namely: social factors, economic factors, educational factors, biological factors and criminal justice systems (Cantor and Land 1985).

The social factors are not just related to society but also to how cybercrime is generally organized. The economic factors examine aspects related to or affecting the material and financial resources. While the educational factors touch upon issues of educational levels of those involved in crime, the biological factors probe race or gender. Lastly, the criminal justice system–related factors are concerned with law enforcement and punishment. In summary, these factors determine and contribute to whether someone gets involved in crime or not.

1.2.7. Nature of Cybercrime

The nature of cybercrime depends on a country's sociocultural environment, technological advancement and geopolitical atmosphere. According to Aguilar-Millan et al. (2008), organized crime involves the illicit flow of goods and services in one direction and the flow of criminal proceeds in the other. Just as the business world has benefited from globalization, so has organized crime. It has also been noted that, in recent years, organized crime groups have committed most of the cybercrimes. From the standpoint of organized criminal groups, a part of the fascinating character of the Internet stems from the fact that cyberspace is characterized by less governance and weak rule of law. The unregulated cyber world offers an opportunity to organized crime groups to mark their victims since their chances of getting caught are few. Organized crime is successful where laws are confusing or lax, or when law enforcement is not prepared or structured to retaliate. Both developing and post-communist countries desperately need foreign investment to survive, and if they cannot guarantee investors some protection against fraud, extortion and corruption, the money is likely to be taken elsewhere. When high-risk rates are assigned to a country and huge sums of investment money are diverted to their neighbours, governments react and start taking these issues seriously.

Ideological hacktivism sees organized crime as an easy way to make money. Political and religious groups use cybercrime as a tool for terrorist activities. These cybercrime activities are supported by global networks of organized crime groups that hire and direct hackers. Due to this radical change in the nature of cybercrime, lawmakers and criminal defence lawyers have started developing solutions related to these areas so that they can reflect and adequately address these changes. These include solutions for new cyber-crimes, such as cyber extortion, information theft, fraud, identity theft, exploitation of children, intellectual property theft, phishing and vishing.

In comparison to other countries, the nature of cybercrime is mostly unorganized in India. Countries such as China and Russia, followed by those in Europe, however, show more incidents of organized cybercrime. United States and Europe have witnessed rampant growth of organized cybercrime, since financial traffic there is very high. Traditional organized criminal groups such as the Italian Mafia, Yakuza from Japan, Chinese gangs, Colombian cartels and Russian and Malaysian organized crime groups also engage in cybercrime. They have apparently got teams of professional hackers working for them and have streamlined their engagements from traditional criminal activities to cybercrime while spreading their tentacles globally (Bell 2002; Foreign Policy 2005; Ismail 2008; Katyal 2001; Parker 1998; The Economist 2009).

The rate at which cybercrime has been growing is alarming and a cause of concern for all. The nature of cybercrime activity itself is such that the criminal can mastermind an impact in any part of the world without being present at the site of the crime. This reinforces the fact that the anonymity of cyberspace has indeed rendered all boundaries meaningless. And this is what makes cybercrime a complex and dangerous threat in today's times.

The effect that cyberattackers can create by disrupting critical infrastructure is no less than the kind of havoc that terrorists cause in the tangible world. Identity thefts, financial frauds, fraudulent access to corporate information such as intellectual property, gaining access to confidential state and military secrets and recruiting a host of criminals and the like to spread acts of physical violence are just some of the many heinous activities that cyberattackers indulge in.

The evolution of new technologies and social media like Facebook and Twitter has made personal information easily available and easy to steal or compromise. There is a need to spread awareness on commonly used modes of cybercrime, such as phishing, identity theft, botnets, DoS attacks, DDoS attacks and so on. The problem assumes greater proportions when individuals, terrorist groups, gangs of criminals or countries, no matter how small they may be, can easily challenge and pose a threat to the bigger powers in the virtual world, and this has the potential to eventually translate into a physical attack as well. It is important to understand the nature of cybercriminal activity and the risk that ensues, so that protection programmes can be suitably planned. Protection has other vital components, such as the profiling of cyber-criminals, awareness building and systematic analysis and study.

1.3. CHALLENGES TO CYBERSECURITY

Dwight D. Eisenhower, 34th President (1953–61) of the US said, 'We will bankrupt ourselves in the vain search for absolute security.'

Attacks motivated by politics are not new, but these are encountered frequently and regularly today. They will be far more numerous going forward. According to the McAfee (2011a) Threat Predictions report:

> In addition to defacement (the primary activity of hacktivists) and distributed denial-of-service (DDoS, the latest 'fashionable' activity) attacks, new kinds of sophisticated attacks are expected to make themselves felt. Information theft and its disclosure specifically aimed at discrediting political opponents are predicted to increase. More groups will repeat the WikiLeaks example, as hacktivism is essentially conducted by people claiming to be independent of any particular government or movement. Whether governments drive these manipulations and activities covertly or not is open to debate, but it is

likely enough that states will adopt a privateer model. Hacktivism as a diversion could be the first step in cyberwarfare.

Everyone in the realm of information security—from journalists to researchers—will have to be vigilant to recognize the difference between hacktivism and the beginning of a cyberwar.

Threats are intertwined—meaning almost every threat comprises multiple components for attacking, infecting and compromising data (Trend Micro, 2010b). At the same time, newer threats related to cloud computing, mobile telephony and social networking are just about emerging. There are incidents of phishing attacks through hacking of shared virtual servers. Botnets are managed and run as an enterprise organization manages its network. Sites offering free domain name registrations are used for registering free domains and phishing attacks. Cybercrime is becoming more organized as revealed by recent incidents, such as infection by Stuxnet, the computer worm, and attacks against Estonia, Georgia, the Pentagon, NASA and websites of the Indian Government (discussed later in the book).

1.4. EFFORTS TO PROMOTE CYBERSECURITY

Considering the growth of cybercrime, the commitment of governments, businesses and the global community to fight it is not surprising. Collaboration (cross-border, public–private and government–private) is needed to shut down the affected domains, freeze payment accounts that are suspected of fraud, isolate bad networks and so on. The mission of The Society for the Policing of Cyberspace (POLCYB), Canada is 'to promote cybersecurity through enhancing and developing global international partnerships to prevent, detect, and combat cyberspace crimes'.

To meet the challenge posed by new kinds of cybercrimes and criminal profiles, many countries have also reviewed their domestic criminal laws so as to prevent computer-related crimes. Governments are also making legislations ensuring that every company from large organizations to midsized and small ones have Internet policies and security solutions in place. However, legislations enacted by different countries cover only a few classified computer-related offences. Given dynamic and fast-changing technologies, new types of offences may come up frequently. The United States Government

Accountability Office reported that efforts to address cybercrime included activities associated with protecting networks and information, detecting criminal activity, investigating crime and prosecuting criminals (USGAO 2007).

Cybercrime will make people reluctant to enter and trust the electronic world. This will hinder interchange of information between people, businesses and governments, impacting everything from education to commerce. Therefore, we need to understand cybercrime in greater detail and take adequate protection measures so that the users feel safe online.

The organized action against malicious programs is not necessarily keeping pace. McColo, a company in San Jose, California, was believed to have hosted some of the command and control infrastructure for several of the world's largest identified botnets, which controlled hundreds of thousands of zombie computers involved in e-mail spam, spamvertising, malware, get-rich-quick scams and the like. Thanks to the efforts of security researchers who regularly collect data on malicious Internet activity, McColo was finally disconnected from the Internet when years of investigation culminated in a complete shutdown, eliminating an unbelievable 50–75 per cent of the world's junk e-mail in a single day. This is the kind of organized action which can be effective against cybercrime. Also, as part of organized action, it is important that a knowledge repository of best practices on cybersecurity be built and shared across organizations.

It is known that cybercriminals are more organized today than ever before. Therefore, our response to them must also take on new structure and focus. Individuals, organizations, law enforcement and IT solutions providers must all join hands to study and meet the evolving challenge posed by cybercrime, specifically in the design of new strategies and solutions, which will become necessary in key areas—people, process, policies and technology.

TWO

IDENTIFYING CYBERCRIME MOTIVES

————◆————

One of the most crucial elements that can help comprehend why individuals within the computer community do what they do is motivation. Motives are more or less consistent in the entire hacker community. Money-based motives are usually confined to those who are identified as 'blackhats' and are associated with organized crime. Blackhats also include those individuals involved in corporate or national espionage. Instead of being driven by curiosity, hackers today are driven by money. 'They're trying to get anything of value that they can market' (Horn 2006).

Patrick Gray, director of X-Force operations at Internet Security Systems, says, 'The stereotypical image of the lone hacker sitting up in a loft somewhere, eating Ding Dongs, drinking Jolt cola until it comes out of his ears, and just hacking away, is gone' (quoted in Bednarz 2004). The popular image of a hacker as young, intelligent, socially inept and male is largely inaccurate (Bednarz 2004).

In the twentieth century, large-scale cybercrime centred on or around one-man operations, who exploited weaknesses in computer operating systems or networks. In most cases, these crimes were committed by computer nerds who felt challenged to prove that they could beat the system. The term 'hacker' was coined for just such an individual, but rarely was there any element of financial gain in this criminal behaviour. While a great deal of financial damage could result from such endeavours, not to mention potential security risks, this one-man band of criminals lacked the motive and intent of traditional criminal gangs. In short, cybercrime was in its infancy and largely seen as a practical joke or game by those who committed it. Criminal defence tactics then were also largely based on the fact that no real intentional damage had been done and, in a large number of cases, the penalty for the crime involved showing how the hacker had manipulated the computer system.

Recent trends show a change in the threat landscape; the threats are increasing in sophistication and becoming more organized. Criminal gangs have introduced a professional element to the world of cybercrime. The geeks who would exploit weaknesses in computer operating or networking systems have now evolved into criminal gangs making use of computer networks to take unsuspecting users for a ride while raking in their money. Upcoming trends and the nature of cybercrime today redefine new attacks as 'targeted' and 'opportunistic'. The mere mention of the phrase 'targeted attack' is enough to generate concern among organizations the world over. An organization singled out by an attacker with sufficient resources often finds it difficult to mount an adequate defence on time.

The evolution of cybercrime from 'mischievous virus-writing' to 'financially or politically motivated attacks' is a trend likely to continue. The WikiLeaks scandal and the subsequent distributed denial-of-service (DDoS) attacks on organizations which had withdrawn their support illustrated a fundamental change in the motivations behind committing cybercrime. A virus unleashed in 2010, called the Stuxnet worm, illustrated this change by targeting the systems used in industrial applications and nuclear facilities.

2.1. CLASSIFICATION OF MAJOR CYBERCRIME MOTIVATIONS

Cybercrime may be motivated by intrinsic or extrinsic motivation. While intrinsic motivation includes enjoyment-based motivation, obligation or community-based motivation, ideology or community-based motivation, entrance or acceptance into social group, and others, extrinsic motivation results in organized or targeted, and financially motivated, cybercrimes.

The theory of intrinsic motivation is based on the premise that the human need for competence and self-determination is linked with interest and enjoyment (Deci and Ryan 1985). According to Ryan and Deci (2000a: 56), intrinsically motivated individuals undertake activities for 'inherent satisfactions rather than for some separable consequence'. They argue that 'when intrinsically motivated, a person is moved to act for the fun or challenge entailed rather than because of external products, pressures or rewards'.

2.1.1. Ego

This motive is shared by the entire hacking community. Interestingly, it is also the power of one's ego that seems to entice one to 'undertake this objective in the face of the real threat of discovery and apprehension and the subsequent serious legal ramifications' (The Honeynet Project 2004: 513).

2.1.2. Enjoyment-Based Intrinsic Motivation

Central to the concept of intrinsic motivation is the notion of having fun or enjoying oneself when participating in a forbidden activity (Deci and Ryan 1985). Csikszentmihalyi (1975), one of the first psychologists to study the enjoyment dimension, emphasized that some activities were pursued for the sake of enjoyment derived from doing them. Shapira (1976) argues that this category of motivation is related to fulfilling a challenging task albeit without an external reward. Maverick hackers, for instance, attack websites because of the perceived challenges they propose rather than a desire for financial incentives.

Entertainment

This is one of the early motivators of the hacking counterculture and is still a primary motivator today. This motivation has probably the least impact on the intended targets because the objective is more amusement than destructive actions. However, any form of entertainment via the Internet that displays child pornography, or that engages in cyberstalking with the intent to sexually assault an individual, adult or child is anything but harmless. It is this possibility that system security professionals need to be aware of. According to *Business Week* (2006):

> Anyone who has responsibility for systems security, incident response teams, business continuity planning and IT hiring must understand the implications of online behavior and computer use beyond purely technical considerations. They must understand how to identify cyber deviant behavior, how to

identify the perpetrators, how to protect the innocent and how to reduce organizational vulnerability.

Mischief

In this case, the motives behind hacking are generally more mischievous than anything sinister. For example, IT students who are learning about operating systems at a college might happily penetrate the college's security system to prove that it can be done, or to gain access to exam questions and answers.

For example, in November 1997, Matthew Bevan, a 23-year-old programmer obsessed with the X-Files and the search for alien spacecraft, and Pryce, his teenaged accomplice, walked free after a three-year-long case against them collapsed. They had penetrated United States Air Force computers, partly motivated by a belief that a captured alien spaceship was being held secretly at a remote Nevada airbase. They were traced not by infowar techniques but by traditional police methods, when Pryce boasted to an undercover informant about his activities on an Internet chatline and gave him his London phone number. They were charged with three offences under the Computer Misuse Act, 1990, but eventually it was decided that they in fact presented no threat to national security and the case was dropped (Heathkote and Langfield 2004: Chapter 26).

Revenge for Being Laid Off: The Maroochy Shire Incident, 2000

Having been turned down for a job by the municipal government of his community, Vitek Boden, a computer expert in his 40s decided he would take his revenge. Using a notebook computer and a radio transmitter, he seized control of a wastewater facility on 46 separate occasions, and over the course of two months spilled 264,000 gallons of sewage into nearby streams and rivers. He was later arrested and served prison time on charges of computer and environmental crimes.

This incident occurred over a period of three months, from February to April 2000, at Maroochy Shire, a rural area of great natural beauty and a tourist destination, located about 100 kilometres north of the Queensland state capital of Brisbane, Australia.

The sewage spill was significant. It polluted over 500 metres of open drain in a residential area and flowed into a tidal canal. Cleaning up the spill and its effects took days and required the deployment of considerable resources. 'Marine life died, the creek water turned black and the stench was unbearable for residents,' said Janelle Bryant, investigations manager for the Australian Environmental Protection Agency. The total loss due to unauthorized spillage amounted to one million dollars (Bloomberg Businessweek 2010).

2.1.3. Obligation or Community-Based Intrinsic Motivation

Principles can be major intrinsic motivators is the way Lindenberg (2001) puts it. Though individuals may, owing to social pressures, act appropriately and in a manner acceptable to the groups within which they coexist, often, it is the aim of being inconsistent in their actions while adhering to the norms of the group that triggers their action.

Hackers are known to owe allegiance to diverse entities such as nations, territories, terrorist organizations and associations of hackers or even to profess adherence to other ideological groups. For instance, the Zapatista Movement in the Chiapas state of southern Mexico was most definitely the first high-profile group that used aggressive cyber tactics to pull down the web servers of Mexican officials and successfully pursue their political goals (Lee 2000). Similarly, another group termed the Electrohippies Collective (http://www.fraw.org.uk) was notorious for encouraging its members to attack the web servers belonging to the World Trade Organization (WTO). It has been found that strong emotions in favour of the obligation/community goal prevail when individuals within the 'reference community' cut down on personal gain seeking at the expense of their fellow group members (Lakhani and Wolf 2005).

2.1.4. Ideology or Community-Based Intrinsic Motivation

One's ideology is shaped by different factors, such as geopolitical orientation, sociocultural influences, religious beliefs, personal history and views, all of which impact how individuals see the world and the causes they cling to. An example of ideology in use today is political activism. Redirection of political websites, social networks, or even domain name system (DNS) servers (like those in China to support free speech), are all instances of hacking to support some political cause. The issue of supporting a cause by action was once limited in physical scope and ability. Now, however, with the advent of the Internet, it has far-reaching implications. There are instances where people utilize their cyber skills to destroy or alter systems in government, military, corporate and/or civilian networks in support of their protest or cause.

The hacker population in the Middle East is perhaps the most politically and ideologically motivated segment in the region as well as its largest and most prolific group. Hackers of all persuasions typically identify, to varying degrees, with the more controversial among the region's political and religious issues, like potential Islamic activism issues in 2009, the Israel–Palestine conflict, the Arab–Iranian dispute, the Kurdish separatists' conflicts against nationalists and various religiously motivated issues. This kind of hacktivism—witnessed in the overwhelming response of Muslim hackers against the 2008 republication of the infamous Jyllands-Posten cartoon caricatures of Islam's Prophet Mohammed—is expected to continue making an online presence, particularly when religious and political tensions between the Islamic world and the West, for example, are running high.

Looking forward, Central Asia is primed to become an important and new source of criminal and ideologically motivated hacking. Internet access and the role of the Internet in general are spreading in the former Soviet republics of Central Asia. The Central Asian republics have a long-shared history with Russia, including linguistic commonality and scripts in variants of the Russian Cyrillic alphabet. They also retain deep economic and significant political ties with Russia, which shows the political- and religion-based terrorist nature of cybercriminals in these regions (iDefense 2008).

WikiLeaks is an online not-for-profit organization that publishes submissions of private, secret and classified media from anonymous news sources, news leaks and whistleblowers. Its website, launched in 2006, claimed a database of more than 1.2 million documents within a year of its launch. This was followed by the release of a number of significant documents, which have become front-page news items. The WikiLeaks website (WikiLeaks 2011: http://wikileaks.org/About.html) says its goal is 'to bring important news and information to the public.... One of our most important activities is to publish original source material alongside our news stories so readers and historians alike can see evidence of the truth'. In this case, what may be a breach for one party may actually be genuine community service for another, driven as they are by ideological motivations.

WikiLeaks also tries to ensure that whistleblowers and journalists are not jailed for e-mailing sensitive or classified documents. The online 'drop box' (currently not functioning) was designed to 'provide an innovative, secure and anonymous way for sources to leak information' to the journalists at WikiLeaks (http://wikileaks.org/About.html).

2.1.5. Entrance or Acceptance into Social Group

The hacker community is organized around groups. One cannot penetrate the social structure of a certain group unless one possesses the necessary levels of technical expertise. 'Field observations of groups within the community support the idea that hacker groups are very status homogeneous—that is, individuals within a group tend to have technical computer skills that are similar in nature' (The Honeynet Project 2004: 517). Entrance to the various social structures within the community are only accomplished by evidence of coding a particular exploit, defeating strong security defences, number of 'owned' machines (zombies) or exploiting application frameworks, to name a few.

Status or Prestige

The most powerful force in any social structure, the status hierarchy, of the hacker community depends solely on one's technical skills in coding, understanding of network protocols and system internals. One's status within the hacker community can cause conflict where individuals or groups may have to fight for higher ranking or prestige. This yields a concerted effort to 'disrespect' the other group or individual in an attempt to establish a superior status position. Interestingly enough, this same sense of status can be the driving motivation for insider attacks or threats. Insider employees may deem themselves to be superior in their programming or network expertise. When confronted with conflicting views within the corporation that challenges this belief (for example, a superior not accepting an employee's advice), the need to re-establish this 'superiority' or status by a demonstration of skills may render necessary an attack against an organization's information infrastructure.

2.1.6. Extrinsic Motivation

A number of studies mention how human behaviour is driven and manipulated by extrinsic behaviour. The most widely held economic theory maintains that human behaviour is a result of 'incentives applied from outside the person' (Frey 1997). So, while the advantages accruing to the individual may be immediate or delayed, the quantity of financial incentive and the degree of motivation which drive hackers may co-vary positively.

Many security researchers suggest that there has been a rise in professional cybercrime (Antonopoulos 2009). Peter Tippett of Verizon Business noted, 'Today's online data thieves don't just run automatic scanners and jump on any network hole they find. They're more likely to first choose a target that has data they can turn into cash, and then figure out how to break in' (Larkin 2009). It is more likely then that hackers who fall within the extrinsically motivated category will be more amenable to attacking the system networks of organizations that hold a higher potential in terms of accruing financial incentives. Consider for instance online casinos, banks and e-commerce hubs, which are the preferred sites for most cyber extortionists.

2.1.7. Financial Motivation

Earlier, in the hacker community, there was a strong norm against illegally accumulating large sums of money or other financial resources. However, this changed over the past decade. As evidenced by the dramatic rise in credit-card theft, extortion and personal identity loss, the pseudo-currency of the blackhat community was stolen credit-card numbers. Hackers have even built their own encrypted instant message (IM) program to enable them to communicate without law enforcement spying on their communication. 'CarderIM is a sophisticated tool hackers are using to sell information such as credit-card numbers or e-mail addresses, part of an underground economy dealing in financial data,' says Andrew Moloney, business director, financial services for the RSA, part of EMC Corp. (quoted in *PCWorld* 2007).

Tragedies continue to attract scammers. Earthquakes and other disasters are always moneymaking opportunities for cybercriminals.

A Case of Financially Motivated Cybercrime: Citibank, 1994

The first financially motivated cybercrime occurred when a Russian hacker named Vladimir Levin masterminded a major conspiracy in which his gang, operating from St. Petersburg in Russia, illegally accessed Citibank's central wire transfer department, located in San Francisco in the United States, and transferred 12 million dollars from large corporate accounts to other accounts opened by his accomplices in the United States, the Netherlands, Finland, Germany and Israel (Chawki and Abdel Wahab 2006).

One of the tools allegedly used by the hackers to break into Citibank was 'Black Energy', a $40 piece of software that was capable of launching distributed denial-ofservice (DDoS) attacks to prevent access to a specific website. Designed by a Russian hacker, 'Black Energy' was commonly sold on certain Russian language forums.

Citibank took immediate action to prevent recurrence of this event. It implemented a security system known as the 'Dynamic Encryption Card'. The card looked like a pocket calculator. The user had to turn the card on and enter a personal identification number. The card would then generate a password to enable users to log in to the system. The password could only be used once, thereby heightening security and taking away the responsibility of customers to frequently change their password. In 1994, Citibank was the only financial organization using such a system. The incident led to Citibank's hiring of Stephen R. Katz as the banking industry's first chief information security officer (CISO) (Kabay 2008).

Another Case of Financially Motivated Cybercrime: TJX, 2007

The Massachusetts-based retail company TJX, which owns well-known chains such as TJ Maxx and Marshalls, was taken for a ride by a group of cyber fiends with a fetish for electronics in another incident of cybercrime in 2007 (Computerworld 2007; Kabay 2008; Infoworld 2007; Computer Business Review 2007).

During the interrogations, a Miami hacker, Albert Gonzalez confessed to having masterminded the hacking of the TJX companies during which 45.6 million credit- and debit-card numbers were stolen over an 18-month period ending in 2007. Some of these card details were then used to fund a multimillion-dollar spending spree from Walmart's stock of electronics equipment. Gonzalez and 10 others sought targets while war driving and seeking vulnerabilities in wireless networks along the U.S. Route 1 in Miami. They compromised cards at BJ's Wholesale Club, DSW, Office Max, Boston Market, Barnes & Noble, Sports Authority and TJ Maxx.

The indictment referred to Gonzalez by the screen names 'cumbajohny', 'soupnazi', 'segvec', 'kingchilli' and 'stanozlolz'. The hacking was an embarrassment to TJ Maxx, which discovered the breach only in December 2006.

The company initially believed the intrusion began in May 2006, but further investigations revealed breaches dating back to July 2005. One of Gonzalez's co-conspirators was Stephen Watt, known in the hacker world as 'Unix Terrorist' and 'Jim Jones'. Watt worked at Morgan Stanley in New York city and wrote the sniffer program.

2.1.8. Targeted versus Opportunistic Attacks

Cybercrimes may broadly be classified into three categories: targeted, opportunistic (random) and opportunistic (directed). There is a fundamental shift in the objective of cybercrime from being random, experimental and opportunistic to being more organized, targeted and direct. This shift is mainly due to the perverse incentives, earning huge sums of money in very little or no time with very little labour, that are created by the IT market and global economic trends. Apart from money being involved directly in the commission of cybercrimes, there is also rise in intangible losses, like loss of confidence and shift of customer accounts.

Targeted Attacks

These use specific tools against specific cyber targets and are executed by skilled hackers equipped with the expertise to do serious damage. Some of them are motivated by financial gains. Targeted attacks are also initiated by terrorists, rival companies, ideological hackers and government agencies. These attacks commence with some reconnaissance on the part of attackers, which may include, or instance, researching publicly available information about the company and its employees from social networking sites. This information may then be used to create specifically crafted phishing e-mail messages, often referred to as 'spear phishing', that target the company or even specific staff members. These e-mail messages often contain attachments that exploit vulnerabilities in client-side applications, or have links to websites that exploit the vulnerabilities in web browsers or browser plug-ins. A successful attack gives the attacker access to the enterprise's network.

A landmark case came to light in August 2004, when six hackers were found guilty of being involved in the denial-of-service (DoS) attacks against their business rivals and convicted by a Californian court (Leyden 2004). While monetary losses in a targeted attack are substantial, reports suggest that gambling sites, for instance, pay out millions of dollars in extortion money each year. Targeted web attacks are therefore not limited to the networks of large organizations.

Opportunistic Attacks

Such attacks involve the release of virtual 'worms' and 'viruses' that attack network systems across the Internet and bring them down. Though they attack indiscriminately, they remain comparatively less dangerous than targeted attacks and have smaller financial fallouts. Compared to the physical world, it is difficult to detect opportunism in cyber world. The Verizon report (2008) indicates a higher concentration of cybercrime in opportunistic (direct) and finance-related cybercrime. The next category is opportunistic (random) and mischievous cybercrime.

Examples of Targeted and Political Attacks

The Estonian Case, 2007: In 2007, disruptions of Internet service in Estonia, formerly a political division of the Russian-dominated Soviet Union, prompted talks of those events as possibly the first-ever cyberwars. The exact nature of the disruptions and the hand behind them proved hard to identify.

On 30 April 2007, the government moved the Bronze Soldier—a memorial commemorating the Soviet liberation of Estonia from the Nazis—from Tõnismägi Park in central Tallinn to the Tallinn Military Cemetery. This decision sparked rioting among the Russian-speaking community, which comprised around 26 per cent of Estonia's population in 2007.

The cyberattacks on Estonia occurred within the overall climate of tension between ethnic Estonians and the country's Russian minority population. To ethnic Estonians, the Bronze Soldier symbolized Soviet oppression. But to the Russian minorities, its relocation represented further marginalization of their ethnic identity.

In May 2007, a series of cyberattacks were launched against the Estonian government and its commercial websites. Some attacks defaced the websites and replaced the pages with Russian propaganda or bogus information. Up to six sites were rendered inaccessible at various points, including those of the Foreign and Justice ministries. Most of the attacks were launched using botnets comprising many thousands of ordinary computers.

Estonia's computer emergency response team (CERT-EE) acted swiftly and, in collaboration with partners from the international community, weathered a very serious attack with little damage. The attack was primarily defended through filtering—blocking connections from outside Estonia. For example, Estonia's second largest bank, SEB Eesti Ühispank, blocked access (from abroad) to its online banking service while remaining open to local users.

Three weeks after the attacks ended, one researcher identified at least 128 separate attacks on nine different websites in Estonia. Of these 128 attacks, 35 were reportedly against the website of the Estonian police, another 35 were reportedly against the website of the Ministry of Finance, and 36 attacks were against the Estonian Parliament's, Prime Minister's and general government websites (Thomas 2008). It was further estimated that some of the attacks lasted more than 10 hours, exceeded 95 Mbps and peaked at about a million packets per second. While this may seem like a lot, other attacks considered 'big' by security experts usually peak at about 20 million packets per second, five times more than the attack against Estonia. This has led experts to conclude that the attack was not optimized for maximum impact on and damage to the network, but rather to make a statement and prove a point (OECD 2008a). The hackers rained down a data load equivalent to downloading the entire Windows XP operating system every six seconds for 10 hours. Hannabank, Estonia's largest bank and one of the prime targets of the attack, lost around one million dollars over the course of the attacks, and the members of Parliament could not access their e-mail for four days (Landler and Markoff 2007; Thomas 2008; Tikk et al. 2010).

The Georgian Case, 2008: This was a case of cyberattack coordinated with a military attack (Tikk et al. 2010).

In August 2008, a cyberattack by civilians, in which computer networks were assaulted, was coordinated with physical attacks conducted by the national military forces of Russia, against Georgia, on the dispute over South Ossetia. On 5 August 2008, three days before Georgia invaded South Ossetia, the websites of the OSInform news agency and OSRadio were hacked. The OSInform website, 'osinform.ru', retained only its header and logo, while its content was replaced by a feed to the Alania TV website content. Alania TV, a Georgian government-supported television station aimed at audiences in South Ossetia, denied any involvement in the hacking of the websites. The cyberattack changed the content of the websites of the Parliament of Georgia and the Georgian Ministry of Foreign Affairs, and compared the then Georgian President Mikheil Saakashvili to Adolf Hitler. It also led to denials of service to numerous Georgian websites. The Georgian spokesperson in the United Kingdom held the Russian Business Network (RBN) website responsible for this. Traffic to key servers in Georgia was intercepted and rerouted by Russian-based servers. Shadow servers reported that command-and-control servers were being used to launch the attacks. According to the reports, the Russian military was not directly involved in this, but the hackers were informed of the military operations so that they could plan their attack accordingly. Cyberattacks occurring at the same time as the military attacks could not have been a mere coincidence.

The cyberattacks on Georgia in August 2008 shut down normal business operations (electronic financial transactions were closed for 10 days). In addition to security and economic well-being, cyber aggression can adversely affect a stable international order, since the cumulative damage from cyberattacks on critical infrastructure can ignite panic, cause a loss of confidence, create uncertainty and destroy trust in modern society. Sustained disruptions to basic services could lead to a mob mentality.

The main effect of the attack was the denial of service and unavailability of websites while the tools employed for the purpose, the web servers, were flooded with 'packets' and a software designed for adding functions to websites, so that it would request random, non-existent web pages. Russian-based servers 'AS12389 Rostelecom', 'AS8342 Rtcomm' and 'AS8359' were controlling all the traffic to Georgia's key servers. German hackers managed to route traffic directly to Georgia through Deutsche Telekom's 'AS3320 DTAG' server for a few hours and this traffic was intercepted and rerouted through 'AS8359 Comstar', located in Moscow.

According to the U.S. Cyber Consequences Unit Report (Thomas 2009; www.usccu.us), 'Many of the cyberattacks were so close in time to the corresponding military operations that there had to be close cooperation between people in the Russian military and the civilian cyberattackers.'

According to Thomas (2008):

When the cyberattacks began, they did not involve any reconnaissance or mapping state, but jumped directly to the sort of 'packets' that were best suited to jamming the Web sites under attack. This indicates that the necessary reconnaissance and the writing of the attack scripts had to have been done in advance.

2.1.9. Combination of Motivations

Human behaviour is often not driven by one or two factors but by a combination of many elements and multiple motivations—there are different forms of intrinsic and extrinsic motivations at play, says Lindenberg (2001). So people who want to enjoy themselves while making a little money on the side will be more likely to choose opportunities that offer a substantial economic reward. While hacking an e-commerce website and getting a reward in the bargain sounds enticing to some, other hackers may just want to have some fun (Lakhani and Wolf 2005). Consider, for example, hackers who protested India's nuclear weapons' tests in 1998. While some of them fought on ideological grounds, they admitted that they had attacked the website for the sheer thrill of doing so (Denning 2000).

External forces come in several flavours and their impact can motivate or even demotivate one in any place. Economic as well as geopolitical forces may be the catalysts that turn one towards crime in the first place. Romania, for instance, is a country whose unemployment rate is high among the educated and the technically trained, and is not surprisingly considered a 'hotbed' of blackhat hacker activities. Around 40 per cent of Romanian citizens live below poverty levels; thus, money is a major motivator for these blackhat hacking groups (Horn 2006).

Hirshleifer (1998) lists various items that are, and have been, motives and/or objectives of cybercriminals. These include motives such as curiosity, destruction of digital property (which may be a threat to corporate resources, intellectual property and the company image), corporate or national espionage, disruption of corporate services, manipulation of data and information (for personal or professional gain), prestige, ego and others.

As early as the mid-1990s, Rasch (1996: chapter 11) noted the involvement of a wide range of individuals with varied motivations for cybercrimes:

> Computer criminals are not of a discrete type. They range from the computer world equivalent of a juvenile delinquent, the hacker or cyberpunk, to the sophisticated white-collar embezzler attacking financial institution computers, and include cyber terrorists, extortionists, spies, petty thieves and joyriders.

For years, profit-motivated cybercrime exploited the geographic flexibility of the Internet, migrating from the United States and western Europe to eastern

Europe and Asia, where digital crimes were equally lucrative and far harder to prosecute (Greenberg 2007).

2.2. MAJOR TRENDS IN MOTIVATIONS FOR CYBERCRIME

Today's Internet attacks are organized and designed to steal information and resources from consumers and corporations. New social networking technologies like Web 2.0 (Facebook, Twitter and others) are also threat concerns. Cybercriminals the world over are driven by similar knowledge of technology. The key difference lies in the 'motivations behind the crime' (*Times of India* 2008).

Technological advancement, sociocultural environment and the geopolitical atmosphere impact greatly on the nature of cybercrime, leading to its growth. Cybercrime activity is seen to gradually shift from random to directed and thereafter, to being politically motivated. An analysis of the nature of cyber activity shows that in India, cyber activity is more mischievous or random and less organized.

Developed countries report higher opportunistic activity, both as a source and a destination. Many a time, cybercrimes are organized and financially motivated, as the financial traffic is high in developed countries. Countries such as China report higher concentrations of targeted and politically motivated cybercrimes (Verizon 2008). Reports also suggest that politically and ideologically motivated crime is prevalent in the Middle East and South East Asia (Symantec Corporation 2010d). Malicious cyber activity including ideological hactivism and militant Islamic use of online resources are major concerns. Some developed countries are seen as a source of cybercrime activity where attacks are motivated mostly by revenge and malicious intent. Holding network administrators hostage by stealing passwords, sacked or disgruntled workers crashing databases, sending hate e-mails are the sorts of crimes seen recently. These are non-threatening crimes though cleaning up after them proves annoying.

The ecology of cybercrime is different in Russia. The country's present socio-economic and geopolitical situation makes it more prone to politically motivated hacking (hactivism). Many legitimate Russian businesses now find DDoS attacks and network penetrations to be effective tactics against competitors. Such countries regard the cyber underground as a political and strategic asset, one to be cultivated and wielded in the pursuit of national interests (iDefense 2008).

Apart from Russia, China is also among the countries reporting high rates of cybercrime, both the organized and politically motivated varieties. The threat of cyber espionage—both strategic and corporate—is expected to grow in frequency and severity, thus remaining the most troubling feature of the Chinese cyber environment (iDefense 2008). The governments in western and eastern Asian countries reveal new instances of apparent Chinese cyber espionage.

It is to be noted however, that the Chinese hacking community has continued its shift away from patriotic motivations, which are already without much force other than the brief catharsis during political crises. Motivations are realigned firmly towards a desire for financial and prestige gains (iDefense 2008).

To sum up, a better understanding of the motivation behind cybercrime will help in handling it better. Since cybercrime is getting organized, it will require organized action to deal with it. The security solutions have to match up to newer threats at all times.

THREE

HOW CAN YOU BE AFFECTED BY CYBERCRIME?

3.1. INTRODUCTION

Considering the dynamics of the cyber environment at the global level, cybercrime can be classified as: crimes where the computer is used as a tool or instrument, such as fraud; crimes where the computer is the object of the crime, such as hacking and release of viruses; and crimes where the computer is incidental to the crime, such as when it is used as a medium for storage of records of criminal transactions.

3.2. CATEGORIES OF OFFENCES

Cybercrime exists in many forms. The various data elements that are targeted in different types of cybercrime attacks include account information, credit-card number, date of birth, driver's licence, medical information, name, social security number and so on. In many incidents, there exist a combination of these elements, some of which are very common to different parts of the world.

As per Information Security Media Group's survey of 150 organizations worldwide, the types of cybercrimes faced by respondent organizations in 2010 were relating to credit/debit card (82 per cent); cheque (63 per cent); phishing/vishing (48 per cent); Automated Clearing House (ACH)/wire (account takeover) (37 per cent); third-party point of sale (POS) skimming (32 per cent) (ISMG 2010).

It is possible to distinguish four different categories of cybercrimes: computer-related offences, content-related offences, offences against the confidentiality, integrity and availability of data and computer systems, and copyright and trademark Offences. In addition, there are also the so-called 'combined offences' (Gercke 2011a).

3.2.1. Computer-Related Offences

Some cybercrimes existed before the emergence of the computer. The computer only provided a new tool by which a crime could be perpetrated. Examples of this type are identity theft, fraud and cyber espionage.

Theft and Fraud

Cyber fraud implies illegal access to a computer system, illegal data acquisition and misleading information (Gercke 2011a). Illegal data acquisition is very often not criminalized because older regional and international legal frameworks do not contain provisions for it. Misleading information includes information that is listed in search engines and can influence consumers and business partners in their decisions; a mere posting that an e-commerce company is involved in fraudulent activities can, for example, negatively influence the sales of an online store. Cybercriminals set up websites to manipulate search engines and then charge companies to remove the posting/s.

Financial theft and misuse committed using computers are the most frequent crimes and they include misuse of credit cards and making unauthorized financial transactions. Cyber theft and fraud may be of different kinds. The theft of a customer's credit- or debit-card information, automated teller machine (ATM) frauds, financial data theft, identity theft and mobile frauds are major ones in the financial fraud category. Technological development today enables digitalization and the alteration of contents of various kinds of paperwork and documents, which are used in legal traffic, and forgery of data in its electronic form.

As per observations made by researchers in the OECD report (OECD 2008b), over the past five years, information theft, and in particular, online identity (ID) theft has grown. According to a report by Javelin Strategy and Research (2010), total financial losses from ID fraud in 2009 were 54 billion dollars, an increase from 48 billion in 2008. Although malware does not always play a direct role, ID theft using malware has become increasingly common with the rise of back-door 'Trojans' and other stealthy programs that hide on a computer system and capture information covertly. Online ID-theft attacks using malware can be complex and may use multiple Internet servers to distribute spam and malware, compromising the users' information systems, and then logging the stolen data to another website controlled by the attacker or sending it to the attackers' e-mail accounts.

Hacktivism (Hack + Activism)

'Hacktivism' refers to 'the use of computers and computer networks as a means of protest to promote political ends' (http://en.wikipedia.org/wiki/Hacktivism). These tools include website defacement, redirection, denial-of-service attack, information theft and so on. Hacktivism can be understood as the writing of code to promote a political ideology: promoting expressive politics, free speech, human rights and information ethics through software development. Acts of hacktivism are carried out in the belief that a proper use of code will be able to produce results similar to those produced by regular activism or civil disobedience. Hacktivist activities span many political ideals and issues. Hacktivists believe in translating political and ideological thought into code. This means anyone should be able to write a code and express himself. With access to data and activism surrounding this term and the emergence of WikiLeaks and the hacktivism group, Anonymous, it is difficult to ignore this phenomenon. Simultaneously, the boundary between hacktivism and cyberwarfare continues to blur.

Recently, the group Anonymous launched several, major, distributed DDoS attacks against websites of copyright protection societies and adult film industries such as SGAE (Spanish agency) and HADOPI (French government agency). In November 2010, the WikiLeaks disclosure of more than 250,000 diplomatic cables of the United States State Department upset many people. WikiLeaks, as well as its supporters and detractors, were victims of numerous DDoS attacks from people supporting one of the two camps. Also in November 2010, Phayul.com, a leading news portal of the Tibetan diaspora, was victimized by a DDoS attack that rendered the website slow or inaccessible.

Cyber Espionage

Corporate espionage has been recognized as a crime under existing criminal laws. The computer and the Internet are new tools for espionage. An instance of how they may be used is explained when one comprehends the ease with which industrial secrets, copyrights and patented information may be down-loaded and sent over the Internet to a competitor. This has the potential to cause huge damage. An innovation, which is yet to hit the market, may be stolen and exploited. It may even be sold for huge sums of money. Networks and connectivity only make it simpler.

According to Schiller (cited on http://en.wikipedia.org/wiki/Cyber_spying):

> Cyber spying or cyber espionage is the act or practice of obtaining secrets without the permission of the holder of the information (personal, sensitive, proprietary or of classified nature), from individuals, competitors, rivals, groups, governments and enemies for personal, economic, political or military advantage using illegal exploitation methods on the Internet, networks or individual computers through the use of cracking techniques and malicious software including Trojan horses and spyware.

A Case of Cyber Espionage: IMF, 2011

In 2011, computers of the International Monetary Fund (IMF) were hacked. The data theft from IMF computers by hackers (said to be linked to a foreign government) came in the wake of incidents against companies and governments that illustrated the growth of cyber attacks as an espionage tool. According to a security expert, the IMF hacking resulted in the loss of a 'large quantity' of data, including documents and e-mails.

Earlier in 2011, the Group of Twenty (G20) and Oak Ridge National Laboratory in the United States had also come under cyber attack. It was said that the intrusion was state-based, without specifying which government was thought to be behind it. The Washington-based IMF had approved a record 91.7 billion dollars in emergency loans in 2010 and provided a third of bailout packages in Europe (Bloomberg 2011a).

Exposure to Indecent Content

Other related crimes include polluting the youth through exposure to indecent content and luring young children to reveal details through social networking sites. Such activities have a lot of financial gain associated with them. Distribution of indecent content is the most under-prosecuted crime today. The regulation in this area is also insufficient.

According to the study conducted by Koerner (2000) for U.S. News and World Report, 'More than 40,000 sex-related sites exist on the Internet.' Moreover, pornographic sites bring in the most revenues. He found that 'adult materials account for 69 percent of the US$ 1.4 billion pay-to-view online-content market, far outpacing video games (4 percent) and sports (2 percent)'.

Forgery

Information technology has eased the process of forging while simultaneously making the act extremely hard to discover. This is very good news for forgers but it makes the lives of law-enforcement officers difficult. Apart from classic forgery under the existing legal systems, there may be many new challenges. Can illicit use of a password be criminalized as forgery? Will creating an electronic signal be deemed forgery? The last challenge is that, in many legal systems, there is a 'person' to be deloused; in this case, how would forgery be purported to induce a computer system or a network? Embezzlement is the most common example in this category. It is a kind of financial forgery by a person to whom property has been entrusted. Countries with high financial traffic are more affected with this type of cybercrime. In the United States, embezzlement is a statutory offence.

Cyberterrorism

Cyberterrorism is the premeditated, politically motivated attack against information, computer systems, computer programs and data which results in violence against non-combatant targets by sub-national groups or clandestine agents (Pollit 1997). It is the use of computer network tools to shut down critical national infrastructure (such as energy, transportation, government operations) or to coerce or intimidate a government or civilian population.

Cyberterrorism is defined by the Technolytics Institute as 'the premeditated use of disruptive activities, or the threat thereof, against computers and/or networks, with the intention to cause harm or further social, ideological, religious, political or similar objectives or to intimidate any person in furtherance of such objectives' (Coleman 2003). The term was coined by Barry C. Collin in the 1980s (Collin 1997).

Cyberterrorism means attacks on computers and Internet resources from an ideological motivation rather than an economic one. When such a crime is perpetrated purely from an economic motivation, it is termed cybercrime. Cyberterrorism may include DDoS attacks against government websites and service networks, such as power distribution, banking, public delivery services, and so on. It may be used by individuals and groups to threaten governments and to terrorize the citizens of a country. The Internet is often used as a tool for cyberterrorism in countries having problems with each other, such as Taiwan and China, Israel and Palestine, India and Pakistan, China and the United States, and many other countries.

The National Conference of State Legislatures (USA) defines cyberterrorism as 'the use of information technology by terrorist groups and individuals to further their agenda: this can include use of information technology to organize and execute attacks against networks, computer systems and telecommunications infrastructures, or for exchanging information or making threats electronically' (National Conference of State Legislatures 2006). Examples of cyberterrorism include hacking into computer systems, introducing viruses into vulnerable networks, website defacing, denial-of-service attacks and terrorist threats made via electronic communication.

This transformation in the methods of terrorism from traditional to electronic methods is one of the biggest challenges faced by modern societies. A consolidated effort is needed in terms of awareness building at each level (individual, regional, national, international), as well as support of laws and regulations and international cooperation to tackle the problem of cyberterrorism and cover its various forms. Cyberterrorism is one of the biggest threats of our times and unless individuals, governments and nations cooperate, we will continue to have more and more such cases.

The Stuxnet worm is the latest example of cyberterrorism attacks. It targeted programmable logic controllers (PLCs) that are used in the industrial control systems (ICS). The main purpose of ICS is to regulate the flow, or move the actuators as in a typical chemical plant scenario. The worm targeted specific manufacturer PLCs and it could reprogram them by injecting a malicious code. This at a ground level is very dangerous because industrial systems are the potential targets. The attacks were specific to manufacturers and nuclear power plants of a country. This requires specific knowledge of the technical aspects of the hardware used and this makes sceptics wonder about the involvement of governments in funding the development and propagation of Stuxnet.

Cyberterrorists are greatly interested in gaining publicity in any possible way. For example, information warfare techniques like Trojan horse viruses and network worms are often used to not only do damage to computing resources, but also as a way for the designer of the viruses to 'show off'. This is a serious ethical issue because many people are affected by these viruses and worms. For one, the viruses can consume system resources until networks become useless, costing companies lots of time and money. Also, depending on the type of work done on the affected computers, the damage to the beneficiaries of that work could be lethal. Even if the person did not mean to harm someone with their virus, it could have unpredictable effects that could have terrible results.

Terrorists can communicate, advertise and even conduct their operations online. Our existing legal systems may be able to comprehend these operations in many cases, but certain amendments may be required. Cyberterrorism can be used for religiously motivated issues, such as the Israel–Palestine conflict and the Arab–Iranian dispute or even the Islamic versus the American and European ideological and thought processes.

3.2.2. Content-Related Offences

The data which is processed by computers is often much more valuable than the hardware itself. That is why crimes committed against the content of those computers are of great importance.

Copyright

In many existing laws, information is protected in relation to know-how, trade secrets and against stealing intellectual property rights (IPRs). However, in the case of cybercrimes, information itself may be a product and therefore, require protection.

Copyright issues include the unauthorized copying of computer software (often referred to as software piracy), which is a copyright infringement of software. Most countries have copyright laws which apply to software, but the degree of enforcement varies. Copyright authorization needs to be checked carefully before downloading, uploading or distributing material over the Internet.

The motivations for copyright infringement may vary across individuals and geographies. It includes reasons such as pricing—unwillingness or inability to pay the price asked by legitimate sellers, unavailability and geographical restrictions on online distribution and international shipping of software.

A user can share a file with other users, which they can download through the Internet. However, this may result in infringement of copyright. In the case of music and movies, this sharing may often be illegal. The regulation of files shared and copied through the network is not clear. Under United States law, 'the Betamax decision' (Sony Corporation of America v. Universal City Studios, Inc.) holds that copying 'technologies' is not 'inherently' illegal, if they can be used for substantial non-infringing purposes. This decision predates the widespread use of the Internet and is applicable to most data networks, including peer-to-peer networks, since they can also be used for distribution of correctly licensed files. These non-infringing uses include sending open source software, public domain files and out-of-copyright works. Other jurisdictions tend to view the situation in somewhat similar ways.

The copyright laws of one country may be difficult to enforce outside the country. It is seen that countries where enforcement is poor host file-sharing software. This software may be used by cybercriminals to distribute files in countries where laws are more stringent. In such cases, enforcement becomes difficult. For example, the program Kazaa is owned by the Australian company Sharman Holdings. Incorporated in Vanuatu it was developed by two Dutch software engineers. The online index of bit torrents—The Pirate Bay—is hosted in Sweden with backup servers in Russia.

Stalking, Harassment, Hate Speech

Cyberstalking is a crime in which the attacker harasses a victim using electronic communication, such as e-mail or instant message (IM), or messages posted to a website or a discussion group (http://searchsecurity.techtarget.com/definition/cyberstalking). A cyberstalker relies upon the anonymity enabled by the Internet to allow him to stalk his victim without being detected. Cyberstalking messages differ from ordinary spam in that a cyberstalker targets a specific victim with frequent and threatening messages, while the spammer targets a multitude of recipients with simply annoying messages. Stalking has typically been defined as involving 'repeated harassing or threatening behavior. The goal of the traditional stalker is to exert control by instilling fear into the victim' (Lipton 2011). While cyberbullying and cyber harassment may damage an individual's reputation or livelihood, cyberstalking is more likely to result in severe and immediate emotional or physical harm.

Working to Halt Online Abuse (WHOA), an online organization dedicated to the cyberstalking problem, reported that in 2001, 58 per cent of cyberstalkers were male and 32 per cent female (presumably in some cases, the perpetrator's gender was unknown). WHOA reported that in 2001, cyberstalking began with e-mail messages most often, followed through on message boards and forum messages, but was less frequent in chat rooms. In some cases, cyberstalking develops from a real-world stalking incident and continues over the Internet. However, cyberstalking is also sometimes followed by stalking in the physical world, with all its attendant dangers. According to former United States Attorney General Janet Reno, cyberstalking is often 'a prelude to more serious behavior, including physical violence' (CNN Tech 2000). In 1999, a New Hampshire woman was murdered by the cyberstalker who had threatened her through e-mail messages and indicated through posts on his website that he would kill her.

Stalking and harassment are malicious activities directed at a particular person. They may or may not be deemed criminal activities, depending on the jurisdiction. But when these activities are committed via computers, all jurisdictions may not be able to prosecute them. This poses a serious challenge to every domestic criminal law even if it is updated to cover cybercrimes. The passing of derogatory or offensive remarks about one's gender, race, religious belief, nationality and sexual orientation come under the purview of cyberbullying, which is a common type of cybercrime the world over. The United States and European countries face it as a major cyber problem and they also have laws to punish those who consistently harass someone on the Internet. Cyberbullying is also prevalent in the Middle East and Central Asia.

There are a number of simple ways to guard against cyberstalking. One of the most useful precautions is to stay anonymous, rather than have an identifiable online presence: one should use the primary e-mail account only for communicating with people one trusts and set up an anonymous e-mail account, such as Yahoo or Hotmail, to use for all other communications. Setting one's e-mail program's filtering options to prevent delivery of unwanted messages is another way. When choosing an online name, making it different from your real name and gender-neutral could also be a shield. One should not put any identifying details in online profiles. If one becomes the victim of a cyber-stalker, the most effective course of action is to report the offender to one's Internet service provider (ISP). Should that option be impossible, or ineffective, the best thing to do is to change one's own ISP and all online names. In India, such issues are covered under Sections 66 and 67 of the Information Technology Act, 2000.

Cyberbullying

This is a very sensitive issue for many countries, since standards and definitions vary widely from place to place.

'Bullying is an attempt to raise oneself up by directly demeaning others; the attacker hopes to improve his social status or self esteem by putting others down' (Fertik and Thompson 2010). The term cyberbullying typically refers to online abuses. Discussions about cyberbullying generally revolve around children of school-going age and often call on schools to address the issue. The term bullying in the physical world tends to describe conduct that occurs when someone uses force or coercion to control another person. Such behaviour is seen to be habitual. It can involve tormenting, threatening, harassing, humiliating, embarrassing or otherwise targeting a victim (Lipton 2011).

3.2.3. Computer Sabotage Offences

This type of cybercrime covers crime which affects the security, integrity, confidentiality and reliability of information on computer systems. It includes all unauthorized access and unauthorized modifications.

Unauthorized Access to Computer Systems

Crimes surrounding unauthorized access to computer systems can be divided into two parts: unauthorized access per se and unauthorized access with the intention to commit another crime. In early 2009, some ghost hackers from China were revealed to have compromised 1,295 computers belonging to embassies, banks, news agencies across the world and NATO (Information Warfare Monitor 2009 and Information Warfare Monitor and Shadowserver Foundation 2010). They also managed to hack the computers used by the

Tibetan government in exile at Dharamshala. This type of crime covers the famous 'hacking' and 'cracking' crimes where a person who is unauthorized to enter a particular computer system does so. It also covers the unauthorized interception of data.

Unauthorized Modification

The crime of unauthorized modification is a serious one since it affects the integrity and availability of the computer system. It is exemplified clearly in most terrorist attempts to ruin the critical infrastructure of a particular nation. Viruses are also usual tools in this sort of crime. Modifications can be made by changing, adding or deleting data on the computer system. They can either be temporary or permanent. Singapore law provides for two years' imprisonment for this particular crime.

3.3. CONCLUSION

This chapter discusses the various types of cybercrime. The idea is to make the reader familiar with the various ways in which the security of information and information systems can be compromised. The next few chapters discuss the techniques used in cybercrime.

SECTION II

THREATS AND METHODS

Safety is something a lot of people learn by accident.

◄ FOUR ►

SPAM METHODS

———————◆•◆•◆———————

Cybercrime has evolved from simple crime techniques to larger scams which target the world's largest corporations and government organizations. Of late, cyberattacks are becoming more sophisticated, targeted and organized. Also, there is an increase in the number of attacks on new classes of devices. The availability of attack tool kits has made anyone capable of cybercrime regardless of computer skills. It is critical to inform users of these threats, and the techniques and methods used. Findings of studies show that malicious activities continue to originate in developing countries, and while targeted attacks on enterprises are on the rise, web-based attacks continue to be favoured attack vectors and readily available malicious code kits only cut out the task of neophyte attackers as they mount their attacks (Symantec Corporation 2010d). As cybercrime matures, so does the cybercriminals' business model. According to Wattanajantra (2008), cybercriminals use increasingly novel and creative methods to victimize businesses and consumers. It was estimated that more than two million new malicious programs, such as viruses, worms and Trojans were in existence and these would increase to more than 20 million by 2008. Research estimated that in early 2007, there were up to 45,000 different botnets involved in cybercrimes (Sullivan 2007). Latest technology trends show an alarming rate at which malware and Trojans are being reinvented and modified every day. Recently, although spam volume has seen a decline, phishing incidents continue to be on the rise. This shows an increase in financial motivation for committing cybercrimes. Criminals have many new tools to choose from. Trojans are lately their weapons of choice. They can use them to build botnets to steal passwords and confidential data; to conduct distributed denial-of-service (DDoS) attacks; and also to encrypt data in order to blackmail he victims. One disturbing feature of today's attacks is the intention to maintaining presence on infected machines. Cybercriminals are using a number of techniques to achieve this goal. Some opt to conduct discrete attacks on target-specific organizations. Writing unique malware for a single target is both time-consuming and difficult to deploy. However once launched, these targeted attacks not only almost always succeed but also usually provide the cybercriminal significant returns on investment, making the targeted attacks small but significant for cybercrime (Kaspersky 2008).

Cybercriminals are not only leveraging new technologies to propagate cybercrime, but are also reinventing forms of social engineering to cleverly ensnare both consumers and businesses (Trend Micro 2008). The methods used in cybercrime include spam, phishing, spear phishing, identity theft, virus or worm, malware, sniffing or spoofing, social engineering or insider threat, hacking, structured query language (SQL) injection, botnets, denial-of-service (DoS) or DDoS attacks and web defacement, to name just a few. I have tried to analyse each method and the ramifications associated with it in the subsequent pages.

4.1. INTRODUCTION TO SPAM

Spam commonly refers to bulk, unsolicited, unwanted and potentially harmful electronic messages. E-mail spam is a significant problem, especially for business houses. Employees need to keep their inboxes clear of junk, and advanced mail filtering systems are a necessity in any business which hopes to use e-mail efficiently. Now, spam is catching up on newer media such as mobile telephony and social networking sites.

Spam is a technique preferred by cybercriminals because of the speed of distribution and delivery and the large number of targets which can be achieved in one go. Trojans are used by cybercriminals to bypass Internet Protocol (IP) block lists, which allow them to send spam using distant locations. To send large volumes of spam, spammers take advantage of geographic areas with large networks of available broadband connections. The majority of spam is sent via botnets, which are nothing but networks of personal computers across the globe. This is one of the major reasons for increase in spam in developing countries having a growing broadband user base with developing infrastructure.

One of the most notable and far-reaching incidents related to spam occurred in November 2008 when the plug was pulled on San Jose-based McColo Corporation—known to be one of the world's most disreputable hosting providers (Trend Micro 2010a). With suspected links to the Russian Business Network (RBN) in St. Petersburg, McColo was believed to have hosted some of the command and control infrastructure for several of the world's largest identified botnets such as Srizbi (Zlob), Mega-D, Rustock, Dedler and Storm, which were in turn controlling hundreds of thousands of zombie computers involved in e-mail spam, spamvertising, malware, child pornography, credit-card theft, fraud and 'get-rich-quick' scams. McColo was known to be unresponsive to complaints about its hosted sites, collecting a premium from criminal operators for turning a blind eye when notified of infractions. Thanks to the efforts of some security researchers who regularly collected data on malicious Internet activity, McColo was finally disconnected from the Internet. Years of investigation culminated in a complete shutdown, eliminating an unbelievable 50–75 per cent of the world's junk e-mail in a single day. Researchers had alerted McColo's upstream Internet service providers (ISPs), Global Crossing and Hurricane Electric, of the purported criminal activities occurring at McColo. After reviewing details of the investigation, the ISPs immediately shut down McColo's Internet connections.

After the McColo incident malicious operators use smaller hosting providers, spread out globally, in an attempt to diversify their operations. In this way they can blend in with Internet noise around the world, making it tough to track the servers and almost impossible to take them down, especially because they share rack space with other, legitimate businesses.

McColo was one of the leading players in the so-called 'bulletproof hosting' market—ISPs that would allow servers to remain online regardless of complaints. At the time of termination of its service in November 2008, it was estimated that McColo customers were responsible for a substantial proportion of all e-mail spam then flowing. When McColo was disconnected from the Internet at 1:23 pm on 11 November 2008, the botnets went offline, resulting in a huge drop in spam levels (about 75 per cent) instantly.

Another noted example of spam is the 'Canadian pharmacy' spam, which accounted for an amazing proportion of spam volume. Pharmacy spam leads unsuspecting users to fake websites that supposedly sell pharmaceuticals but are instead made up of a shifting hyperlink in a spam message, generated by one of the world's biggest botnets.

The Canadian pharmacy spam, rogue antivirus (AV) and other cyber scams are often part of an intricate, highly sophisticated and highly organized business model based on the concept of affiliate marketing. Affiliate networks are essentially a way to distribute and sell products using multilevel marketing (MLM) techniques. Products are sold using independent distributors who build and manage their own sales force by recruiting, motivating, supplying and training others to sell products. The distributors' compensation consists of their own sales and a percentage of the sales of their sales group. In an MLM structure, payouts occur at two or more levels—the worker and the person managing the worker receive a portion of the proceeds. One of the best-known examples of a legitimate, successful MLM company is Amway, which sells a variety of health and beauty products. However, in the case of cybercrime, products sold via MLM techniques, are anything but legitimate—click fraud, credit card details, rogue AV, fake pharmaceuticals—are highly lucrative, nevertheless very much illegal.

Spamit and McColo are two significant cases of spam shutdowns that took place over the last couple of years. Spamit, a notorious spammer, responsible for large volumes of 'pharmacy' mail, shut its operations in 2010. The effect of the McColo shutdown was seen in 2009. These spam shutdowns were a result of organized action. But it does not appear that spam volumes reduced for good. Some retooling and consolidation in the botnet space will once again see spam volumes rise (McAfee Labs 2011b).

Spam volumes have reduced since 2007, but at the same time, attacks on newer devices such as smart phones using the Android operating system are gaining momentum. Mobile malware and threats have been around for some time and it is time they were taken as part of the mobile landscape, both in terms of awareness and deployment.

As per estimates, the volume of junk e-mails flooding inboxes each day has seen as much as a 90 per cent decrease in 2010. Spam volumes hit their highest mark in July 2010, when junk e-mails were blasting in excess of 225 billion spam messages per day, after which it has dropped significantly. Spam volumes now range between 25 and 50 billion messages (McAfee Labs 2011b). Studies from Symantec also show a high-water mark in July 2010 followed by a decrease thereafter (Symantec Corporation 2010d). Anti-spam experts from Ciseo Systems are witnessing a similar decline, from 300 billion per day in June 2010 to just 40 billion per day in June 2011 (Kerbsonsecurity. com 2011).

There may be many reasons for this reduction in spam volume, but the need for organized action and consistent efforts by law enforcement officials and security experts is equally important.

4.2. HOW DOES SPAM WORK?

Spam is rarely sent directly by a company advertising itself. It is usually sent by a 'spammer', a company in the business of distributing unsolicited e-mail. An advertiser enters into an agreement with a spammer, who sends e-mail advertisements to a group of unsuspecting recipients. The cost of spam is far less than postal bulk mailings. An advertiser could spam 10,000 recipients for less than $100 as compared to several thousand dollars for a postal mailing (Nolo.com: http://www.nolo.com/legal-encyclopedia/how-does-spam-work-30013.html).

4.2.1 How Do Spammers Collect E-mail Addresses?

Sometimes spammers may buy the addresses—15 million e-mail addresses can be purchased for as little as $129—or they could obtain them by using software programs known as 'harvesters' that pluck names from websites, newsgroups, or other services in which users identify themselves by their e-mail address. To protect against harvesters of e-mail addresses, some websites use software that 'poisons' the harvester—for example, by generating bogus e-mail addresses or directing the harvester to a non-existent site. The use of poisons, filters and blocking software can be costly and only leads to a never-ending cat-and-mouse game since spammers always attempt to circumvent each new round of anti-spam software (Nolo.com: http://www.nolo.com/legal-encyclopedia/how-does-spam-work-30013.html).

4.3. CLASSIFICATION OF SPAM

Spammers generally lure victims by using social engineering techniques such as exciting purchase offers, lottery tickets, jobs and entertainment. They capitalize on human fears, emotions and desires. The subject of spam varies considerably among countries. The most common topics include jobs, lonely women, drugs, credit offers, diplomas, casinos, newsletters, stocks, horoscopes, phishing, marketing and so on.

The McAfee Threats Report for the first quarter of 2010 (McAfee Labs 2011b) identified 20 common categories to classify spam messages. A brief description is given below.

1. 419 Scam: This is a game of winning one's confidence. By doing so the criminal tries to extort money from victims who willingly give it up because of a tragic story or the promise of a reward. Some formal-looking documentation usually completes the process. These types of messages often come from hosts that provide free e-mail accounts, but we see an increasing trend of these messages coming from infected hosts as well.

2. Adult Products: These spam mails advertise pornography, usually DVD movies or download sites. By volume, pornography is not as large a part of the spam world as most people think, but the effect of a single pornographic e-mail on the recipient is exponentially greater than other types of spam, and the chance of it generating a complaint is greater still.

3. Casinos: These e-mails advertise online casinos. They are often associated with botnet activity and require victims to download and install software to play the games.

4. Diplomas: These are sites offering fake diplomas, where clients can request forged documents that 'prove' they have graduated from a certain school. These are not legitimate academic institutions and do not represent actual education. These are often associated with botnet activity.

5. Delivery Status Notification (DSN): They are also called non-delivery receipts (NDRs). These messages may be legitimate, but usually they are spam that bounce back to a forged sender address. Higher ratios of DSN messages could indicate larger volumes of individually maintained e-mail servers.

6. Drugs: This category includes the faux Canadian pharmaceutical spam that are generally hosted in China, 'açai-berry' spam, dietary supplements and so on. These messages are usually associated with

botnet activity, but can also come from hosted web farms that send mail into some other country.

7. Jobs: Many are a form of 419 scams or confidence scams. They victimize the unemployed or under employed and extract money from them through cheque frauds or entice them to launder money or perform activities of questionable legality.

8. Lists: These offer contact lists, such as a list of doctors or dentists, in the recipients' area.

9. Lonely Women: This is very often a kind of a confidence scam. The criminals (probably men pretending to be women) try to get money from victims for plane tickets, customs, food, travel or other expenses. The Russian-bride spam is the most common form of this.

10. Lotteries: These spam may read like this: 'Your e-mail address has been randomly selected from our database to get bags of cash; you just have to send us $3,000 to handle the processing'. This is another form of confidence scam.

11. Malware: This spam includes anything that comes with a virus or Trojan attachment or that urges you to visit an infected website. 'UPS tracking number' and 'Conficker.B Infection Alert' are common examples.

12. Marketing: This implies advertising or selling a product to a recipient who has opted for receiving messages. An example of this is an airline or travel agency sending a list of deals to the recipient. These e-mails are first-party advertising, meaning that recipients should know why they are getting the e-mail. These are different from third-party advertising.

13. Newsletters: This type of spam consists of an informational e-mail that recipients sign up for. A newsletter probably does not sell products directly, but often urges customers with fancy wording and flashy text, for instance an alert from a news company or updates from discussion lists.

14. Phishing: This includes any e-mail that begins the process of extracting personal information from a victim. Banking alerts that require recipients' usernames and passwords are the leading examples.

15. Products: These are any unsolicited spam mail that tries to sell manufactured goods (usually replica purses or jewellery). These mails are

not from a legitimate company and are often associated with botnet activity.

16. Social Networking Sites (SNS): These spam mails are generated by social networking sites and sent to their subscribers. Such sites often send unsolicited e-mails to a user's entire address book, usually without alerting the subscriber. Although such spam-like behaviour is undesirable, our (McAfee Lab's) data collections make no distinction between solicited or unsolicited social networking e-mails.

17. Software: This attempts to sell original equipment manufacturer (OEM) licences as individual licences or attempts to sell hacked or cracked copies of software at heavily discounted prices.

18. Stocks/Shares: These are a part of a 'pump and dump' stock scheme. Someone buys penny stocks and then sends out a bunch of spam that creates a false demand, allowing the spammer to sell the stock for a profit.

19. Third Parties: These lie between marketing and products spam. The company at one end of the spam mails is legitimate, and the recipients have probably inadvertently opted in to allowing partner advertisers to send them mail. E-mail lists can also be purchased from companies that are going out of business or in some cases the privacy statements may allow companies to sell customer e-mail addresses. Free t-shirts, insurance offers and medical devices are all common examples. These spam are often sent from hosting facilities in foreign countries, which makes it more difficult for the victims to complain. Such spammers subscribe to the letter of the United States statute called the Controlling the Assault of Non-Solicited Pornography And Marketing Act, 2003 (CAN-SPAM Act), but completely subvert its intentions by using anonymous domains, malformed and misspelled words and embedded hidden text blocks.

20. Watches: This easily distinguishable message[1] is the most common form of product spam.

---

[1] Easily distinguishable message: Some of the most popular fonts used by designers, scanning for Content Types in a MIME Formatted Message, the patient ID, and that ID has a pattern that is readily distinguishable. Ads for fake designer goods including watches have always been common in spam, especially in the build-up to Christmas and the New Year.

Spam is created in a variety of different styles and with varied complexities. Some spam is plain text with a uniform resource locator (URL) and some is cluttered with images and/or attachments. Some comes with very little in terms of text, perhaps only a URL. It should also be noted that spam is distributed in a variety of different languages. It is quite common for spam to contain random text added to messages. This is done in an attempt to thwart spam filters that typically try to deduce spam based on a database of words that are frequently repeated in spam messages. Any automated process to classify spam into one of the categories above would need to overcome this issue. For example, the word 'watch' may appear in the random text included in a pharmaceutical spam message, posing a challenge as to classify the message as pharmaceutical spam or in the watches category. Another challenge occurs when a pharmaceutical spam contains no obvious pharmaceutical-related words, but only an image and a URL. Spammers use a variety of ways to get past the automated anti-spam techniques. Spam detection services often resist classifying spam into different categories because it is difficult to do (for the reasons above). The purpose of spam detection is usually to determine whether the message is spam and whether to block it or not, rather than to identify its subject matter. In order to overcome the ambiguity faced by using automated techniques to classify spam, most companies prefer to have a real person classify unknown spam manually. Though time consuming, the results are much more accurate. An analyst can read the message, understand the context of the e-mail, view images, follow URLs and view websites in order to gather the bigger picture around the spam message (Symantec Corporation 2010a).

Spammers try to ensure that their botnets are not concentrated in one country or region, but are spread across different parts of the world. It is expected that spam will become more culturally and linguistically diverse as emerging economies begin to experience increased economic growth and broadband usage.

According to another report, most of the spam is in English. This shows that the spammers still prefer English. The same report also indicates that out of every four spam attachments, three are malicious in nature (Symantec Corporation 2010a).

4.4. SPAM AND BOTNETS

There is a correlation between botnets and spam due to changes in spamming techniques in the last few years. Attackers find it convenient to tie up with spammers so that they can use their e-mail lists to send mass quantities of spam—which often contain other malware as an e-mail attachment—through botnets. For example, the second most common malicious code family reported between January and June 2006, 'Bomka', was a Trojan download-able from a link provided in a spam e-mail that used social engineering tech-niques to persuade the user, stating that the link was the site of a video clip. The problem of spam and malware is also cyclical and self-sustaining. Information systems compromised by malware are used to distribute spam. A proportion of the spam so distributed is designed to spread malware to new victims, whose information systems are then used to perpetrate further mali-cious activities online (OECD 2008a).

With the convergence of spam and malware, a growing proportion of spam messages are moving away from these more direct scams. Sending out malicious attachments continues to be widely practised, but even more preva-lent is the mailing of links to poisoned web pages. Operating in the same man-ner as any other scam, victims are tricked into clicking a link in a mail which leads them to a site that attacks their system with exploits (Sophos 2011).

These examples of the three internet companies—Atrivo, ESTDomains, McColo—prove that the security community working together can severely disrupt cybercriminals' activities on a global scale (Sophos 2009). Indeed, the shutting down of McColo has had more of an impact on global spam levels (even if temporarily) than any hacker arrest by the authorities has ever achieved.

The shutdown of McColo especially affected Srizbi, the world's largest botnet, with around 500,000 infected nodes. The botnet was reported to be capable of sending around 60 billion spam messages in a day. This was more than half of the global total of 100 billion messages then being at the time. Spamhaus.org reportedly finds roughly 1.5 million computers, infected with either the Srizbi or Rustock botnet, sending spam in an average week (Krebs 2008).

There are hundreds of affiliates that operate 'pay-per-install' or 'installs for cash' programs, in which a criminal organization enlists an army of workers to drive traffic to malware-serving websites. These workers are then paid a commission for every 'install achieved'. By using affiliate marketing, crime leaders distribute tasks and responsibilities amongst a wide network of workers, increasing their reach and their ability to contact consumers. Additionally, these networks keep the criminal organizations, or the brains of the operation, away from the day-to-day work, to minimize the risk of being caught.

The rogue antivirus software is perhaps the most prevalent today in the world of cyber scams. It encompasses several classes of scam software—usually with limited or no benefits—and is sold to consumers using unethical marketing practices. Queries for normal search terms lead unsuspecting parties to legitimate websites that have been compromised as part of a plot to manipulate search engine results. When predetermined keywords are searched, victims encounter fake web pages—some of which have been booby-trapped with malicious content—that redirect them to a scareware page that may read something like this: 'Your computer is running slower than normal, maybe it is infected with viruses, adware or spyware.'

One is then prompted to download fake antivirus programs. Rogue antivirus programs are usually Trojans or other malware disguised as files to protect a computer. This selling approach is designed to cause shock, anxiety or the perception of a threat, generally directed at an unsuspecting user. Cybercriminals may also use spam to convince persons that a virus has infected their computer, suggesting that they download (and pay for) antivirus software to erase it. Usually the virus is entirely fictitious and the software is non-functional or a malware.

These cybercriminal ventures are amazingly lucrative, with profits now aggregating to millions per year. In some countries, spam is treated just like any other business and spammers do not understand why the rest of the world sees spam as a nuisance when, to them, it is simply business (Trend Micro 2010a).

4.5. HOW TO PROTECT AGAINST SPAM

- Do not provide anyone with your e-mail address unless it is absolutely necessary.
- Do not get lured by contests paying you huge amounts of money or benefits.

- Spammers can obtain addresses from forums, white page sites, chat rooms, and bulletin boards. Try not to distribute or post your e-mail everywhere on the Internet.
- Do not forward chain letters. Spammers collect e-mail addresses from them.
- Do not unsubscribe from spam. Spam often contains an unsubscribe link. Clicking on this link will bring you even more spam. (Akner 2010)

FIVE

MALWARE TOOLS

———•◦•———

In God we trust. All others, we virus scan...

—Author unknown

Malware is a general term for a piece of software inserted into an information system to cause harm to that system or other systems, or to subvert them for use other than that intended by their owners. In short it is 'malicious software' designed to carry out annoying or harmful actions or to damage or carry out other unwanted actions on a computer system. In Spanish, 'mal' is a prefix that means 'bad', making the term 'bad ware'. Malware can gain remote access to an information system, record and send data from that system to a third party without the user's permission or knowledge, conceal the fact that the information system has been compromised, disable security measures, damage the information system and otherwise affect the data and system integrity.

'Trust is essential to business, security just gets in the way.'

Ronald Reagan said, 'Trust ... but verify.'[1]

[1] Trust, but verify is a form of advice given which recommends that while a source of information might be considered reliable, one should perform additional research to verify that such information is accurate, or trustworthy. The term was a signature phrase adopted and made famous by U.S. President Ronald Reagan. Reagan frequently used it when discussing U.S. relations with the Soviet Union. The phrase was originated by Russian leader Vladimir Lenin.

Benito Mussolini said, 'It's good to trust others but, not to do so is much better.'[2]

CIFAS, a United Kingdom-based fraud-prevention service defines malware as:

> Malware is malicious software that infects a victim's computer. It can capture private information stored on an individual's computer and send it to fraudsters, who can use that information to impersonate the individual and commit fraud. Malware can also hijack your web browser, redirect your search engine attempts, bombard your screen with pop-up advertisements and even monitor your web activity. Most malware programs will reinstall themselves even after you think they have been removed. (CIFAS 2010)

Malware is commonly described as viruses, worms, Trojan horses, back doors, keystroke loggers, root kits or spyware. These terms correspond to the functionality and behaviour of the malware (for example, a virus is self-propagating, a worm is self-replicating and so on).

A virus is a program, which once inserted into another program, spreads destructive program routines that could destroy the contents of the memory, hard disks and other storage devices. It is usually an executable program that 'infects' computer files, by inserting a copy of itself into the file. A virus program code cannot work without being inserted into another program—for instance, 'Melissa', 'I Love You'. A worm, on the other hand, is a distinct program that can run unaided also; for example, Code Red, Nimda.

A Trojan horse is a harmful piece of software that looks legitimate. Users are typically tricked into loading and executing it on their computers. Adware and spyware are two more forms that an antivirus can tackle. Adware, or advertising-supported software, is any software package which automatically plays, displays or downloads advertisements to a computer after the software is installed on it or while the application is being used. Spyware is a type of malware that is installed on computers and collects little bits of information about users without their knowledge.

Experts usually group malware into two categories: 'family' and 'variant'. 'Family' refers to the distinct or original piece of malware, while

---

[2] It is the quote of Benito Mussolini who was great dictator of Italy. It is the English translation of famous Italian proverb.

'variant' refers to a different version of the original malicious code or family, with minor changes. Over the last 20 years, malware has evolved from occasional 'exploits' to a global multimillion-dollar criminal industry (OECD 2008a).

5.1. MALWARE: A BRIEF HISTORY

Viruses and worms date back to the early days of computers when most viruses were created just for fun and worms to perform maintenance on computer systems. Malicious viruses did not surface until the 1980s. In 1986, 'Brain' appeared and propagated when the user 'booted up' her computer from a floppy disc. Two years later, in 1988, the Morris worm received significant media attention and affected over 6,000 computers. Although other types of malicious software appeared in the mid-1980s, the landscape of the late 1980s and early 1990s predominantly consisted of viruses. Until about 1999, most people associated viruses with mere instances of teenagers trying to hack into the Pentagon's systems, as seen in the 1983 movie 'Wargames'. It was only during the mid-1990s that the scenario began to change with the growth of the Internet and personal computer usage, the rise in social networking and the adoption of electronic mail systems. The so-called 'big impact worms' began to reach the public in novel ways. The increased use of e-mail brought high-profile mass-mailer worms such as Melissa (1999), 'I Love You' (2000), 'Anna Kournikova' (2001), 'SoBig' (2003) and 'Mydoom' (2004) into the limelight. They made the headlines and entered the public consciousness. These types of worms doubled their number of victims every one or two hours, rapidly reaching peak activity within 12–18 hours of being released. This marked a parallel rise in organized, sometimes coordinated attacks. The explosive growth of online financial transactions resulted in increased security incidents and in the appearance of new types of malicious software and attacks. Today, mass worms and virus outbreaks are becoming scarce while stealthy malware such as Trojans and back doors are on the rise. Many of the attacks are on a small scale mainly to stay 'below the radar' of the security and law enforcement communities. The goals of the attackers are financial gains. These new trends help explain why malware is now a booming business? (OECD 2008a).

It is important to note that not all spam contains malware and it is often difficult to determine how much spam directly contains it. Manual analysis conducted by the Information and Communication Security Technology Center (ICST) in Chinese Taipei over the course of two years, on 417 suspect e-mails, found that of those, 287 (68 per cent) contained malware attachments (OECD 2008b).

5.1.1. The Morris Worm, 1988

The Morris worm, named after its creator Robert Tappan Morris, then a student at the Cornell University, emerged even before most people knew there was an Internet. It was created not to cause any disruption but to measure the size of the Internet by propagating itself across the network. One of its side effects was that it slowed computers down to the point of becoming redundant. It affected about 6,000 computers, which were around 10 per cent of all the computers using the Internet in those days. This was quite a high number for that time.

The worm was created by Robert Morris in 1988. Morris was studying at the Massachusetts Institute of Technology (MIT) at that time and although this program was not intended to be a virus, it halted the working of all the computers it went into. He is now an associate professor in the same university. He sent the virus making it look as if it was sent by the MIT. The virus exploited weaknesses in passwords, in Unix and 'finger' and took advantage of the exploits in Unix's sendmail, fingerd, rsh/rexec and so on. The 'finger' program was a utility that allowed users to obtain information about other users, while the sendmail program was a mailer designed to route mail in a heterogeneous internetwork. The actions of the Internet worm exposed some specific security flaws in standard services provided by Berkeley Software Distribution (BSD–derived versions of Unix, and only affected Digital Equipment Corporation's (DEC's) 'VAX' (Virtual Address eXtension[3]) and Sun Microsystems's 'Sun 3' systems. The worm had a design flaw. The critical error that transformed it from a potentially harmless intellectual exercise into a virulent denial-of-service attack was its spreading mechanism. This incident

---

[3] Virtual Address eXtension (VAX) was an instruction set architecture (ISA) developed by Digital Equipment Corporation (DEC) in the mid-1970s.

however, motivated the world to think seriously about information security. During the Morris appeal process, the United States Court of Appeals estimated the cost of removing the virus from each installation to be in the range of $200–$53,000 (Hafner and Markoff 1991).

5.2. BROAD CHARACTERISTICS OF MALWARE

Although it is not the only means by which information systems can be compromised, malware provides attackers convenience, ease of use and the automation necessary to conduct attacks on a scale that was previously inconceivable (OECD 2008a).

Malware is multifunctional and modular. There are many kinds of malware that can be used together or separately to achieve a malicious person's goal. New features and additional capabilities can be easily added to malware to alter and 'improve' its functionality and impact. Malware can insert itself into a system, compromise the system, and then download additional malware from the Internet that provides increased functionality. It can be used to control an entire host or network, it can bypass security measures such as firewalls and antivirus software and it can use encryption to avoid detection or conceal its means of operation.

Malware is available online at a nominal cost, thus making it possible for almost anyone to acquire. There is even a robust underworld market for its sale and purchase. Furthermore, it is user-friendly and provides attackers with a capability to launch sophisticated attacks otherwise beyond their skill level. Malware is persistent and efficient. It is increasingly difficult to detect and remove and is effective at defeating built-in information security countermeasures. Some forms of malware can defeat strong forms of multi-factor authentication while others have been able to undermine the effectiveness of digital certificates. Malware can affect a range of devices because it is nothing more than a piece of software. It can affect devices such as personal computers (PCs) or personal digital assistants (PDAs) or servers across different types of networks. All these devices, including the routers that allow traffic to move across the Internet to other end points, are potentially vulnerable to malware attacks. Malware is part of a broader cyberattack system. It is used both as a primary form of cyberattack and to support other forms of malicious activity and cybercrimes such as spam and phishing. Conversely, spam and phishing can be used to further distribute malware.

Malware is no longer just a fun game for script kiddies[4] or a field of study for researchers. Today, it is a serious business and source of revenue for malicious individuals and criminals all over the world. Malware, together with other cyber tools and techniques, provides a low-cost, reusable method of conducting highly lucrative forms of cybercrime.

Viruses can cause havoc on a computer's hard drive by deleting files or directory information. Spyware can gather data from a user's system without the user knowing it. This can include anything from the web pages a user visits to personal information, such as credit-card numbers.

5.2.1. The Melissa Virus, 1999

A 30-year-old man launched the email computer virus known as 'Melissa' on 26 March 1999, a Friday. Named after a topless dancer from Florida, the virus spread rapidly around the world over the weekend, swamping the e-mail systems of thousands of computers including those at government agencies. Melissa targeted users of Microsoft Outlook and spread over the Internet like fire. The virus came in the form of an e-mail, usually containing the subject line 'Important Message,' and appeared to be from a friend or colleague. The body of the e-mail message said, 'Here is that document you asked for ... don't show it to anyone else.' It had a winking smiley face formed by punctuation marks. Attached to the message was a Microsoft Word document file. If the user opened that file, the virus dug into the user's address book and sent infected documents to the first 50 addresses.

Investigators traced the origin of the virus to a New Jersey resident, David L. Smith (Beer 1999). The virus was reported to have caused 80 million dollars worth of damage in North America alone and about $1.1 billion worldwide. Some estimates say at least 100,000 computers were infected and 300

---

[4] Script kiddie refers to an inexperienced malicious actor who uses programs developed by others to attack computer systems and deface websites. It is generally assumed that script kiddies are kids who lack the ability to write sophisticated hacking programs on their own and that their objective is to try to impress their friends or gain credit in underground cracker communities (OECD 2008a).

organizations reported infections by it. As per the United States Department of Defense (DoD) fund and Computer Emergency Response Team (CERT) claims, 233 organizations and 81,285 computers had Melissa infections and one site reported receiving 32,000 copies of mail messages containing Melissa on its systems within 45 minutes. Several antivirus software makers posted patches on their websites that detected and rejected the Melissa virus (Richard 1999).

5.3. HOW MALWARE WORKS

A virus might attach itself to a program such as a spreadsheet program. Each time the spreadsheet program runs, the virus runs too, and it has the chance to reproduce (by attaching to other programs) or wreak havoc. An e-mail virus travels as an attachment to e-mail messages, and usually replicates itself by automatically mailing itself to dozens of people in the victim's e-mail address book. Some e-mail viruses do not even require a 'double-click'—they launch the moment the infected message is viewed in the preview pane of the client's e-mail software.

Although malware can attack in multiple ways, the technology (spyware, Trojan, root kit) and the attack vector (fake software, e-mail attachments, direct hacking) remain the same.

Here are a few instances of how malware works.

5.3.1. Trojan Horse

Trojan horse malware is a classic example of a 'malicious' social engineering technique. It gets its name from the ancient tale of the huge wooden horse that the Greeks constructed and left at the gates of Troy as a gift. Today's Trojan horse also works by bypassing security defences. For instance, a user downloads a calculator program and installs it. The calculator works fine. In a few days the user starts to have problems with her computer and when she browses the Internet, she starts getting annoying pop-ups. The malicious 'pop-up' program was most likely hidden away inside the calculator program. The installation also may have implanted itself inside programs that already existed on the computer. This makes it all the more difficult to remove it.

5.3.2. The Trojan Hydraq, 2010

Trojan Hydraq, also known as 'Aurora', was first discovered on 11 January 2010, when it was used as part of a targeted attack, likely in an attempt to gain access to a corporate network and steal confidential information. Hydraq entered computers via e-mail attachments or was downloaded via malicious websites. It allowed attackers to compromise systems by exploiting a zero-day vulnerability in the client-side software. Once executed, the Trojan installed a back door that allowed an attacker to control the computer and perform a variety of compromising actions which included modifying, executing and deleting files; executing malicious files; and most importantly, gaining access to the compromised corporation's network—which then opened up the target to additional attacks. As with other common Trojans, Hydraq would attempt to remotely contact its command and control server via a number of uniform resource locators (URLs) in order to receive updates and further instructions (Symantec Corporation 2011c).

The motivation of the virus was to take control of corporate networks and steal confidential and sensitive information from corporations. The number of infections from Hydraq was limited due to the nature of the targeted attacks—only a small number of corporations were targeted since attackers preferred to avoid attracting attention by limiting their attacks and, thus, remained concealed in a small volume of computers for as long as possible, rather than risk exposing themselves by compromising too many systems at once. The Trojan Hydraq thwarted antivirus sensors because it contained an obfuscation technique called 'spaghetti code' in which blocks of codes of the Trojan are rearranged to avoid detection. However, once a targeted attack is discovered, it becomes less effective due to increased awareness and the adoption of increased security measures, such as updating patches and sanitizing infected machines. As such, the life of Hydraq was short-lived, peaking in January 2010 and subsequently tapering off after February 2010.

5.3.3. Root Kit in E-mail Attachment

Let us take another example. A user's friend sends her a funny video. When she opens it he gets a security warning, but nevertheless she wants to see it. So she proceeds to get past the warning. However, nothing happens and the user thinks nothing of it. Later when she meets her friend, she comes to know that her friend did not send her any such video. What actually happened in the background when she clicked on the video was that malware was installed. There is no way one can find out the intent of such attacks. One may not even notice anything. The computer could be used as a botnet drone to attack websites or other computers.

Spyware is the name given to a specific type of malware that can be installed on computers. It collects little bits of information about users at any given time—without their knowledge. Spyware programs can collect various types of personal information, such as Internet-surfing habits, including sites that have been visited. It can also interfere with a user's control of the computer, such as installing additional software and redirecting web-browser activity.

In case of spyware, when one clicks on a link in search results and click on the download, one immediately starts getting pop-ups. One may close the pages but still get weird errors. One may think nothing harmful can come of it since one simply 'drove by' the website and never installed anything. However the computer might have had a software flaw that let the website install spyware without the owner's permission. There was no warning because of the flaw in the programming of the web browser. There is a possibility that spyware is now resident on the system. Information on what one types in web forms, login pages, chat and the sites one visits could all be sent to the hacker's website.

Cybercrooks manipulate search results from search engines such as Google, Bing and Yahoo to lure victims to their malicious pages. Once a victim is lured to the desired webpage, they are redirected to rogue or poisoned sites. Through these sites, cybercriminals infect users' machines with malware or push fake goods and services to users while attempting to steal personal information.

5.3.4. The Zeus Family

The rapidly growing Zeus family is a classic example of one of the biggest increases in malicious URLs and websites. Zeus' ease of use and prevalence among cybercriminals has proved that there has been a distinct shift to truly malicious servers using automated domain registration practices. Once a Zeus machine is tracked it is easy to find dozens more. In one particular case, a Zeus command server which was identified yielded another 160 malicious domains carrying on everything from social networking to media sharing infections and other credential phishing activities. According to McAfee Threats Report: First Quarter 2010 (McAfee 2010a), the Zeus URLs are found primarily in the United States, with around 40 per cent in Europe alone.

The Zeus malware kit is primarily designed to steal users' online banking login credentials. It is made up of many, many small botnets linked by their use of the same crimeware. Zeus has proliferated partly due to the availability of Zeus toolkits, which allow cybercriminals to rapidly create Zeus variants in a matter of minutes. It is the handiwork of organized criminals from eastern Europe that has now entered the underworld cybercriminal market as a commodity (Trend Micro 2010b). Zeus may arrive as an attachment or link in a spammed message or be unknowingly downloaded via compromised websites. Most Zeus botnets target bank-related websites.

5.4. MALWARE TRENDS

According to McAfee (McAfee Labs 2011b) the volume of malware is showing an increasing trend. In December 2010 the figures were well above the 50 million mark. According to another report, 95,000 malware pieces were reported every day in 2010, nearly double the number of malware pieces tracked in 2009 (Sophos 2011). This implies that one unique file was being analysed every 0.9 seconds, 24 hours a day, each day of the year. This is a clear indication that the malware threat is continuing to grow at an alarming rate. The functionality and sophistication of malwares has constantly been on the rise. Hackers are not just producing malware for notoriety—they are producing it for large financial gains.

Over the last decade, there has been a proliferation of malware. Today, estimates of the number of known computer threats such as viruses, worms, Trojans, exploits, back doors, password stealers, spyware and other variations of potentially unwanted software range in the millions.

Ever since criminal malware developers began using client and server polymorphism (the ability for malware to dynamically create different forms of itself), it has become increasingly difficult to exactly identify how many threat variants there are. Polymorphism implies that there can be as many threat variants as the infected computers can produce. According to a Microsoft study in 2011, about 50,000 different and unique threat families were reported (Microsoft Corporation 2011). Many of these reported families were duplicates or polymorphic versions of the key threat families.

India has also experienced a surge in malicious activity recently. Malicious activity generally tends to increase in countries experiencing rapid growth in broadband infrastructure and connectivity, and right now India's broadband infrastructure and user base is growing steadily.

Trojans are the favourite cyber weapon of cybercriminals. Data-stealing and generic Trojan malware is typically designed to send information from the infected machine, control it, and open back doors on it. Traditional viruses come next in terms of malware. Even though viruses may seem like a thing of the past, recent cases of their revival stem from the appearance of a few but highly active families with new variants aimed at infecting a large number of users. New viruses such as 'Sality' or 'Viking' have Trojanlike features and are capable of stealing user information. Worms are the third most detected malware (The Slammer Worm, http://www.spamlaws.com/slammer-worm.html).

5.4.1. The Slammer Worm, 2003

The Slammer worm, more commonly known as the SQL Slammer worm, was infamous for its denial-of-service (DoS) attack on various Internet hosts. The attack, which occurred on 25 January 2003 at 5:30 pm, infected more than 75,000 machines within 10 minutes. Despite the name, the Slammer worm did not use the SQL language as its method of exploitation. Instead, it exploited a buffer overflow condition in the Microsoft-branded structured query language (SQL) server and other database products.

The Internet Storm Center (The Slammer Worm, http://www.spamlaws. com/slammer-worm.html) and other sites monitoring Internet traffic reported significant performance issues throughout the globe, similar to the impact of the 'Code Red Worm' that struck in 2001. Yonhap (http://www.spamlaws. com/slammer-worm.html), a news agency in South Korea, reported that several Internet services worldwide were shut down for sometime on 25 January 2003. The Slammer worm was also detected throughout most of North America, Asia and Europe. The overall impact was somewhat mitigated by the fact that the worm struck over the weekend.

The exploitation of the Microsoft SQL server desktop engine (MSDE) substantially increased the number of infected systems. This, combined with the fact that many home PC users were unaware of MSDE's presence, essentially worsened the impact.

According to several analysts the propagation of the worm followed an exponential path with a doubling rate of 8.5 seconds in the earlier stages of the attack. This was contained only because of the failure of several networks due to the DoS attack caused by Slammer's traffic. A router is designed to delay or temporarily halt traffic when it becomes too much to handle. The Slammer worm caused these routers to crash instead, forcing neighbouring routers to remove them from their routing table. This process spread from router to router, causing the flooding of multiple routing tables, which eventually caused other routers to fail. The routers were soon restarted, announcing their status and sparking another wave of updates in various routing tables. Shortly thereafter, large portions of Internet bandwidth were consumed as the routers were in constant communication with one another, trying to update their tables. Since the Slammer worm was small in size, it was able to get through the network, bringing the Internet to a standstill.

The Slammer worm was more of a network scare than a threat to personal users. Home computers typically were not vulnerable to infection unless they had MSDE installed on their system. The Slammer worm was so small that it contained no code allowing it to be written to a hard disk. This meant that it had to stay resident in the memory, making the infection fairly easy to remove. Symantec Corporation and several other security vendors offered free utilities that effectively remove the worm. Slammer had spread across the globe in 30 minutes. While nothing was actually destroyed by this attack, the revenue lost was estimated to be around one billion dollars (Moore et al. 2005). South Korea was the hardest hit, where 27 million people lost Internet and cell-phone usage. In Australia, the American Express website had to be closed for several hours and Bank of America customers were unable to use 13,000 automated teller machines. The United States had the most traffic and several businesses and government agencies were negatively affected.

The growing use of Internet infrastructure and broadband has led to a significant increase in malicious activities across all countries. The easy availability of resources, highly skilled professionals and a prosperous society are other factors for most cybercrimes. It is for these reasons that developed countries such as the United States and European nations show high instances of cybercrime both as a source and a destination. Countries which mastermind cybercrimes use highly sophisticated techniques like SQL injection, phishing and Trojans for financial gains. Growing economies such as India are used as a medium because of the vast pool of computers. Botnets through these countries are also the origin of minor cybercriminal incidents such as identity thefts for individual financial gains.

The frequency with which a link is clicked is an indication of the success of using shortened URLs that lead to malicious websites. These shortened URLs are observed more on social networking sites and lead to attack toolkits when clicked. A favoured method to distribute an attack from a compromised profile is to post links to malicious websites from that profile so that they appear in the news feeds of the victim's friends. The use of shortened URLs for this purpose specifically helps because the actual destination of the link is obscured from the user.

According to a Trend Micro report, most malicious websites are seen to be in the adult entertainment category. Education is another industry that has been hit hard by infections. This has probably been due to a large number of students using old and out-of-date software and security, and possibly visiting suspect websites (Trend Micro 2010b).

Let us examine some cases.

5.4.2. The Koobface Worm, 2008

A malware that uses social networking sites to infect users in a concerted attack is a threat. Current variants of the Koobface worm can not only send direct messages from an infected user's account on a site to all of that user's friends in the network but are also capable of updating status messages or adding text to profile pages (Koobface Facebook Trojan on the March Again, http://www.webologist.co.uk/internet-security/koobface-facebook-trojan-on-the-march-again). Moreover, in addition to possibly giving attackers access to an infected user's social networking site account, some threats could also infect the user's computer. The Koobface worm attempts to download fake antivirus applications onto the compromised computers. These threats are a concern for network administrators because many users access their social networks from computers at workplaces.

Koobface cybercriminals have also been known to encrypt their command and control communications to avoid being monitored and taken down by security researchers and the authorities.

The first version of the Koobface worm was detected in December 2008 and a more potent version appeared in March 2009. The main intention of the Koobface worm was to gather login information for File Transfer Protocol

(FTP) sites, Facebook and other social media platforms, but not any sensitive financial data. It used compromised computers to build a peer-to-peer botnet. A compromised computer would then contact other compromised computers to receive commands in a peer-to-peer fashion. The botnet was used to install additional 'pay-per-install' malware on the compromised computer, as well as hijack search queries to display advertisements. Its peer-to-peer topology was also used in showing fake messages to other users with the purpose of expanding the botnet.

5.4.3. The Stuxnet Worm, 2010

Another interesting case to examine is that of the Stuxnet worm. First spotted in June 2010, Stuxnet was a new kind of worm aimed at industrial control computers running software from the Germany company Siemens (*Business Week* 2010; Matrosov, Rodionov et al. 2011). Its robust capabilities and a high concentration of infections in Iran led to speculation by security researchers in Germany and the United States that it had been created by a nation state—the United States or Israel being the most likely candidates—and was aimed at sabotaging Iran's nuclear programme.

The worm initially spread via Microsoft Windows, and targeted Siemens' industrial software and equipment. While it was not the first time that hackers had targeted industrial systems, it was the first discovered malware that spied on and subverted industrial systems, as well as the first to include a programmable logic controller (PLC) root kit.

The worm initially spreads indiscriminately, but includes a highly specialized malware payload that is designed to target only Siemens supervisory control and data acquisition (SCADA) systems that are configured to control and monitor specific industrial processes.

Variants of Stuxnet targeted five Iranian organizations, with the probable target widely suspected to be the uranium enrichment infrastructure in Iran. Symantec noted in August 2010 that 60 per cent of the infected computers worldwide were in Iran (Fildes 2010; Symantec 2010). Siemens stated on 29 November 2010 that the worm had not caused any damage to its customers, but the Iran nuclear programme, which uses embargoed Siemens equipment procured clandestinely, had been damaged by Stuxnet (CBS News 2010; 'An Overview of the Industrial Worm Called StuxNet', http://embeddedsw.net/doc/Stuxnet_white_paper.html).

5.4.4. The Conficker Worm, 2008

Conficker, also known as 'Downup', 'Downadup' and 'Kido', was a computer worm that targeted the Microsoft Windows operating system (Microsoft Corporation 2012a). First detected in November 2008, it made use of the flaws in the Windows software and launched dictionary attacks on administrator passwords to propagate, while forming a botnet. It was unusually difficult to counter this worm because of its combined use of many advanced malware techniques. At its peak, the Conficker had infected an estimated seven million government, business and home computers spread across more than 200 countries, making it a large worm infection.

The motivation behind it was to mobilize a large number of compromised or infected computers into a kind of peer-to-peer network. This would allow the perpetrators to run malicious applications on them. The conficker worm was also known to piggyback with anti-virus products offered free for download at some websites. However, in reality, the antivirus carried malware and spyware with it and once the user installed the anti-virus, the computer system was compromised and became a part of the infected network.

Five variants of the Conficker virus have been known to exist and have been dubbed Conficker A, B, C, D and E. They were discovered on 21 November 2008, 29 December 2008, 20 February 2009, 4 March 2009 and 7 April 2009 respectively. The Conficker Working Group (CWG) uses the names A, B, B++, C and E for the same variants respectively.

Recent estimates of the number of infected computers have been notably difficult because the virus has changed its propagation and update strategy from version to version (Neild 2009). The estimated number of infected computers ranged from almost 9 million to 15 million (UPI 2009).

5.5. CAN MY COMPUTER ALSO GET INFECTED?

If it is a computer and it accepts some information from external sources, then yes, there is a chance of it getting infected by malware. Unfortunately, there is no specific method by which the malicious code (viruses and worms) may be detected. There are many forms of harm caused by such code. It can vary from computer system slowdown to malfunctioning. In some instances, it can corrupt the data present on the computer and render it useless.

Let us assume for a minute that antivirus software is installed and is working. But there are chances of a virus infection if the antivirus is not updated regularly.

It is not always easy to tell if your computer has been infected by a virus. It is the practice of writers of programs for viruses, worms, Trojans and spyware to go to great lengths to hide their code and conceal what their programs are doing on an infected computer. It is very difficult to provide a list of characteristic symptoms of a compromised computer because the same symptoms can also be caused by hardware and/or software problems. Here are just a few examples:

- Your computer behaves strangely, that is, in a way that you have not seen before.
- You see unexpected messages or images.
- You hear unexpected sounds, played at random.
- Programs start unexpectedly.
- Your personal firewall tells you that an application has tried to connect to the Internet (and it is not a program that you started).
- Your friends tell you that they have received e-mail messages from your address and you have not sent them anything.
- Your computer 'freezes' frequently, or programs start running slowly.
- You get lots of system error messages.
- The operating system will not load when you start your computer.
- You notice that files or folders have been deleted or changed.
- You notice hard-disk access (shown by one of the small flashing lights) when you are not aware of any programs running.
- Your web browser behaves erratically, for example, you cannot close a browser window.

5.5.1. What Is to be Done if Your Computer Is Infected?

Do not panic if you experience any of the above. You may have hardware or software problems, rather than a virus, worm or Trojan. Certain things you can do immediately are:

- Disconnect your computer from the Internet. If the computer is connected to a local area network, disconnect it from the network.

- If your operating system will not load, start the computer in Safe Mode or boot from a 'rescue CD' supplied with the computer.
- Make sure your antivirus signatures are up to date. If possible, do not download updates using the computer you think is infected, but use another computer (for example, a friend's computer). This is important: if your computer is infected and you connect to the Internet, a malicious program may send important information to a remote hacker, or send itself to people whose e-mail addresses are stored on your computer.
- Scan the whole computer using the antivirus program.
- If a malicious program is found, follow the instructions the antivirus program suggests: options such as disinfect infected objects, quarantine objects that may be infected, and delete worms and Trojans. The antivirus scan also creates a report file that lists the names of infected files and the malicious programs found on the computer.
- If your Internet security software does not find anything, your computer is probably not infected. Check the hardware and software installed on your computer (remove any unlicensed software and any junk files) and make sure you have the latest operating system and application patches installed.
- Make sure you apply security patches to your operating system and backup your data regularly. It should be kept in mind that a robust antivirus cannot all alone save your computer from being infected. Any software that gets installed on the operating system is bound by the security flaws that inherently exist in the code. Regular update of operating system with patches along with a good antivirus is a winning combination.

At the workplace, one should not attempt to tackle the virus infection oneself. In most cases, there are persons with specialized skills in the information technology department of the organization to handle this sort of work. It would be better to act fast. The more time that is wasted, the greater the possibility is that the attacker has gained access to all the information available on the computer.

If an infection happens at home, if nothing else works, the only option left is to reinstall the operating system. However reinstalling the operating system would require erasing the data on the computer. So taking a backup of the data is a must.

5.6. HOW CAN WE PROTECT OURSELVES FROM MALWARE?

All this said and done, how can we protect our computers and the valuable data in them? This can be done by installing genuine licensed antivirus software that has a fair ranking in the antivirus rankings that are published every year by leading labs the world over.

'Antivirus is a software used to prevent, detect, and remove malware, including computer viruses, worms, and Trojan horses. Such programs may also prevent and remove adware, spyware, and other forms of malware' (http://en.wikipedia.org/wiki/Antivirus_software).

Here, why am I stressing on 'genuine and licensed'? This is because pirated or illegally downloaded antivirus products can cause harm rather than protect the computer. In plain English, one is unsure about the source of the software program and there is at least one method to bypass the activation procedure or validation mechanism of the trusted developer of the antivirus software. In this process, there is a fair chance that the pirated antivirus program could itself open a 'back door' for gaining access to the computer.

If an antivirus program is already installed and updated periodically, there are fewer chances for a virus to infect a computer. Even if some virus tries to infect the computer, the antivirus will promptly detect it and thus protect the computer system from possible infection.

Along with a resident antivirus, there are some other things which are important to keep the computer safe, up and running. There are several flaws and potential workarounds to circumvent the operating system safety procedures. From time to time, small chunks of software called 'patches' are released by the software vendors to fix a particular software problem. These patches can be located on the vendor's website. Typically, most operating system vendors push the updates through online systems, which identify the necessary updates, and then the user is given choice to install the patches according to the order of importance or priority. It is an important point to note that these patches should only be downloaded from authorized and legitimate websites. Else, the whole purpose of securing the application or the operating system is lost.

One must update the operating system from time to time and use only genuine software. Pirated or counterfeit software are themselves vulnerable to attacks because the vendor does not offer any updates for them. Also, merely installing an antivirus program is not enough. One must go through the features of the software and see how to enable and disable some functions like firewalls, enhanced protection, enhanced scan and so on. One must remember to keep changing the passwords of the computer on a regular basis.

At the corporate level, while education and awareness are the best ways to stay safe from cybercriminals and malware attacks, there are also a range of technologies one can employ to help maintain security and privacy. They include (OECD 2008a):

1. Antivirus software: This is a must-have for just about any computer system. It can detect, block and remove malicious codes; cover root kits and scripts in web pages, identify exploit attempts and other malicious activities as well as traditional file-based threats.

2. Gateway malware and content filters: A close watch should be kept for malware being downloaded at the gateway level. Malicious URLs as well as file transfers using cloud lookups should be blocked. Quality web filtering solutions enable enforcement of corporate browsing policies. Management and reporting systems help corporate administrators monitor company networks and ensure compliance with policies.

3. Anti-spam software: These are a must, especially for business houses. Anti-spam software filters e-mails to remove spam, phishing scams and messages with malicious attachments and links to malicious web pages. Good-quality software must combine strong detection with an insignificantly small number of false-alarm rates. It should also provide traceability and archiving to ensure blocked messages can be retrieved in case of problems.

4. Encryption software: This is vital in any business working with sensitive customer data, and in many places where internal data might be valuable or compromising if lost. Data should be kept in encrypted form whenever possible, particularly during transfer and on portable systems or devices. Fail-safes and administrator overrides are also useful in case of lost passwords or abuse by rogue employees.

5. Patching and vulnerability monitoring: All software must be kept up to date. With the latest security fixes some may offer automatic updating, but in corporate environments internal testing may be needed first. Solutions are available to coordinate and enforce

patching policies across a network. Tools are available to scan for vulnerable and out-of-date software.

6. Device and network control: It is necessary to enforce rules regarding systems and devices which can connect to company networks. To ensure network integrity, company networks need to be isolated from all potential sources of infection, and should also be protected from methods of data theft.

7. Data loss prevention: Sensitive information can be specifically 'walled in' and prevented from moving off designated systems where it is needed. This stops malware or rogue employees from stealing company or customer information.

8. Removable media: The USB flash drive is now the preferred method for sharing files between people at the same physical location. There should be a clear policy on the use of the USB drive. Most organizations have limited the usage of portable media like USB drives to safeguard confidential information from being compromised.

The current response and mitigation systems are mainly reactive strategies. There is a need for more structured and strategic coordination at the national and international level with the involvement of all stakeholders to adequately assess and mitigate the risk of malware. No single entity has a global understanding of the scope, trends, development and consequences of malware and thus the overall malware problem is difficult to quantify. Data on malware is not consistent and terminology for cataloguing and measuring the occurrence of malware is not harmonized. Although its economic and social impacts may be hard to quantify, malware, whether used directly or indirectly, can harm critical information infrastructures, result in financial losses and erode trust and confidence in the Internet economy. It is important for policymakers to keep in mind the limitations of ongoing actions against malware and to explore ways to strengthen incentives for market players to fight this phenomenon. This is possible only if all concerned communities work together across borders successfully (OECD 2008b).

SIX

PHISHING WAYS

Phishing is a high-tech scam that frequently uses spam or pop-up messages to deceive people into disclosing their credit card numbers, bank account information, social security numbers, passwords or other sensitive information. Phishing attacks use e-mails and/or malicious websites to solicit personal information by posing as trustworthy organizations. The attacker is said to be actually 'fishing' for information.

According to the anti-phishing working group, APWG (2011a), 'A phishing attack is defined as a phishing site that targets a specific brand or entity. One domain name can host several discrete attacks against different organizations.'

For example, an attacker may send an e-mail seemingly from a reputable credit-card company or financial institution that requests account information, often suggesting that there is a problem. When users respond with the requested information attackers use it to gain access to their accounts.

Phishing attacks may come from other types of (legitimate) organizations, like charitable institutions. Attackers use phishing techniques to take advantage of current events such as natural disasters (tsunami), epidemics (swine flu, malaria, dengue), economic concerns (global meltdown), festivals (greetings, wishes, gifts) and so on.

Phishers are especially attracted to cheap domain names which can be obtained in bulk and can avoid red flags by banks and credit card companies. The target institutions include banks, e-commerce sites, networking services, ISPs, lotteries, government bureaus, postal services and the like.

A phisher breaks into a web server that hosts a large number of domains—
a 'shared virtual server' in industry parlance. Once a phisher breaks into such
a server, she first uploads a single copy of the phishing content. She then
updates the web server configuration to add that content to every host name
served by that web server so that all websites on that server start displaying
the phishing pages via a customized subdirectory. There is a standard capability for every web server, which allows webmasters to set up shared 'info'
pages, administrative facilities and 404 ('not found') pages. In this way the
phisher can infect dozens, hundreds or even thousands of websites at a time.
The compromise is at the system administrator level as the web configuration
file is tampered. The probability of such phishing attacks is rather low if you
are on a dedicated server rather than on a virtual server. An interesting finding
is that at least a third of all phishing attacks involved hacking of shared virtual
servers. This would pose fundamental questions about virtualization space.
This type of attack involves a large number of attacks and domain names, but
these phishing attacks have shorter uptime than average (APWG 2011a).

6.1. PHISHING TRENDS

According to an APWG report in 2011, the average uptime of a phishing
attack was 54 hours and 37 minutes in 2011 as compared to 73 hours in 2010
(APWG 2011a). This decrease could be due to multiple complaints coming to
the hosting company in case of a virtual server attack. Financial services continued to be the most targeted industry sector followed by payment services in
terms of phishing attacks (APWG 2011a). Banking information was the most
sought after information in phishing uniform resource locators (URLs). Of the
top 200 organizations observed, the most frequently spoofed were banks,
which accounted for 56 per cent of phishing attacks blocked in 2010. It is not
surprising that banks are spoofed by phishing URLs more than any other category. Phishing URLs spoofing banks attempt to steal a wide variety of information that can be used for identity theft and fraud. Attackers seek information
such as names, government-issued identification numbers, bank account
information and credit-card numbers. Cybercriminals are more focused on
stealing financial information that can earn them large amounts of money
quickly as opposed to goods that require a larger time investment, such as

scams (Symantec Corporation 2011a). According to Trend Micro (2012a), PayPal and eBay were the most commonly phished sites in 2011.

According to APWG, there were at least 112,472 unique phishing attacks worldwide in 2011, in just four top-level domains (TLDs). '.TR', '.IMFO', '.COM' and '.NET', '.TK' surfaced as the TLDs which offered free registrations for phishing activities (APWG 2011a).

There has also been an increase in the number of free web hosting services utilized for developing phishing sites. According to the Symantec Corporation (2010), as many as 118 different web hosting services served as a home for 2,150 phishing sites in December 2010.

The United States, China and Brazil figured amongst the top countries where the use of malware and phishing hosting is the highest in the world (Symantec Corporation 2010d: 7).

6.1.1. Avalanche, 2008

Avalanche is the name given to the world's most prolific phishing gang, and to the botnet infrastructure it uses to host phishing sites. This criminal enterprise perfected a system for deploying mass-produced phishing sites, and for distributing malware that gave the gang additional capabilities for theft (APWG 2010).

During the second half of 2010, Avalanche reduced its phishing activities significantly and completely disappeared. However, reports (APWG 2010) suggest that the people behind Avalanche switched to distributing the notorious Zeus Trojan. Zeus is a sophisticated piece of malware used by many different gangs of cybercriminals. The Avalanche gang began incorporating Zeus into its phishing and spamming campaigns in 2009. Zeus is crimeware or malware designed specifically to automate identity thefts and facilitate unauthorized transactions.

The Avalanche infrastructure is still in existence as of this writing, but its activities are stealthier, more focused on malware distribution and control, money mule recruitment, and other illicit activities. Recent law enforcement actions and continued takedown efforts by industry do seem to have had an effect on the operation (APWG 2010).

Avalanche used spam e-mail purporting that it came from trusted organizations such as financial institutions or employment websites. Victims would be deceived into entering personal information on websites which were made to appear as though they belonged to these genuine organizations. Victims would also be asked to install software by e-mail or at the websites. The software was actually malware which could log keystrokes, steal passwords and credit-card information, and allow unauthorized remote access to the infected computer. The Internet Identity's Phishing Trends report for the second quarter of 2009 (Internet Identity 2009) said that Avalanche members 'have detailed knowledge of commercial banking platforms, particularly treasury management systems and the Automated Clearing House (ACH) system. They are also performing successful real-time "man-in-the-middle" attacks that defeat two-factor security tokens'.[1]

Avalanche had many similarities to a previous group 'Rock Phish'—the first phishing group to use automated techniques—but has been described as being greater in scale and volume. One of the techniques Avalanche used was to host its domains on compromised computers which were part of a botnet. Since there was no hosting provider, it was difficult to take the domain down. It required the involvement of a responsible domain registrar. In addition, Avalanche used fast-flux domain name system (DNS),[2] causing the compromised machines to change constantly.

Avalanche attacks also spread the Zeus Trojan horse, enabling further criminal activity. Many of the domains which Avalanche used belonged to national domain name registrars in Europe and Asia, unlike other phishing attacks, where the majority of domains belonged to United States registrars. It appears that Avalanche chose registrars based on their security procedures, returning repeatedly to registrars who did not detect domains being used for

---

[1] In a 'man in the middle' attack, an attacker can intercept and control the communication between the sender and the receiver without their knowledge. In such an attack, even advanced authentication mechanisms such as two-factor authentication may not be of much help.

[2] 'Fast Flux' Domain Name Server (DNS) is a technique to hide the actual sites for malware in a network. In this technique, the domain name for a site is linked to multiple IP addresses which are a part of a botnet. The IP addresses change rapidly and randomly through changing DNS records thus masking the actual malware/phishing sites.

A cybercriminal can use this technique to prevent identification of his key host server's IP address. By abusing the way the domain name system works, the criminal can create a botnet with nodes that join and drop off the network faster than law enforcement officials can trace them.

fraud, or which were slow to suspend abusive domains. Avalanche frequently registered domains with anything between one and three registrars, while testing others to check if their distinctive domains were being detected and blocked. They targeted a small number of brands (such as specific financial institutions) at a time, but rotated these regularly. A domain which was not suspended by a registrar was often reused in a later attack. The group created a phishing 'kit', which was pre-prepared for use with many brands.

Avalanche attracted significant attention from security organizations. As a result, the uptime of the domain names it used was half that of other phishing domains. In October 2009, the Internet Corporation for Assigned Names and Numbers (ICANN), the organization which manages the assignment of domain names, issued a situation awareness note encouraging registrars to be proactive in dealing with Avalanche attacks. The United Kingdom registry, Nominet, changed its procedures to make it easier to suspend domains, because of attacks by Avalanche interdomain. A Spanish registrar began requiring a confirmation code to be delivered by mobile phone in April 2009, which successfully forced Avalanche to stop registering fraudulent domains with them. In November 2009, security companies managed to shut down the Avalanche botnet for a short time. Thereafter, Avalanche reduced the scale of its activities and altered its modus operandi. By April 2010, the number of attacks by Avalanche had decreased to just 59 from a high of more than 26,000 in October 2009, raising concerns that a more damaging successor may be on the way (APWG 2010).

6.2. SPEAR PHISHING

Spear phishers target select groups of people who have something in common (Symantec Corporation 2011a). These may include things like working at the same company premises, having accounts in the same bank, attending the same college, ordering items from the same website and so on. The e-mails are apparently sent by organizations or individuals from whom the potential victims would normally get e-mails, so they believe that the e-mail is genuine.

This makes spear phishing attacks much more deceptive than other phishing attacks. The threats posed by spear phishing are numerous. It can trick a user into downloading malicious codes or malware by clicking on a link in the e-mail. The malware can be installed on the computer once the link is clicked and go completely unnoticed. Such malware can take control of a user's computer. Several such computers can then be organized into enormous botnets, which can be used for launching denial of service attacks.

At first, the criminals need some inside information about the potential targets, to make their e-mails look genuine. This information is obtained by hacking into an organization's computer network or sometimes by thoroughly studying and understanding company websites, blogs and social networking sites. Once this is done, legitimate looking e-mails are sent to targeted people. Most unsuspecting users are convinced that the e-mail is from a genuine source. Finally, users are asked to click on a link inside the e-mail that takes them to a fake but genuine-looking website, where they are asked to provide passwords, account numbers, user IDs, access codes, personal information numbers (PINs) and such other personal information.

6.2.1. Picture-in-Picture, 2010

One particularly interesting phishing scam identified in 2010 used the 'picture-in-picture' (PiP) technique to disguise the message as a portable document format (PDF) file. The phishing e-mail claimed that the recipient was entitled to a refund, and included a hypertext markup language (HTML) attachment, which when opened loaded a fake website hosted on a compromised web server. The website was noteworthy because it used a PiP attack to disguise the page to make it appear as though it was a PDF document being displayed within a web browser using a plug-in (Symantec Corporation 2011a: 62).

The PiP scam took advantage of inefficient 'spam checkers' of an e-mail application and 'document verifiers' within the PDF reader. The recipient of the e-mail would be unaware of the potential threat lurking in the attachment, disguised as PDF. For instance, an incoming mail with a message for tax refund had a form as an attachment, which a user had to fill with confidential information. The form had two layers of imagery to disguise it as a PDF form. When the user opened the form, instead of PDF, it actually opened a website on a compromised server. Thus all the information which a user had entered, understandably in a PDF mode, was actually being transmitted through a frame-based HTML form, to unscrupulous elements. The information required to be filled was confidential since it not only included tax-related fields, but also bank account-related information for tax refunds.

The key motivation behind the incident was the confusion created by an announcement from the United Kingdom's tax collecting agency HM Revenue & Customs (HMRC) that six million people had submitted incorrect tax claims and that the HMRC would soon start sending letters to those people for a tax refund or payment, as applicable. The fraudulent message from HMRC accounted for 10.8 per cent of all phishing e-mails globally. It affected six million citizens in the United Kingdom and they also lost their confidential information.

Spammers also use spear phishing to target webmail services. There have been instances when businesses and institutions have received warnings about problems with webmail services, which turned out to be a lead to phishing pages. Once compromised, webmail accounts can become fertile ground for disclosing personal data, conducting identity thefts and corporate espionage.

Spear-phishing attacks can target anyone. While the high profile, targeted attacks that received a high degree of media attention such as Stuxnet and Hydraq attempted to steal intellectual property or cause physical damage, many spear-phishing attacks simply prey on individuals for their personal information. In 2010, for example, data breaches caused by hacking resulted in an average of over 260,000 identities being exposed per breach—far more than any other cause. Breaches such as these can be especially damaging for enterprises because they may contain sensitive data about customers as well as employees, which even an average attacker can sell to the wrong persons (Symantec Corporation 2011a).

6.3. HOW TO PROTECT AGAINST PHISHING

It is essential to keep in mind that most companies, banks and agencies do not request for personal information via e-mail. If a doubt arises, the concerned bank or the related officials may be informed. Phishing filters these days come embedded in Internet browsers in the form of plug-ins. It is advisable to enable and use them. A URL should always be entered manually rather than by clicking on the link provided in an e-mail. One should avoid giving personal information or information about one's organization, including its structure or networks, unless one is certain of the recipient's identity and her level of authority to have the required information. Personal or financial information should never be revealed via e-mail, and e-mails that ask for such information should never be responded to. Antivirus software, firewalls and e-mail filters should be installed and regularly updated.

It is advisable to look for a trusted symbol from an external agency (for example, VeriSign) on the website if one is about to transact through the website. If one believes that one's financial accounts may be compromised, the concerned bank or financial organization should be informed immediately and the accounts that may have been (or are expected to have been) compromised should be closed. Any unusual activity or transaction in the account should be investigated into and the issue should be reported to the nearest police station having jurisdiction of that area.

SEVEN

IDENTITY THEFT METHODS

Identity theft is a term used to refer to all those types of crimes in which one wrongfully obtains and uses personal data belonging to another in some way that involves fraud or deception, for economic gain. It is a practice by which some people with malicious intentions steal personal information such as bank account numbers, phone numbers and credit-card numbers for purposes like impersonation, opening new bank accounts, undertaking fraudulent transactions and even applying for loans.

Identity theft continues to be a high-profile security issue, particularly for organizations that store and manage large amounts of personal information. On the one hand, the compromises that result in the loss of personal data undermine customer and institutional confidence, and on the other, they damage an organization's reputation. They also prove to be costly for individuals recovering from the resulting identity theft.

The extent of damage caused by identity theft can be massive. Criminals stand to benefit from the victim's money and can even go to the extent of destroying their credit standing, and in turn the individual's future. Many a time, it is difficult and takes a long time for the victim to recover from the losses. Identity thefts could include stealing phone numbers, social security numbers, driver's license and identifiers from cheques. They may also involve burglars breaking into a home and stealing important documents such as tax returns, passports, birth certificates, social security cards and so on. Again, hacking into computers to steal information, buying stolen records from a co-worker, and gathering personal information from a newspaper article, or 'Who's Who' book are also forms of such theft.

Some statistics on identity theft are presented below (Javelin Strategy and Research 2010):

- In the United States, 11.1 million adults were victims of identity theft in 2009.
- The total fraud amount was 54 billion dollars.
- The average victim spent 21 hours and $373 out of her pocket trying to resolve the crime.
- In the United States, 4.8 per cent of the population were victims of identity fraud in 2009.
- 13 per cent of identity fraud crimes were committed by someone the victim knew.

7.1. HOW DOES IT WORK?

With the arrival of the Internet, identity theft has become much easier. As everyone knows, most companies have a database of their customers. If an attacker gains access to such a database, there is a possibility that a large amount of user data can be stolen. This data can be used for any sinister purpose. It must be noted that there are dedicated individuals and firms dealing with selling and buying customer data such as names, contact numbers, e-mail addresses and postal addresses. The list does not stop here. Buying habits of persons can also be revealed. It should also be noted that there is no hard and fast rule about the profile of the person whose data would be stolen. It often depends upon the availability of information.

Identity theft can occur within an organization, for instance, through transactions such as purchases made in a store. The means used could include Trojan horses, key logger software, viruses, malware or spyware on a computer. Identity theft could happen through a data breach, where a business or organization that accesses personal information such as a hospital, school, departmental store or a company is compromised. Phishing or vishing techniques may be used, in which someone pretends to be a bank or trusted source and tricks a customer into providing personal and confidential information through e-mails, calls or text messages. Such theft could also happen through social networking sites where personal information can be found and communication with fraudulent individuals can occur.

Figure 7.1 shows the number of complaints of identity theft and other fraud received by the United States Federal Trade Commission (FTC) for the years 2000–08.

Figure 7.1
FTC Consumer Complaint Data: Identity Theft and Other Fraud for 2000–10

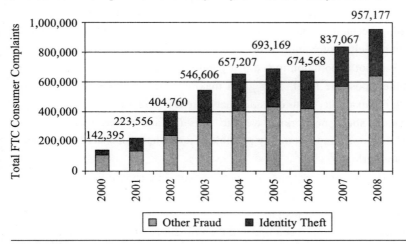

SOURCE: Finklea (2010).

7.2. IS THERE A WAY TO KNOW IF YOU ARE A VICTIM OF IDENTITY THEFT?

Loss of identity cannot just be discovered by some simple litmus test. But there can be patterns which suggest that there has been a compromise of information leading to loss of identity. These can be:

- Unusual activity in the bills.
- New bills from the services to which you never subscribe.
- Rejection of credit card or its blockage.
- Denial of use of your accounts or login details.

These are some preliminary signs to suggest that your identify may be stolen.

7.3. HOW TO PROTECT ONESELF AGAINST IDENTITY THEFT

These days, a large number of websites (especially social networking web-sites) have a plethora of information about users. The registration is free of cost, hassle-free and the experience is entertaining. All these make people supply their personal information in some form or the other. One must give as little information as possible while registering for an e-mail account, online shopping account, social networking website and so on. It is advisable to restrict oneself to providing information only for the fields marked as compul-sory. It is not uncommon to see that people usually update their accounts to the fullest possible level. This gives maximum information about the indi-vidual. For example, let us consider that there is a field for entering one's pet's name on a social networking website. It is fun and it may make one look 'cool'. But it is almost certainly possible that one has just shared a password-reset answer!

While updating contents or contact details, one should be sure to enable privacy options and be selective about showing such information only to a trusted circle of known people.

Once a profile has been updated the possibility of it being compromised always exists. Hence it would be futile to subsequently delete or remove the information. Trust is another important factor to consider. One should do busi-ness or transactions with only the persons whom one knows.

People hardly ever read through the privacy policy of the website that they have registered on. This should not be so. It is important to read and understand the disclaimers and the information-sharing policies of the web-site. It should be noted that whenever there is a change in the privacy policy, all the settings might be reverted to default settings and this might result in exposure of information.

There are almost always some built-in security features in web browsers. It is important to go through these settings and enable them. However much one tries to protect information, once it is online, it is not impossible to obtain it. So, one should act with discretion.

7.4. MY IDENTITY IS STOLEN. WHAT SHALL I DO NOW?

It is not an easy process to recover from identity theft. As it is always said, prevention is better than cure. In case of an unfortunate instance of identity theft, found below are the steps that may be followed.

- Immediately inform the financial organization or bank about the theft and get the account closed or the login credentials changed.
- Report the incident and request that the credit card be blocked.
- Inform the police station in your jurisdiction about the theft and file a case.
- Identity information is not always stand-alone. So as a precautionary step, harden other login credentials and keep other accounts safe.

Loss of driving license, passport and such documents should be immediately reported to the local police and a complaint should be filed.

EIGHT

DENIAL-OF-SERVICE ATTACK

———•◆•———

A denial-of-service or DoS attack is said to have taken place when some or all of the services are denied to legitimate users. By 'hammering' a web-site with too many requests for information, an attacker can effectively clog the system, slowing performance or even crashing the site. This can happen with e-mail services, search services, online banking services and the like. Usually, this happens when the attacker floods the network with information or when the number of requests for service exceeds the permissible limit of that particular service. At first the network becomes slow and after a while, it reaches a saturation point such that no new service requests can be handled. For example, logging into an e-mail account or accessing search results is no longer possible.

8.1. DISTRIBUTED DENIAL-OF-SERVICE ATTACK

Distributed denial of service (DDoS) is a method of carrying out a denial-of-service attack through a large number of connected computers. Once the attacker gains control over a group of computers, she can engage the group into specific activities like spamming, sending a huge number of requests to a website or taking up so much of a shared resource that nothing remains for other users.

For instance, sending an extraordinary amount of e-mails to someone could fill the computer disk where the mail resides. This implies that people using the computer will not be able to receive any new e-mails until the disk has been cleared.

8.2. HOW IT WORKS

Figure 8.1 describes how denial-of-service and distributed denial-of-service attacks work.

Figure 8.1
How Denial-of-Service Attacks Work

In a denial-of-service attack, a hacker compromises a system and uses that system to attack the target computer, flooding it with more requests for services than the target can handle.

In a distributed denial-of-service attack, dozens or even hundreds of computers (known as zombies) are compromised, loaded with DoS attack software and then remotely activated by the hacker to conduct a coordinated attack.

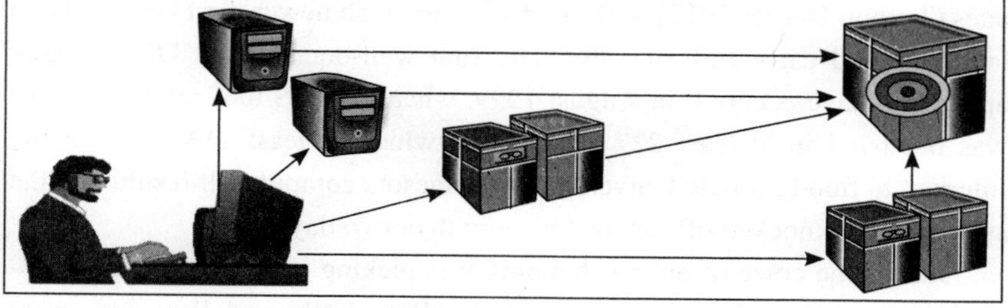

SOURCE: Whitman and Mattford (2009: 65).

8.3. TRENDS IN DENIAL-OF-SERVICE ATTACKS

The United States was the most targeted country with respect to denial-of-service attacks in 2010 (Symantec Internet Threat Report 2011a). Both the number and volume of distributed denial-of-service attacks are on the rise, according to new reports from DDoS mitigation companies Prolexic and Arbor Networks (Arbor Networks 2011; Constantin 2012; Prolexic 2011). The trend is towards shorter attack duration, but a bigger packet-per-second attack volume. There was a 136 per cent year-on-year increase in attack bandwidth in 2011. This trend is also reflected in a new report from Arbor

Networks which interviewed 114 representatives of different market segments about their experience with DDoS attacks in 2011 (Constantin 2012). More than 40 per cent of respondents said they experienced attacks that exceeded a bandwidth of 1 Gbps in 2010, while 13 per cent said they were the targets of at least one attack that exceeded 10 Gbps. Both Prolexic and Arbor Networks recorded an increase in the number of so-called Layer 7 DDoS attacks,[1] which target particular Internet facing applications[2] rather than load balancers[3] or Internet gateways.[4] DDoS attacks on applications focus on sending bad traffic using those applications' protocols. The attacks are very effective using relatively low bandwidth and just a few hosts. The number one motivation for DDoS attacks in 2011 was rooted to political and ideological conflicts (Arbor Networks 2010).

8.3.1. The Web Denied: Attacks in 1999 and 2000

Denial-of-service attacks under a number of guises have been around for decades (Techno Diaries 2012). DDoS attacks are much newer, first being seen in late June and early July of 1999. The first well-documented DDoS attack appears to have occurred in August 1999, when a DDoS tool called 'Trin00' was deployed in at least 227 systems, of which at least 114 were on the Internet, to flood a single University of Minnesota computer. It resulted in the system being knocked off the air for more than two days.

Just as the craze of online shopping was picking up steam, several high-profile sites, including Yahoo, Amazon, eBay, CNN and Buy.com, were

[1] The term 'Layer-7' attack is basically an attack targeted at the application Layer-7 of Open Systems Interconnection (OSI) Model. These attacks are difficult to detect. They are conducted by exploiting flaws in the application logic and making it consume all resources, for instance, by sticking the application in CPU-intensive loops, making the application consume all local resources or simply having the application layer consume all bandwidth.

[2] Internet facing means a system with a port, typically Ethernet, directly connected to an Internet modem or network interface unit.

[3] A load balancer is an equipment that helps to improve the network/application traffic by distributing the workload across multiple servers and therefore, decreasing the overall burden placed on each server. A load balancer is used to improve the concurrent user capacity and overall reliability of applications.

[4] An internet gateway is a modem or router or any other peripheral device that allows you to access the Internet.

overcome by denial-of-service attacks that prevented the sites from responding to legitimate traffic. Investigators arrested a Canadian teenager using the pseudonym 'mafiaboy', who was later identified as Michael Calce, as the person behind the first attack against Yahoo, to win street credibility. A rival gang then went after Buy.com, and the attacks escalated from there (Bloomberg Businessweek 2010).

The first well-publicized DDoS attack took place in February 2000. On 7 February, Yahoo became the victim of a DDoS attack during which its Internet portal was inaccessible for three hours. On 8 February, Amazon, Buy.com, CNN, and eBay were all hit by DDoS attacks that caused them to either stop functioning completely or slowed them down considerably. On 9 February, E*Trade and ZDNet suffered DDoS attacks. Analysts estimated that during the three hours that Yahoo was down, it suffered a loss of e-commerce and advertising revenues that amounted to about $500,000. According to bookseller Amazon.com, a widely publicized attack on its website resulted in a loss of $600,000 during the 10 hours for which it was down. During their DDoS attacks, Buy.com went from 100 per cent availability to 9.4 per cent, while CNN's users went down to below 5 per cent of normal volume, and ZDnet.com and E*Trade.com were virtually unreachable. Schwab.com, the online venue of the discount broker Charles Schwab, was also hit, but refused to reveal exact figures of losses. One can only assume that to a company that does two billion dollars of business weekly in online trades, the downtime loss must have been huge.

In a DDoS attack, the attacking packets come from tens or hundreds of addresses rather than just one, as in a 'standard' DoS attack. Any DoS defence that is based upon monitoring the volume of packets coming from a single address or single network will then fail, since the attacks come from all over. Rather than receiving, for example, a thousand gigantic pings per second from an attacking site, the victim might receive one ping per second from 1,000 attacking sites.

One of the other disconcerting things about DDoS attacks is that the handler can choose the location of the agents. So, for example, a handler could target several North Atlantic Treaty Organization (NATO) sites as victims, and employ agents that are all in countries know to be hostile to NATO. The human attacker, of course, might be sitting in Canada.

Like DoS attacks, all of the DDoS attacks employ standard transmission control protocol/Internet protocol (TCP/IP) messages but employ them in some non-standard ways. Common DDoS attacks have such names as 'Tribe Flood Network', 'Trin00', 'Stacheldraht' and 'Trinity'.

8.3.2. Attack against Root Servers, 2002

Another DDoS attack occurred on 20 October 2002 against the 13 root servers that provide the domain name system (DNS) service to Internet users around the world (EC-Council 2009: 6–17). They translate logical addresses such as 'www.yahoo.edu' into a corresponding physical IP address, so that users can connect to websites through more easily remembered names rather than numbers. If all 13 servers were to go down, there would be serious problems in accessing the Web. Although the attack only lasted for an hour and the effects were hardly noticeable to the average Internet user, it caused 7 of the 13 root servers to shut down, demonstrating the vulnerability of the Internet to DDoS attacks. If left unchecked, more powerful DDoS attacks could potentially cripple or disable essential Internet services.

8.3.3. Attack against Georgia, 2008

In the weeks leading up to the five-day South Ossetia war, 2008, a DDoS attack was directed at Georgian government sites containing the message: 'win+love+in+Rusia' (Hollis 2011). This effectively overloaded and shut down multiple Georgian servers. The websites targeted included the website of the Georgian President, Mikhail Saakashvili, and the National Bank of Georgia. The attack rendered them inoperable for 24 hours. While the sword of suspicion was placed on Russia for orchestrating the attack through a proxy, the Russian government denied the allegations, stating that it was possible that individuals in Russia or elsewhere had taken it upon themselves to start the attacks.

8.3.4. The Michael Jackson Incident, 2009

On 25 June 2009, the day Michael Jackson died, the spike in searches related to Michael Jackson was so big that Google News initially mistook it for an automated attack (Pitman 2009). As a result, for about 25 minutes, when some people searched Google News they saw a 'We're sorry' page before finding the articles they were looking for.

8.3.5. The WikiLeaks Incident, 2011

In August 2011, a high-profile denial-of-service attack was launched on the WikiLeaks website (Hoffman 2011a). The motivation for the apparent cyber-attack came after current and former American officials said that they were concerned about the recently released 134,000 cables over the protection of the source and would create an embarrassment for the Obama administration as well as endanger United States foreign policy goals. The attacks involved the WikiLeaks website (London) and the United States government. During its prior releases, WikiLeaks had exercised diligence in maintaining the privacy of individuals mentioned by name in the United States diplomatic cables. However, the WikiLeaks site apparently suffered a data breach when Julian Assange, founder of WikiLeaks, shared a passphrase, required to decrypt a batch of cables taken by former colleague Daniel Domscheit-Berg, with an external source. The Internet was used as the tool for the attack on the WikiLeaks website and denial of service was the technology used.

8.3.6. Attack against South Korea, 2011

On 4 March 2011, there were distributed denial-of-service attacks on South Korean websites, including those of government agencies, prominent busi-nesses and the United States forces in South Korea (McAfee 2011c). The attacks lasted 10 days, after which the malware was designed to self-destroy. The command and control (C&C) servers were distributed across multiple geographies and included nations like the United States, Taiwan, Saudi Arabia, Russia, India, South Africa, Thailand, Hong Kong, Australia, South Korea, Mexico, Poland, Israel and Turkey.

Like most DDoS attacks, these attacks would have started with compro-mised hosts. Investigations suggested that two South Korean file-sharing sites were used to inject the malicious code into files, which were downloaded onto personal computers (PCs). Infected hosts were controlled by remote C&C servers. There were multiple C&C servers distributed across geographies that were compromised targets themselves. All these C&C servers triggered cyber-attacks from infected PCs (zombie PCs) that targeted major military websites and some non-military websites also. In the end, the bots were configured to delete and overwrite key files and finally damage the master boot record to render the host unusable.

The DDoS attack left major websites in South Korea including those of the Presidential office, government ministries and major financial institutions temporarily unavailable. The attack hit 29 institutions on the first day itself but no significant tangible damage was reported. However, the larger, intangible impact was that the credibility and trust in government websites (especially the military ones) was shaken by the attacks.

8.3.7. The Megaupload Cyberattack, 2012

This cyberattack was the largest-ever cyberattack by the hacker collective Anonymous (The Conversation 2012; Williams 2012). It brought down the websites of several large organizations, including the United States Department of Justice and the Federal Bureau of Investigation (FBI). The attacks started on the morning of 20 January 2012 and appeared to be in retaliation against the forced shutdown of the popular file-sharing website, Megaupload. The file-sharing website, which allowed users to freely exchange large videos and audio files, was shut down overnight and its operators were charged with criminal copyright infringement. They were accused of deliberately ignoring requests from film and music firms to remove pirated material, while making more than 175 million dollars from membership fees and advertising.

The attacks were perpetrated by a collective of more than 5,000 Internet users, apparently using more than 27,000 computers to set up a distributed denial-of-service attack.

The websites of the Motion Picture Association of America (MPAA), Warner Music Group, Universal Music and the Recording Industry Association of America (RIAA) were also taken down (The Conversation 2012).

8.4. HOW TO PROTECT AGAINST ONE

- Updating the computer operating system with patches regularly (only from the vendor's site).
- Installing an antivirus and keeping it updated.
- Configuring applications, services and operating systems with denial of service in mind.
- Staying current with patches and security updates and strengthening the TCP/IP stack against denial-of-service.

- Making sure the application is capable of handling high volumes of traffic and that thresholds are in place to handle abnormally high loads.
- Reviewing the application's failover functionality and using an intrusion detection system (IDS) that can detect potential denial-of-service attacks. (Microsoft Corporation 2003)

In the event a DoS or DDoS attack occurs, the symptoms, such as slower performance of network resources, overwhelming spam in the e-mail account, non-availability of website and so on, will become apparent (Microsoft Corporation 2003). In such a situation it is prudent to inform the network administrator and the Internet service provider immediately after the symptoms appear. The faster one acts the better. There may be chances that the attack can be stopped without progressing to further severity. It should always be remembered that attempts to take care of these attacks could be more damaging than helpful.

NINE

DAMAGE BY BOTNETS

———•◦•———

The term botnet is an abbreviation of 'bot-network' where 'bot' stands for robot, an automated tool. It is in fact a computer that can control and be controlled by many computers arranged in a network by a person with malicious intent. This usually happens when an attacker gains access to a computer system and tries to control other interconnected computers.

Bots have a wide range of functionalities and most of them can be updated to assume new capabilities by downloading new codes and features. Attackers can use bots to perform a variety of tasks, such as set up denial-of-service (DoS) attacks against an organization's website, distribute spam and phishing attacks, distribute spyware and adware, propagate malicious codes and harvest confidential information that may be used in identity theft from compromised computers. All of these acts can lead to serious financial and legal consequences.

Large botnets such as Zeus—which commandeered as many as two or three million computers worldwide—have been used to steal banking information and login data for years. A recent development has been the launching of attack toolkits by botnet creators. Botnet codes are built into the kits, enabling the creation of a host of smaller botnets. Earlier, when there were only a few large botnets in existence, it was easier to track them and understand how they operated. However, nowadays there exist dozens of smaller botnets engaging in criminal activities. The availability of botnet toolkits has not only increased their numbers, but also allowed more variations, thus complicating the task of analysing their behavioural patterns and providing protection against them. The new, smaller botnets also aim to gather bank account information, much like the larger Zeus botnets. The number and variety of these smaller botnets makes it challenging for security professionals to track their movements.

Botnets are personal computers, which have been compromised to carry out malicious activities without the owner's consent and are the most common medium used by cybercriminals. Computers become the nodes in a botnet. Attackers illicitly install malware that secretly connects the computers to the botnets of hundreds of thousands or sometimes millions of machines. An estimate suggests that about 10 million computers worldwide are 'hijacked' everyday and connected to botnets (Wolfe and Wade 2008). Two recent examples are the Conficker network of seven million machines and the Spanish-based Mariposa network of 12.7 million machines (OECD 2011).

Virtually all spam comes from compromised computers (called bots or zombies) that have been successfully attacked and now, without the knowledge of their owners, are sending out large volumes of spam, adware and spyware; launching distributed DoS attacks; organizing hacking attempts; or stealing confidential information. It should be understood that even if a computer is not behaving abnormally, it could be a part of a botnet. The main objectives of a person using a botnet are recognition in the hacker community and some financial gain. It is an accepted fact that the more the number of computers in a botnet, the greater the respect the person behind its initiation commands. It is a usual practice to rent out botnets to other persons to launch attacks similar to those discussed earlier.

These botnets sit at the heart of the cybercrime infrastructure, allowing criminals to perpetrate spam, phishing, identity theft, click fraud[1] and advance fee fraud.[2] It is clear that their controllers, known as 'bot-herders', work hard

---

[1] Click fraud is an arrangement between the webmaster and an advertiser where the latter pays for the number of clicks that have been made on an advertisement. In a click fraud, there is a malware concealed behind the online advertisement. A person clicking on such an advertisement becomes victim of a cyberattack.

[2] Advance fee fraud is a rising type of Internet crime causing Internet users to lose significant amounts of money. The expression 'Advance Fee Fraud' (AFF) describes fraud cases in which criminal fraudsters convince a victim that the victim has won a prize or been selected for a business deal with easy money to be gained and the only condition to obtain the gain is that the victim has to pay a small amount of money in advance. When the victim pays the fee, it will not bring him closer to receiving the gain. In fact, he only risks losing more money as the fraudster will be encouraged to re-contact the victim to request the payment of additional fees for the same transaction.

to sustain, maintain and grow them for financial gains. Most of the unsolicited e-mail is sent by botnets.

The existence of botnets poses a significant threat to the security of the Internet. They are the result of the efforts of resourceful and sophisticated cybercriminals for whom they have a great deal of value. A number of different and dynamic factors are responsible for the existence of botnets. For instance, Internet users not applying the fundamentals of good security practices; deceptive creativity of criminals evidenced by social engineering attacks; potentially unwanted software; use of pirated software; weak passwords and security policies and so on. The continued sophistication of cybercriminals can be seen in the way they develop specialized botnets to launch cybercrimes.

Bot-Infected Computers

Bot-infected computers are compromised computers that are controlled remotely by attackers. Typically, the remote attacker controls a large number of compromised computers through a single, reliable channel in a botnet, which is then used to launch coordinated attacks.

A bot-infected computer is considered active on a given day if it carries out at least one attack on that day. This does not have to be continuous; rather, a single such computer can be active on a number of different days. A 'distinct' bot-infected computer is a distinct computer that was active at least once during the period.

The explanations used by the fraudsters for demanding the additional fees are creative but still credible and may include the advance payment of bank fees for money transfers, payment of courier services to send the check, legal fees to have an attorney or notary prepare documents needed for the money transfer, or the advance payment of taxes on the prize.

To make their deception more convincing, the fraudsters are known to create fake companies and provide them with domain names, phone numbers and email addresses. Enforcement against AFF is complicated by the fact that fraudsters commit their crime across borders and although the aggregated cases add up to very large crimes, the individual cases may not be large enough to meet the threshold for initiating an international investigation (http://affcoalition.org/).

Metaphisher (2006) is one of the most sophisticated botnets to date. The botnet operated for several months where it stole credentials so that criminals could exploit bank accounts, eBay accounts and other similar targets for financial gains. What made this bot different from the others was its ability to defeat two-factor authentications. The redundant command and control (C&C) centres and drop points for stolen data also added to the sophistication of this threat. Finally, the number of malicious actors working on the bot and the way they worked mirrored a professionally developed project with output that maximized profitability for the group. Metaphisher was just one of several emerging attacks involving multiple fraud rings (iDefense 2006). It successfully undermined the secure sockets layer (SSL) and the tax deduction and collection account number system to steal thousands of accounts to leverage for other attacks, spam and fraud (iDefense 2006).[3]

9.1. WHAT ARE BOTNETS USED FOR?

Botnets are mostly used for the following purposes:

1. To locate and infect other information systems with malware.
2. To conduct distributed denial-of-service (DDoS) attacks.
3. To sell or rent out as a service.
4. To send spam, which can distribute more malware.
5. To steal sensitive information from each compromised computer that belongs to the botnet.
6. To host a malicious phishing site, often in conjunction with other members of the botnet to provide redundancy.
7. Many botnet clients allow the attacker to run any additional code of their choice, making the botnet client very flexible to adding new attacks (OECD 2008b). This includes sending spam, organizing hacking attempts and even organizing detailed denial-of-service attacks.

[3] MetaFisher bots are programmed to steal passwords, personal ID numbers and other information from compromised users who visit specific banking websites in the United Kingdom, Spain and Germany and infected the United States banking system.

9.1.1. The Zeus Botnet, 2007

First spotted in July 2007, the Zeus botnet became more widespread in March 2009. It consists of a network of compromised computers built via techniques such as phishing. It tries to entice recipients of an e-mail message to click on links to software that infects the computer. The Zeus Trojan-controlled machines are scattered across 196 countries (Bloomberg Businessweek 2010).

The five countries with the most significant instances of infected machines are Egypt, the United States, Mexico, Saudi Arabia and Turkey. Altogether, 2,411 companies and organizations are said to have been affected by the criminal operations running the Zeus botnet. Federal Bureau of Investigation (FBI) investigators say its purpose is to steal money from the owners of affected computers by capturing their keystrokes, stealing banking information like account name and password, credit-card credentials and other financial information (Null 2010).

Any individual criminal or small or medium-sized criminal organization could be involved in these types of attacks. It is less likely that a country-run organization, a terrorist group or any organized sector criminal agency could be behind this Trojan.

In October 2010, the FBI disclosed that it had detected an international cybercrime ring that had used Zeus botnets to steal over $70 million dollars from bank accounts in the United States. This spurred an FBI crackdown on the Zeus Trojan and Zeus botnets that led to the arrest of over 100 cybercriminals (http://www.veracode.com/security/botnet). The thieves mainly targeted small businesses, municipal governments and churches, and managed to steal about 70 million dollars in the past. This botnet uses the 'Man-in-the-browser'[4] keystroke for logging in and grabbing forms[5] for collecting information. It is

---

[4] This is a type of threat that takes advantage of the vulnerabilities in the web browser to affect the web pages. MITB works on some weakness in the browser and therefore beats the security mechanisms such as Public Key Infrastructure, digital signature and two or three factor authentications which are transaction verification mechanisms. MITB is one of the biggest threats to online commerce and online banking.

[5] This is a malicious code–based method to capture data that a user fills in the web forms. This may involve capturing passwords and other sensitive data in online transactions.

spread mainly through 'drive-by' downloads[6] and phishing schemes. It is also known as 'Zbot', 'WSNPOEM', 'NTOS' and 'PRG'.

This malware only targets the Microsoft Windows operating system. Every criminal can control which information she is interested in and fine-tune her copy of ZeuS to steal only that. However, in general, it targets bank websites and online payment websites. An international police investigation led to the arrest of more than 100 people in the United States, United Kingdom and Ukraine in connection with this botnet's operations (Null 2010).

9.2. HOW DO THEY WORK?

Computers become nodes in a botnet when attackers illicitly install malware that secretly connects the computers to botnets of hundreds of thousands, or sometimes millions, of machines.

Botnets get their origin from criminals who are very tech-savvy and well versed in computer programming and software creation. Once the computers are compromised, they can communicate over the Internet, which means a botnet can be a group of zombie computers that is formed anywhere in the world.

Botnets essentially hold a computer captive for the purpose of criminal activity. There are literally millions of botnets formed on the Internet on a regular basis. What is worse is that the bots and the codes that make up a botnet are made available online. Bot herders can easily combine the codes to create a major denial-of-service attack to bring down networks and websites.

Figure 9.1 is a diagrammatic representation of how a typical botnet works.

A botnet propagates itself in a somewhat unusual way, as it actively searches and infects vulnerable websites by running active server pages. Once it finds a potential target, it performs structured query language (SQL) injections on the website, inserting an iFrame, which redirects the user visiting the

---

[6] Drive-by download broadly refers to the injection of malicious code without the knowledge of the victim. For instance, a user may download a programme and become target of malicious code. The attacks are almost exclusively launched through compromised legitimate websites which are used by attackers to host malicious links and actual malicious code.

Figure 9.1
How a Typical Botnet Works

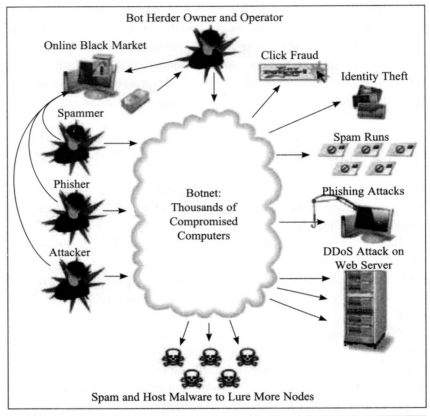

SOURCE: Microsoft Corporation (2012b).

site, to a site hosting malware. While bots are typically used for spam or rogue ware campaigns, they are also increasingly being used for DDoS attacks.

9.2.1. The Asprox Botnet, 2008

The Asprox botnet (discovered around 2008), also known by its aliases 'Badsrc' and 'Aseljo', was a botnet mostly involved in phishing scams and performing SQL injections into websites in order to spread malware.

Since its discovery the Asprox botnet has been involved in multiple high-profile attacks on various websites in order to spread malware. The botnet itself consisted of roughly 15,000 infected computers as of May 2008. However, the size of a botnet is highly variable since the controllers have been known to deliberately shrink (and later regrow) their botnets in order to prevent more aggressive countermeasures from the information technology (IT) community.

A botnet usually attacks in waves—the goal of each wave being to infect as many websites as possible—thus achieving the highest possible spread rate. Once a wave is completed the botnet lies dormant for an extended amount of time, most likely to prevent aggressive counter reactions from the security community. The initial wave of the Asprox botnet took place in July 2008, infecting an estimated 1,000–2,000 pages (Cyber insecure.com 2008; Poremba 2008). An additional wave took place in October 2009, infecting an unknown number of websites (Dave 2010; Trustwave 2010). Another wave took place in June 2010, increasing the estimated total number of infected domains from 2,000 to anything between 10,000 and 13,000 in a day (Dave 2010; Trustwave 2010). The Asprox incident in 2008 led to 50,000 hosts losing millions of dollars. The first reported financial loss was from Walmart. Similar incidents took place with Sony PlayStation, Adobe's Serious Magic website and several government, healthcare and business-related websites (Wilson, 2010).

The total amount of global spam in circulation decreased towards the end of 2010, with a number of major botnets reducing their output (Symantec Corporation 2011a). A primary reason behind this could be the shutdown of the Spamit affiliate programme in the fall of 2010. Spamit was the largest known pharmaceutical spam affiliate responsible predominantly for the 'Canadian Pharmacy' brand and the largest botnets sent related to pharmaceutical spam.

9.2.2. The Rustock Botnet, 2010

Rustock was the largest malicious botnet observed in 2010 and had more than one million bots under its control. It was followed by another equally malicious botnet called 'Cutwail' which also controlled many hundreds of thousands of bots. The volume of spam coming from the United States increased during the first half of 2010, accounting for 8 per cent of all global spam and spam from Rustock dominated the country. Rustock had a significant spam output of over 44 billion e-mails sent per day, translating to almost half of all spam e-mails sent by botnets in 2010 (Symantec Corporation 2011a). This was almost double its output by volume in 2009. It continues to be the largest botnet for spam, with an estimated size of between 1.1 and 1.7 million bots under its control during 2010 (Symantec Corporation 2011a).

Cybercrime is now getting more and more organized with cybercriminals supporting each other in their attack methods. For instance, Cutwail may spam messages containing the variants of the 'Bredo' malware and get paid per machine that they infect with the Bredo variant. These infected machines, which are part of the Cutwail botnet, report back to the Bredo botnet master. The same thing may happen between Zeus and Bredo. The criminals behind Zeus may pay the criminals behind Bredo to install their (Zeus) malware on infected machines. Zeus malware is capable of stealing bank account information, among other things. This results in an ongoing cycle of money moving from one group to another. Money is extracted from the affected user. Thus each time the malware is installed through the botnet, the criminals behind the botnet get paid.

The Rustock Botnet Takedown, 2010

The Rustock botnet was taken down by Microsoft on 16 March 2011. TrendLabs data showed more than a 95 per cent decrease in Rustock spam on 16 March, at around the same time the botnet was taken down. Microsoft published advertisements in Russian newspapers offering a $250,000 reward to anyone who gave information that would lead to the identification, arrest and conviction of the Rustock gang members. Microsoft's lawyers used novel legal arguments to convince a federal court in Seattle that it had the right to seize Rustock's servers, which set an important legal precedent for future cases (Trend Micro 2012a).

Rustock accounted for 36 per cent of all spam globally in 2010, including over 60 per cent of all spam in August and October. Legal action taken at the end of the first quarter of 2011—based, in part, on trademark abuse in spam—was used to seize Rustock's C&C servers and cut off its communication with its related bots. The result of the operation was a significant decrease in Rustock-related malicious activity that, combined with other botnet shutdowns, resulted in noticeable decreases in overall malicious activity from botnets during that quarter. This was especially true in the United States, where the majority of Rustock bots had been located (Trend Micro 2012a).

Discussions on botnets would be incomplete without a reference to the Conficker worm infection, which made use of the flaws in the Microsoft Windows operating system. Tackling this worm was difficult because it used a sophisticated mechanism to evade detection by antivirus software. It used administrator passwords (obtained by using a method called dictionary attack) to gain access to computers and linked them into a very big network. This helped the perpetrators of this worm to control the computers in the network.

9.2.3. The Mariposa Botnet, 2008

Mariposa, or butterfly in Spanish, referred to a network of about 13 million compromised systems, scattered across more than 190 countries worldwide, managed by a single C&C server in Spain (Leyden 2010). This malware, created by a set of cybercriminals, had the capability of spreading itself through various channels like universal serial bus (USB) drives, Internet messengers and peer-to-peer (P2P) technologies to remote computers. The computer infected by the malware was called the Mariposa botnet. It caused millions of dollars of damage in 2008 and 2009 before being detected and eliminated. The software was engineered to gain access to and maintain control over the victim machine. Infiltrating a user's computer was not difficult. Using a variety of software exploits and social engineering tactics, an attacker could find a way to distribute his malware to his victims.

This botnet has been dubbed one of the biggest networks of zombie computers in cyberspace alongside the Conficker and Zeus botnets. The Mariposa botnet was in existence as early as December 2008, and became better known in May 2009. However, in March 2010 came its shutdown and the subsequent arrest of three of its main perpetrators. The administrators of Mariposa also offered illegal services such as hacking servers to take control; encrypting bots to make them invisible to security applications; and creating anonymous virtual private networks (VPN) connections to administer bots.

Though it originated in Spain, eventually 190 countries were impacted by it, including Mexico, Brazil, Korea, Columbia, Russia, Egypt and Malaysia among others. The highest infection ratios were found in countries where education on computer security is not such a high priority. In other countries the infection rate was much less.

Botnet infections include the following (Gartner 2002; Microsoft Corporation 2010):

1. RCBot—lowers security settings.
2. Hamweq—spreads via removable drives, such as USB memory sticks. It contains an Internet relay chat (IRC)-based back door, which may request the machine to participate in DDoS attacks.
3. Rimecud—downloads malware to the affected computer which is designed to send spam messages and to download more malware.
4. Alureon—a Trojan and root kit which is designed to steal data by intercepting a system's network traffic and searching it for user-names, passwords and credit-card data.
5. Virut—infects executables and screensaver files and attempts to download additional malware; also injects an 'iFrame' object into HTML-based files; disables Windows file protection in order to infect essential protected Windows system files.

There are other cases where organized action by government and software companies has helped in the control of botnets. The shutdown of the Kelihos and Coreflood botnets are cases in point.

9.2.4. The Kelihos Botnet Takedown, 2011

In September 2011, Microsoft convinced a federal judge in the United States to allow it to block all of Kelihos' C&C servers' Internet protocol (IP) addresses without first informing their owners. The 'cz.cc' domain owner was explicitly named in the complaint. Shutting the domain down took hundreds of thousands of Kelihos' sub-domains offline, setting an example for all other rogue second-level domains (SLDs) to be more accountable for abuse incidents. Such types of attacks occurred mainly due to infected servers of Internet service providers (ISPs). The shutdown affected a total of 49,007 different IP addresses identified as infected by Kelihos (Trend Micro 2012a). The basic means or tools for such attacks are spam and viruses, and the objectives are theft of financial or important information, collecting e-mail addresses and sniffing user credentials from the network stream. Extreme spamming could even choke the network, causing loss of data and increasing the hop count[7] of transmission packets.

[7] Hop count is a measure of the distance between source and destination in a network. Here, each 'hop' refers to an intermediate router through which data must pass to cover the distance.

9.2.5. The Coreflood Botnet Takedown, 2011

In April 2011, the FBI was able to debilitate the Coreflood botnet after it was granted a temporary court order that allowed it to replace known Coreflood C&C servers with servers that it controlled (Trend Micro 2012a). As a result, each time a Coreflood bot contacted an agency-controlled server for instructions, that server would note the IP address of the bot and instruct it to stop operating. This would disable the bot until the next time the compromised computer rebooted. Using the logged IP addresses, the FBI worked with various ISPs to notify users that their computers were compromised and assisted them in the removal of the malicious code. The shutdown was facilitated by the United States Department of Justice and the FBI. The FBI took over the C&C servers and operated them until mid-June 2011. This event has been marked as the first time the United States government took over a botnet's C&C infrastructure and pushed a command to its bots to make them inaccessible to the botmasters.

9.3. ADVANCED PERSISTENT THREATS

Advanced persistent threat (APT) is a term used to refer to threats which persistently and effectively target a specific entity. It usually refers to a group, such as a government, with both the capability and the intent to persistently and effectively target a specific entity. The term is commonly used to refer to cyberthreats, in particular Internet-enabled espionage. Individuals, such as an individual hacker, are not usually referred to as an APT as they rarely have the resources to be both advanced and persistent even if they are intent on gaining access to, or attacking, a specific target. 'Lurid' may be categorized as a case of APT. The Stuxnet computer worm discussed earlier is considered a case of state terrorism. The Iranian government may consider the Stuxnet creators as an APT.

9.3.1. Lurid Advanced Persistent Threat Cyberattacks, 2011

Lurid was discovered as an ongoing series of targeted attacks which were known to have successfully compromised 1,465 computers in 61 different countries. It had victims in diplomatic missions, government ministries, space-related government agencies, as well as other companies and research institutions (Villeneuve and Sancho 2011).

The countries most impacted by this attack were Russia, Kazakhstan and Vietnam, along with numerous other countries from the Commonwealth of Independent States (in the former Soviet Union). This particular campaign comprised over 300 malicious targeted attacks that were monitored by the attackers using a unique identifier embedded in the associated malware. An analysis of the campaigns revealed that attackers targeted communities in specific geographic locations, as well as specific victims.

The attackers used a C&C network of 15 domain names and 10 active IP addresses in all to maintain persistent control over the 1,465 victims. The Lurid downloader, often referred to as 'Enfal', belonged to a well-known malware family. It was, however, not created with a publicly available toolkit that could be purchased by any aspiring cybercriminal. This malware family had in the past been used to target both the United States government and non-governmental organizations (NGOs). However, there appeared to be no direct links between this particular network and earlier ones.

Targeted malware attacks such as these are described as advanced persistent threats in which a target receives an e-mail that encourages her to open an attached file. The file sent by the attackers contains a malicious code that exploits vulnerabilities in popular software such as Adobe Reader (.pdf) and Microsoft Office (.doc). The payload of these exploits is a malware that is silently executed on the target's computer. This allows the attackers to take control of the computer and to obtain data. The attackers may then laterally move throughout the target's network and often maintain control over compromised computers for extended periods of time. Ultimately, the attacks locate and extract sensitive information from the victim's network. The main motivation behind this incident is to take control of computers in government ministries and diplomatic missions as well as space-related government agencies and research institutions and to obtain data (Villeneuve and Sancho 2011).

9.4. HOW TO PROTECT ONESELF AGAINST BOTNETS

Most networks use multiple firewalls and a layered security approach for protection against botnets (Spam Laws: http://www.spamlaws.com/how-botnets-work.html). Patching the operating system and installing the updates regularly can be a good measure to counter the problem of botnets. It is always good to have an antivirus installed and updated from time to time, to safeguard against an attack from, or inclusion in, a botnet. Other steps that can be taken to prevent botnet attacks are:

- Full-Fledged Security Systems: Many companies and organizations deploy full-fledged network security systems covering all levels of the network, right from individual computers to the servers, local area networks and external connectivity to the Web. They also install intrusion detection systems and protection at the gateway to e-mail servers.
- Disabling Unused Ports: Another effective measure is shut down all unused ports not required for specific applications on the network. These are mainly those ports which are used for file transfer protocol (FTP) applications and Internet relay chats, which are the prime applications hackers use to get the bot computers to communicate with the bot herder.
- Isolation: This involves isolating the infected computer from the network as soon as an attack is detected by the security system. The infected computer is used to educate the organization on the security breach, so that a patch can be developed to repair the vulnerability.
- Educating Users: Companies and organizations must educate users on how to browse with care, at the same time stressing on the need to be wary of opening e-mail attachments that may contain botnet software.

Despite all this, we have to accept that there will always be a sizeable portion of the Internet-using community, many of them consumers, who we are unlikely to educate on Internet security best practices. For a variety of reasons they will continue to not use antivirus and firewall software, they will not install security updates and latest versions of software. Those people are a fertile ground for cybercriminals to infect with malicious attacks and recruit into botnets. And they in turn pose a security threat to the broader Internet-using community.

TEN

HACKING AND STRUCTURED QUERY LANGUAGE INJECTION

———◆———

The traditional meaning of the word 'hacking' is the reconfiguring or reprogramming of a computer system, which is not authorized or permitted by the computer administrator. Many hacking attempts are done using readily available tools on the Internet.

A hacker is an unauthorized user who attempts to or gains access to an information system. Hacking is a crime even if there is no visible damage to the system, since it is an invasion into the privacy of data. There could be many motives behind hacking, varying from mischief to elaborate plans of hacking into complex systems of companies and governments. Over many years in the past, several attempts have been organized by governments and specific task forces to hack into other government systems.

10.1. HACKERS AND THEIR CRITICAL ROLE IN CYBERCRIME

The word hacker in the 1960s referred to a person who was capable of solving technologically complex problems. Till the 1980s, hackers were people who had superior computing skills. Some of the hackers in this period were even glorified by the media.

According to Sandberg (1995), 'Cyber crime-related institutions and related organizations have undergone gradual changes.' In developing countries, high levels of poverty combined with good education levels are seen as potential factors leading young people towards cybercrime. In Russia and eastern Europe, students good at mathematics, physics and computer science find it difficult to get jobs (Bryan-Low 2005). Lack of employment opportunities has led to an increase in cybercrimes. Resourceful hackers now want to get paid well (Sandberg 1995).

Further, the nature of technology, proliferation of communities and organized crime groups which support hacking have contributed to a reduction in the complexity of cybercrime. Most hacking tools are widely available online and require little or no expertise. Less skilful criminals can also secure the help of experienced hackers easily, thanks to the Internet.

In schools, parents and teachers emphasize the use of the Internet as a tool to enhance education. However, awareness of Internet safety, security and cyber ethics is lacking. For cybercriminals, it is an opportunity to build on cybercrime.

10.1.1. The Sony PlayStation Case, 2011

A cyberattack penetrated the PlayStation network in 2011, and personal information of more than 80 million users was compromised. The cost of the breach was over 170 million dollars. Following a criminal cyberattack on the company's data centre located in San Diego, California in the United States, Sony Network Entertainment International quickly turned off the PlayStation Network and Qriocity services, engaged multiple expert information security firms over the course of several days and conducted an extensive audit of the system. The intrusion was discovered between 17 April and 19 April in 2011 and the PlayStation Network was taken down on 20 April. On 26 April, Sony notified the owners of 10 million accounts that their personal information, including credit-card information, had been compromised in the attack.

The tool used in the incident was a very basic technique of hacking, the structured query language (SQL) injection, where a malicious code is infested in the web form to get the desired data. This breach of the Sony Online Entertainment personal computer (PC) games network was discovered after a review of the PlayStation Network intrusion. Sony said it occurred a day earlier than the PlayStation break-in, between 17 April and 19 April. The names, addresses, e-mails, birth dates, phone numbers and other information of 24.6 million PC games' customers were stolen from its servers. Sony also said the financial records of users from an outdated 2007 database, involving people outside the United States, may also have been stolen, including 10,700 direct debit records of customers in Austria, Germany, the Netherlands and Spain.

Following this incident the company shut down the Sony Online Entertainment service, which was available on PCs, Facebook and the PlayStation 3 console. EverQuest, Free Realms and DC Universe Online were its most popular games.

The incident led to a loss of all administrative details (personal identification information, including passwords, e-mail addresses and birth dates) of Sony Pictures, as well as 75,000 music codes and 3.5 million music coupons (Ogg 2011).

10.2. HOW DOES HACKING WORK?

Hackers crack complex security systems, steal private information and may try to corrupt a company or person's website. All websites and computer-related programs are run by some sort of code. Whatever be the program used to design it, such as 'HTML', 'C++', or 'JavaScript', hackers try to exploit the code and find its weakness. They look for a way to get around the security codes by using special programs or writing their own codes to try and alter the original. Some sites are currently difficult or impossible to be hacked, and these are the sites that hackers target the most, since they present a challenge. Hacking creates a sense of accomplishment, but the stakes are high: hackers face jail terms and heavy fines if caught.

10.2.1. The Washington Post Case, 2011

In 2011, the *Washington Post* reported that a data breach had compromised an estimated 1.27 million accounts on its jobseeker site thus proving that the seemingly endless series of cyberattacks had finally caught up with the media industry as well and that no one was immune (Hoffman 2011c).

The Washington Post said in July 2011 that its 'Jobs' section had experienced a cyberattack by an 'unauthorized third party' in what it described as 'two brief episodes' occurring on 27 and 28 June 2011. The hackers made off with user identities and e-mail addresses but failed to obtain passwords and other personal identification data. The Post warned that the stolen e-mail addresses could be used by the hackers to launch spam attacks or wage targeted campaigns against users. 'We are taking this incident very seriously,' the Post said in its alert. 'We quickly identified the vulnerability and shut it down, and are pursuing the matter with law enforcement. We sincerely apologize for this inconvenience' (Hoffman 2011c).

According to Symantec Corporation (2011a), hacking continues to be the leading cause for identities exposed. Although hacking was only the third most common cause of data breaches that could lead to identity theft in 2010, it was the top cause for reported identities exposed. In 2009, hacking was responsible for more than half of the identities exposed. Breaches such as these can be especially damaging for enterprises because they may contain sensitive data relating to customers as well as employees, which even an average attacker can sell to the criminal underworld.

10.2.2. The Epsilon Case, 2011

The hack into Epsilon was one of the worst data breaches in corporate history, with a cost that could have reached four billion dollars. Epsilon was a provider of marketing and e-mail marketing solutions to many large organizations, seven of which appeared among the top 10 in the 'Fortune 100' list. The Dallas-based company was known to send over 40 billion e-mails a year to more than 2,500 companies and was estimated to possess around 250 million e-mail addresses. The true extent of damage that occurred when these were compromised was difficult to fully grasp. The lessons to be learnt from the Epsilon cyberattack are: pay attention to credible warning signs, and proactively implement the necessary security controls and defences to reduce risk; increase the probability that an attack will be discovered; and minimize the damage. The details of exactly how Epsilon was breached are still murky, but it is worrying that multiple Epsilon customers were compromised from a seemingly single attack (Bradley 2011).

Data stolen by hackers pose future threats to customers in the form of malware circulation or phishing campaigns. Malware and spyware were the tools used for the cyberattack. Spyware can collect almost any type of data, including personal information like Internet-surfing habits, user logins and bank or credit account information. It can also interfere with user control of a computer by installing additional software or redirecting web browsers. Some spyware can change computer settings, resulting in slow Internet connection speeds, unauthorized changes in browser settings or affect other functionalities of the software.

10.3. STRUCTURED QUERY LANGUAGE INJECTION

Structured query language (SQL) injection is a type of attack where hackers inject malicious code into legitimate websites by exploiting security vulnerabilities in the database layer of an application. Whenever a user visits such a website, the malicious code is downloaded to the user's computer. In many cases, users visiting these infected websites are redirected to malicious websites which trigger undetected downloads of malware, Trojans or viruses on the user's computer.

> An SQL query involves a request for some action to be performed on a database. Typically, on a Web form for user authentication when a user enters his name and password into the text boxes provided, those values get inserted into a SELECT query. If the values entered are found to be as expected, the user is allowed access; if they aren't, access is denied. However, most Web forms have no mechanisms in place to block input other than names and passwords. Unless such precautions are taken, an attacker can use the input boxes to send their own request to the database, which could allow them to download the entire database or interact with it in other illicit ways.
>
> The risk of SQL injection exploits is on the rise because of the availability of automated tools. In the past, the danger was somewhat limited because an exploit had to be carried out manually. The attacker had to actually type his SQL statement into a text box. However, automated SQL injection programs are now available, and as a result, both the likelihood and the potential damage of an exploit have increased enormously. (Rouse 2010)

The automation of SQL injections has given rise to the possibility of an SQL injection worm, which is very common nowadays.

For instance, in July 2010, a South American security researcher obtained sensitive user information from the popular 'BitTorrent' site. He gained access to the site's administrative control panel and exploited an SQL injection vulnerability that enabled him to collect user-account information, including Internet protocol (IP) addresses, MD5[1] password hashes and records which torrents individual users had uploaded. The year 2011 witnessed the worst mass SQL injection attacks. Eight million pages were infected during the 'willysy.com' attack and one million pages were infected during an attack targeting ASP.NET sites (Trend Micro 2012a).

---

[1] MD5 is Message Digest algorithm that produces 128-bit hash-value and is used in cryptographic security applications and to check data integrity.

10.3.1. The Citibank Case, 2011

In May 2011 hackers compromised Citibank's extranet web servers through SQL injection techniques, allowing remote command execution. They also used commonly available hacker tools like NMAP and NIKTO, which were uploaded on the compromised web servers, allowing attackers to pivot into the bank's network. According to Citibank's official announcement the impacted customers were only 1 per cent of its total 21 million customers, which translated to a total of 360,083 North American Citigroup credit card accounts. Of those affected, some 217,657 customers were reissued new cards along with a notification letter, while the remaining accounts were either inactive or had already received new cards earlier, the bank added. Customers had their names, account numbers and contact information accessed, but Citibank said that 'data critical to commit fraud was not compromised' and that other consumer banking online systems were not accessed. There was no impact on debit card customers.

As major American lenders come under growing pressure from lawmakers to improve account security, Citigroup Inc. said the cyberattack in May 2011 affected almost twice as many accounts as the bank's figures had initially suggested.

Citigroup had identified 'the majority' of compromised accounts within seven days, adding that the while information on the accounts was accessed by 24 May, it only started notifying customers of the breach on 3 June. According to reports, Citibank may have suffered close to 4.3 million dollars of tangible losses, being the cost of giving replacement cards to all the affected customers (taking cost of replacement card as $20 a piece and multiplying it by 217,657) (Aspan and Soh 2011).

Primarily used to access databases of various types, SQL-injection attacks usually represent a sophisticated class of attacks with a determined aggressor.

10.4. HOW DOES STRUCTURED QUERY LANGUAGE INJECTION WORK?

The structured query language (SQL) injection process works by prematurely terminating a text string and appending a new command. Because the inserted command may have additional strings appended to it before it is executed, the malefactor terminates the injected string with a comment mark

'--'. Subsequent text is ignored at execution time. (http://msdn.microsoft. com/en-us/library/ms161953%28v= sql.105%29.aspx)

Figure 10.1 is a representation of how the process works.

A successful SQL injection attack enables a malicious user to execute commands in the application's database by using the privileges granted to the application's login. The problem is more severe if the application uses an over-privileged account[2] to connect to the database. For instance, if the application's login has privileges to eliminate a database, then without adequate safeguards, an attacker might be able to perform this operation.

The most common vulnerabilities that make data access codes susceptible to SQL injection attacks are weak input validation; dynamic construction of SQL statements without the use of type-safe parameters;[3] use of over-privileged database logins and so on.

10.4.1. The Xbox Live Clans[4] Case, 2012

This incident took place on 24 January 2012. A user with the 'v bulletin'-based forum[5] extracted the usernames and encrypted passwords of 34,000 users on the forum. These usernames were in the form of e-mail addresses used to register on the site, and the passwords were encrypted. The hacker with the username 'alsa7rx' posted all the information on Pastebin—a public paste site (http://pastebin.com/MaQ7ipmv), potentially exposing all the forum's members. The administrators of the Xbox Live Clans website did not officially announce the data breach but has been working on securing its customers. Advice is given to the users of the site to change their passwords. This type of data breach is a much greater threat than it sounds because of the general

---

[2] Privilege in computing means the permission to perform an action such as read, write or delete over a computer system. Sometimes a user may be given more system privileges/permissions than he/she actually requires. If the application is connected to a database through an over-privileged account, an SQL account is made possible.

[3] Using a list of acceptable characters/parameters to constrain input to the database.

[4] xboxliveclans.com is a website which gives information about xbox 360 game forum with xbox news, xbox clans, xbox videos and xbox tournaments.

[5] vbulletin is an application to make web-based community forum using PHP and uses a MySQL database server.

Figure 10.1
How SQL Injection Works

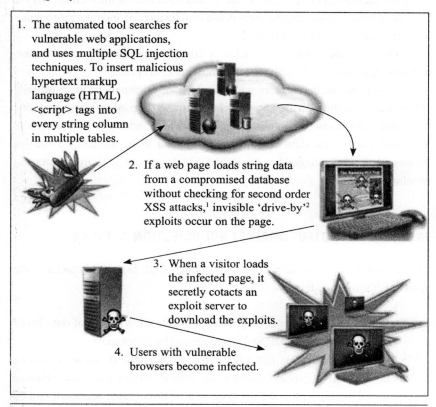

1. The automated tool searches for vulnerable web applications, and uses multiple SQL injection techniques. To insert malicious hypertext markup language (HTML) <script> tags into every string column in multiple tables.

2. If a web page loads string data from a compromised database without checking for second order XSS attacks,[1] invisible 'drive-by'[2] exploits occur on the page.

3. When a visitor loads the infected page, it secretly cotacts an exploit server to download the exploits.

4. Users with vulnerable browsers become infected.

SOURCE: Gartner (2002).

NOTES: [1] Second order XSS attack: Cross-Site Scripting (XSS) is a type of vulnerability in which an attacker may inject malware into web pages viewed by users by exploiting some aspect of web-browser security. A second-order code injection attack can be classified as the process in which malicious code is injected into an application and not immediately executed, but instead is stored by the application (for example, temporarily cached, logged and stored in a database) and then later retrieved and executed by the victim on the computer. For instance, the malware may get activated on some later date. Therefore, second order XSS attacks are special cases of malware injection where the malware may be dormant for some time.

[2] Drive-by exploits: Drive-by exploit broadly refers to the injection of malicious code without the knowledge of the victim. For instance, a user may download a programme or a web-browser plug-in such as Java, Adobe Reader and Adobe Flash and become target of malicious code. The attacks are almost exclusively launched through compromised legitimate websites which are used by attackers to host malicious links and actual malicious code.

human tendency of using the same passwords for more than one site. Also since the usernames in this case are the e-mail addresses of the members of the site, the e-mail accounts of the users could also be hacked and thus more sensitive information could be extracted.

The leaked data, which totalled over 20 MB of accounts, was in the format of e-mail passwords with all of them being encrypted.

It was expected that alsa7rx would make a lot of gamers panic, especially if they had used the website xboxliveclans.com and signed up using the same usernames and password combinations everywhere, which is very common. The total cost of the data breach was calculated to be around 7.3 million dollars (http://hackmageddon.com/2012/02/02/january-2012-cyber-attacks-timeline-part-2/).

10.5. HOW TO PROTECT AGAINST SQL INJECTION ATTACKS

The following are some of the ways to counter SQL injection attacks at the system administrator level:

- Input data should be constrained and sanitized. Validity of data based on type, length, format and range should be checked.
- An account that has restricted permissions in the database should be used. Ideally, 'execute' permissions should only be granted to selected stored procedures in the database and no direct table access should be provided.
- Disclosing database error information should be avoided. In the event of database errors, it should be ensured that detailed error messages are not disclosed to the user. (Meier et al. 2003)

10.6. WEB DEFACEMENT

Web defacement occurs when a hacker changes the front page of a website to something other than what was originally there. A message is often left on the web page stating the hacker's pseudonym. Sometimes, the defacer makes fun of the system administrator for failing to maintain server security. Although most of the time the defacement is harmless, one must remain cautious because it can sometimes be used as a distraction to cover up more sinister actions such as uploading malware.

The Indian Computer Emergency Response Team (CERT-In) has been tracking cases of defacement of Indian websites and suggesting suitable measures to strengthen the web servers of concerned organizations. In all, 14,348 cases of defacements were identified in the year 2010. Most of them were carried out for the websites under the '.in' domain (CERT-In 2011). Totally, 9,772 '.in' domain websites were defaced. Figure 10.2 contains detailed statistics of defacement of Indian websites in 2010.

Figure 10.2
Indian Websites Defaced in the Year 2010

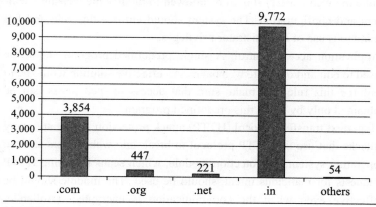

SOURCE: CERT-In (2011: 5).

10.6.1. How Web Defacement Works

The defacer changes the visual appearance of the site or a web page. These are typically the work of system crackers, who break into a web server and replace the hosted website with one of their own.

10.6.2. The Sun Case, 2011

An anonymous group targeted Rupert Murdoch with a series of derogatory hacks against the website of The Sun newspaper while pledging that e-mail leaks and data disclosures were to follow in the near future. The Sun's website was defaced in 2011 by redirecting visitors to a phony homepage, which claimed that News Corp. Chairman and CEO Rupert Murdoch had died of drug overdose in his garden (Hoffman 2011d).

10.6.3. How to Protect against Web Defacement

- On-the-spot prevention: The attack should be identified at the service request level since at this stage the request has not yet been executed.
- Administrator resistance: Most hackers first gain privileged rights and then try to deface the site. Therefore, it is a good practice to restrict the privileges of the administrator account on a web server machine. Instead of the administrator account, only a specific predefined user (like the web master) should be allowed to modify the website's content and configuration. The system should enforce this rule and fail malicious use of administrator privileges.
- Application access control: A single predefined program should be used to edit and/or create web pages. An effective solution would be to enforce this rule and make sure that access to web pages can be obtained only by using this predefined program.
- Hypertext transfer protocol (HTTP) attack protection: There are many attacks that use the HTTP protocol to break into web servers and the operating system. A protection module, which scans incoming HTTP requests for malicious intent, should be used. The module should be effective even when the communication is encrypted. (Hollander 2000)

ELEVEN

SOCIAL ENGINEERING TECHNIQUES

Social engineering is a form of cybercrime in which criminals attempt to obtain confidential information from their victims through deception and persuasion techniques. This data is later used for identity theft or to access sensitive computer systems. Social engineering, in the form of intriguing e-mail messages or which appear to be from legitimate organizations, is often used to convince users to click on a malicious link or download malware.

For example, users may think they have received a notice from their bank, or a virus warning from the system administrator, when they might have actually received a mass-mailing worm. Again, e-mail messages such as e-cards from unspecified friends may try to persuade users to open the attached card and download the malware. Malware can also be downloaded from web pages unintentionally by users. Dumpster diving (where attackers go through dustbins to obtain information) and office snooping are some other forms of social engineering techniques.

A cybercriminal does extensive research on the enterprise and the individual (legal and illicit), which is then used to exploit people. A successful social engineering technique results in the cybercriminal partly or fully circumventing an enterprise's security systems. Even the best security systems prove useless if the person who is responsible for guarding the access codes and the information in an enterprise herself gives it away. Social engineering mainly involves the manipulation of people rather than technology to breach security Gartner (2002).

Figure 11.1 is a pictorial representation of how social engineering works.

Figure 11.1
How Social Engineering Works

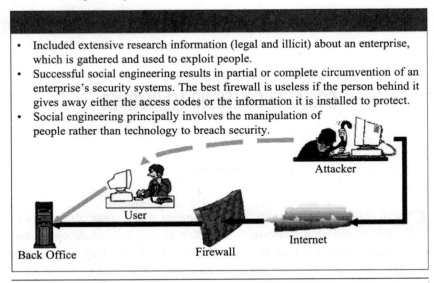

- Included extensive research information (legal and illicit) about an enterprise, which is gathered and used to exploit people.
- Successful social engineering results in partial or complete circumvention of an enterprise's security systems. The best firewall is useless if the person behind it gives away either the access codes or the information it is installed to protect.
- Social engineering principally involves the manipulation of people rather than technology to breach security.

Attacker

User

Internet

Back Office   Firewall

SOURCE: Gartner (2002).

Social engineering is a catch-all term for psychological tricks used to persuade people to undermine their own online security. This could include opening an e-mail attachment, clicking a button, following a link or filling in a form with sensitive personal information. Scams of all sorts, and many of the methods used to spread malware, make use of social engineering techniques, and target human desires and fears, or just plain curiosity, to get past the caution they should be exercising when browsing online.

11.1. COMMON TACTICS

Famous hacker Kevin Mitnick helped popularize the term social engineering in the 1990s, but the simple idea itself (tricking someone into doing something or divulging sensitive information) has been around for a long time. For instance, stealing a company's hold music, spoofing caller identities and so on. Social engineers blend different methods, old and new, to seize passwords, install malware or grab profits.

It is said that in 200 BC, the Hun invaders threatened the security of China. The Chinese emperor constructed the Great Wall to defend against the Hun invaders. In AD 1275, Kublai Khan, a Hun ruler, bribed the gatekeeper to open the gate and this finally led to the invasion. People can be the weakest link. 'You can have the best technology; firewalls, intrusion-detection systems, biometric devices ... and somebody can call an unsuspecting employee and get everything' (quoted by Kevin Mitnick in Abreu 2000).

According to *Sophos Security Threat Report 2011*, the number one goal of a social engineer who uses the telephone as her modus operandi is to convince her target that she is either a fellow employee or a trusted outside authority. But if her ultimate goal is to gain information from or about a particular employee, her first calls or e-mails might go to a different person. The targeting of employees may start with the receptionist or even the guard at the gate who is watching a parking lot. That is why training has to filter down to the staff. The secretary, driver, receptionist and the other people cybercriminals start with are easily accessible. A cybercriminal may use them to get information about people higher up in the hierarchy. A social engineering criminal will study the communication channel in the organization and take cues from the surroundings to win the trust of the people in that organization. She will then use this trust to extract more information.

Successful social engineering requires time, persistence and patience. Attacks are often slow and methodical. The build-up not only includes collecting personal titbits about people, but also collecting other 'social cues' to build trust and even fool others into thinking they are employees, when they are actually not. Another successful technique involves recording the 'hold' music a company uses when callers are left waiting on the phone. A criminal may use this music when an employee from the organization calls up, to make them believe that he is a part of the organization.

Spoofing phone numbers is another tactic used by criminals to HYPERLINK 'http://www.csoonline.com/article/221064/Truth_Lies_and_ Caller_ID' make a different number show up on the target's caller identification system. The criminal could be sitting somewhere else but the number that shows up on the caller identification appears to come from within the company. Of course, unsuspecting victims are more than likely to give private information, like passwords, over the phone if the caller identification legitimizes it. And, of course, the crime is often undetectable later because once dialled, the number goes back to an internal office number.

A cybercriminal may use the news headlines to get access to his victims. He may use this information as social engineering lures for spam, phishing and other scams.

The Trojan horse malware is a classic example of a social engineering technique. Taking its name from the ancient tale of the huge wooden horse that the Greeks constructed and left at the gates of Troy as a gift, today's Trojan horse also works by bypassing security defences. This malware routinely uses the Trojan horse scheme by disguising files as 'free' or cracked software, and may include sex videos or any other hidden means to get past security.

By mid-2010, Facebook recorded half a billion active users, making it not only the largest social networking site, but also one of the most popular destinations on the Web. People have begun to use the Internet differently after the advent of social networking. Young people are less likely to use e-mails today, and are more prone to communicate through Facebook, Twitter or other social sites. It is not surprising therefore, that this massive and committed database has also fallen prey to diverse and steadily growing attacks of scammers and malware purveyors throughout 2010.

One of the more common types of attacks on Facebook users today is 'clickjacking'. These attacks use maliciously created pages, where the true function of a button is concealed beneath an opaque layer showing something entirely different. Often, sharing or 'liking' the content in question sends the attack out to contacts through newsfeeds and status updates, thereby propagating the scam. Clickjacking uses the standard arsenal of social engineering techniques to lure new victims and trick them into clicking on the disguised links. Alongside the usual barrage of lures such as humour, compromising pictures of celebrities and major news and entertainment events, there has also been a rise in increasingly bizarre and often gruesome content.

Clickjacking attacks not only spread social networking link spam, but also regularly carry out other actions, such as granting access to valuable personal information and even making purchases. One of the main financial motivations behind clickjacking is money earned from survey scams.

On the Internet, criminals may target simple typographical errors made by users hoping that the user erroneously lands on a fake site. This site may try to steal information, push malware or sell something to the unsuspecting user.

A survey report by Cisco found that only about one in five websites analysed was malicious by design. This led to the conclusion that most of the web-based malware was being hosted on innocent but compromised websites, unknown to their owners (Sophos 2007; OECD 2008a).

11.2. HOW TO PROTECT ONESELF

Of late, there has been a reported rise in the number of cyber incidents. These are suspected to be the result of social engineering, which involves approaching an individual, either online or in person, and manipulating them into providing personal information that can be used to break into a computer network or assume someone's identity.

To avoid becoming a victim of a social engineering attacks, one must:

- Be suspicious of unsolicited contact from individuals seeking internal organizational data or personal information.
- Never provide personal information or passwords or information about one's organization over e-mail or on the phone.
- Pay attention to website uniform resource locators (URLs) that use a variation in spelling or a different domain (for example, '.com' versus '.net').
- Type web addresses manually to avoid malicious links. Also, it must be remembered that it is very rare for a site to send out a request for a password change or an account update.
- Verify a request's authenticity by contacting the company directly.
- Install and maintain antivirus software, firewalls and e-mail filters.
- Report any incident one suspects to be a social engineering attack to the concerned authority such as Cert-In in India immediately. Change passwords periodically. (http://www.dhs.gov/cybersecurity-tips)

TWELVE

NEWER THREATS

———◆◄●►◆———

This chapter discusses newer threats which affect cyberspace, such as risks associated with social media, mobile security threats and security issues relating to the Cloud.

12.1. SOCIAL MEDIA RISKS

Social networking sites are websites one can use to contact friends, share music, photos and join communities of like-minded people. Social networking websites function like an online community of Internet users. Depending on the website, many of these online community members share common interests in hobbies, religion or politics. With the evolution of new technologies and growing popularity of social media like Facebook and Twitter, we are witnessing an increase in threats related to information security. Social networking sites rely on communication and building connections, which encourages the user to provide a certain amount of information. Sometimes people do not exercise restraint in sharing information as the Internet provides a sense of anonymity; the lack of physical interaction provides a false sense of security and they tailor information for their friends, forgetting that others may also see it. Although social networking and online sites can be quite useful and are extremely popular, it is important to remember that sharing too much information online can be risky.

12.1.1. The Dark Side of Social Media

The increasing use of social media today has resulted in high levels of security risk. Cybercriminals may be drawn to such sites because of the accessibility and amount of personal information that is available. It is easy to steal personal and other information about individuals from social networks. The personal information can also be used to conduct a social engineering attack. Additionally, because of the popularity of these sites, attackers may use them to distribute malicious code.

This security risk is a critical factor for individuals as well as corporations. There are three broad categories of security risk arising from the use of social media: (a) malware infection, (b) data leakages and (c) unwilling attack participation. Social networks with hundreds of millions of users are logical targets of cybercrime. User accounts can be used to create accounts in forums for propagating spam, phishing links, links to fake products or services or even for malicious downloads. Criminals are increasingly using social networking sites to perpetrate identity frauds for financial gains or espionage. Predators target children using social networking sites. Studies indicate that on an average, children have 56 online friends. A majority (that is, about 82 per cent) of them have met more than half of their online friends in real life. About 41 per cent have someone they do not know trying to add them as friends (Ng 2011). These unknown people can be sources of cybercrime.

12.1.2. Trends in Social Media Risks

The recent attacks on Twitter, Facebook and MySpace clearly indicate that cybercriminals are exploiting the viral nature of Web 2.0. Cybercrime is spreading rapidly through social networking sites. According to prior research about Web 2.0 technologies conducted by McAfee Labs, 6 out of 10 organizations experience some sort of security incident because of Web 2.0 technologies in which virus and malware infections are quite common (McAfee 2010b).

Though 2011 was not a very good year for site administrators and regulators, it proved to be a boon for social media spammers and scammers. Survey scams and all kinds of spam leveraging every trending topic imaginable littered social networking sites. Armed with sophisticated social engineering and hacking tactics and tools, spammers and scammers alike continued to wreak havoc among social networkers worldwide. Regulators started demanding that social networking sites implement policies and mechanisms to protect the privacy of their users (Trend Micro 2012a). There is every possibility of new users making mistakes and divulging private information due to lack of awareness, no matter which social network they use.

Spamming is on the rise in social networks. Phishing and malware incidents have also become common. This continues to cause problems for businesses with a large number of corporate houses worried that employee behaviour on social sites could endanger company security (Sophos 2011).

12.1.3. Social Media Security Risk—Classification

Gone are the days when social engineering attacks came from strange e-mail addresses, employed seemingly malicious links or had bad grammar. Today, the attacks are sophisticated, well planned, smartly composed and so well directed that they are almost impossible to track. Hackers 'sneak' in amongst the friends, learn about the interests of the person, gain trust and convincingly masquerade as friends. The Internet and social networks provide ample information for tailoring a well-directed cyberattack. According to Trend Micro (2012a), e-mail addresses, hometown and high school information were the top three publicly available pieces of information on social media. Likejacking attacks,[1] rogue application propagation attacks[2] and spam campaigns were the three most common attacks Facebook encountered.

[1] In a 'likejacking attack' a cyber criminal may conceal malware behind the 'Like' link. A user who clicks on the 'Like' button would unknowingly become a victim.

[2] In a rogue application attack, when a victim clicks on a link, it downloads an application on the user computer. If installed, this application proceeds to post the same spam message on behalf of the victim. Sometimes, such applications may lead to a survey which is a part of affiliate marketing scheme. In such cases, the scammers may earn a commission for each completed survey.

Examples include the rogue applications titled 'Find out who has viewed your profile recently', 'When will you die', etc., attacks targeted at Facebook users. The social networking applications such as Facebook and twitter are more vulnerable to these kinds of attacks. The Facebook is mostly very responsive to such threats and removes them as soon as they are identified. However, such applications propagate very fast on the social networks and generate a lot of traffic before they are stopped.

Survey Scams

In these scams, attackers use newsworthy events and tempting offers, such as tickets to movie premieres, to trick users into clicking links to survey pages. The survey scam' tricks unsuspecting users by tempting them to install an application from a spammed link. To make this application's alleged (often fake) functionality work, users are asked to fill in their personal data. This sends out links to a new stash of contacts, who must also fill in a survey form. Thus, the affiliate systems help the application creators earn money (Sophos 2011). The victims on the other hand, end up with stolen personal data or, worse still, thinner wallets.

Social Media Spam

This uses practically every current topic possible to lure victims (for instance, Lady Gaga's supposed death). The spammers usually take advantage of even the most unfortunate events, such as 'Hurricane Irene' in the United States, to attack as many victims as possible, mostly for financial gains. To make the attacks look genuine, spammers use the names of reputed media companies such as the British Broadcasting Corporation (BBC) as 'senders'. Spammers also make use of links to phishing pages and fake sites that host malware or act as site redirectors. Spamming rides on popular gadget or application releases to get user clicks and spreads by getting automatically reposted on victims' 'walls' or 're-tweets' (Trend Micro 2012a).

Social networks provide convenient platforms for cybercriminals to target their victims by leveraging new feeds to spread spam, promote scams and launch massive attacks. By mining profile information, a hacker can easily launch targeted social engineering attacks and befriend people by impersonating their friends. Facebook, which is the largest social networking platform today, is the most targeted by cybercriminals. It has a major flaw in its application system, which allows any user to create an application that can be installed and run by another user. The scale of malicious activities on Facebook is getting out of control and people are gradually taking note of this fact. A Sophos poll in June 2010 found that most of the respondents wanted Facebook to take steps to prevent 'likejacking' attacks (especially 'clickjacking' by liking something on Facebook) and urged the site to impose stricter controls on the plug-in (Sophos 2011). A 'walled garden' approach may be more suitable to combat this serious problem. Under this approach, a closed or restricted set of information services is provided to users, as opposed to allowing open access to applications and content. Apple's App Store operates in this way. The applications require official approval before they can be uploaded on to the site and shared with others. This has been effective in protecting users from the menace of malicious applications.

Another method is to give users with security concerns the option to secure their own page, allowing only vetted applications to run. However, it is argued that this second approach would only protect the more aware and cautious users, who in any case are less likely to fall for scammers' social engineering tricks. Since it would not do much to reduce the spam flooding from less secure users, a full-spectrum control system is preferable. Nevertheless, one must remember that even officially vetted and approved applications cannot be entirely trusted. There are occasional slip ups, allowing applications like 'user data harvester' to make it to the 'verified' list (Sophos 2011).

Organizational Security Policies

Organizations need to build an internal policy with regard to social networking sites, thus restricting the number of sites that can be accessed from the workplace. Most organizations try to avoid weak passwords by laying down requirements about the length and use of alphanumeric combinations, and requiring employees to change their passwords periodically. However, the rise of social media and 'cloud' computing is exacerbating the password problem and making it easier to make predictable guesses about passwords.

12.1.4. Social Media—How to Play Safe

The popularity of social networking sites continues to increase, especially among teenagers and young adults. The nature of these sites introduces security risks, so you should take certain precautions. As a general rule, you should never put anything on social networks that you would not feel comfortable telling a total stranger. After all, you never really know who is going to read your information, or what they could possibly do with it (US Computer Emergency Readiness Team: http://www.us-cert.gov/cas/tips/ST06-003.html).

Limit the Amount of Personal Information You Post

Do not post information that would make you vulnerable, such as your address or information about your schedule or routine. If your connections post information about you, make sure the combined information is not more than you would be comfortable with strangers knowing. Also be considerate when posting information, including photos, about your connections.

Remember That the Internet Is a Public Resource

Only post information you are comfortable with anyone seeing. This includes information and photos in your profile and in blogs and other forums. Also, once you post information online, you cannot retract it. Even if you remove the information from a site, saved or cached versions may still exist on other people's machines.

Be Wary of Strangers

The Internet makes it easy for people to misrepresent their identities and motives. Consider limiting the people who are allowed to contact you on these sites. If you interact with people you do not know, be cautious about the amount of information you reveal or agreeing to meet them in person.

Be Sceptical

Do not believe everything you read online. People may post false or misleading information about various topics, including their own identities. This is not necessarily done with malicious intent; it could be unintentional, an exaggeration or a joke. Take appropriate precautions and try to verify the authenticity of any information before taking any action.

Evaluate Your Settings

Take advantage of a site's privacy settings. The default settings for some sites may allow anyone to see your profile. You can customize your settings to restrict access to only certain people. However, there is a risk that even this private information could be exposed, so do not post anything that you would not want the public to see. Also, be cautious when deciding which applications to enable, and check your settings to see what information the applications will be able to access.

Use Strong Passwords

Protect your account with passwords that cannot easily be guessed. If your password is compromised, someone else may be able to access your account and pretend to be you.

Check Privacy Policies

Some sites may share information such as e-mail addresses or user preferences with other companies. This may lead to an increase in spam. Also, try to locate the policy for handling referrals to make sure that you do not unintentionally sign your friends up for spam. Some sites will continue to send e-mail messages to anyone you refer until they join.

Use and Maintain Antivirus Software

Antivirus software recognizes most known viruses and protects your computer against them, so you may be able to detect and remove the virus before it can do any damage. Because attackers are continually writing new viruses, it is important to keep your definitions up to date.

12.2. MOBILE SECURITY THREATS

Recent technological developments have enabled seamless integration between traditional desktops and mobile devices. The ever-increasing programmable electronic devices, right from television set top boxes to smartphones, are potential targets for cybercrime. Mobile devices are mini-computers with vulnerabilities that can and will be exploited. They, like other electronic devices are fairly flexible, provide reprogramming functionalities and are frequently networked with other devices. Therefore, convergence of technology has its pros and cons. On the one hand, it allows users to literally browse the Web 'on the go' while on the other hand, it widens the playing field for attackers, who are constantly looking to proliferate their ware. Unfortunately, a majority of the users do not realize that most of the threats such as phishing attacks which they face online using traditional devices can also hound their mobile experiences (Ng 2011).

Today, an increasing number of consumers are using mobile devices and tablets in their daily lives as well as at work. Enterprises must now support more devices than ever before, in effect extending their corporate firewalls and services to places they may not be prepared for. Sensitive data stored on mobile devices is usually the focus of attacks. Even legitimate applications are not safe. Trojans, for instance, are inserted by modifying legitimate applications. Attackers usually target a mobile's inherent billing features, which subscribe the victim to premium services (Ng 2011).

12.2.1. Trends in Mobile Security Threats

Threats to mobile devices (primarily smartphones) are not new anymore. Of late, cybercriminals seem to have renewed their interest for many reasons. They have a window of opportunity to exploit a variety of mobile platforms. Speculations about threats targeting smart devices have been made ever since the first smartphone was launched. While early smart devices such as the Symbian and Palm were also targeted, threats to these devices never became widespread and many remained proof of concept only. There has been an increase in attention, both from threat developers and security researchers alike, with the growing popularity and demand for smartphones and tablets and their increasing connectivity and capability. Although in comparison to the threats that target personal computers (PCs), immediate threats to mobile devices remain relatively low, new developments in the field cannot be undermined. It is estimated that 30 per cent of malicious software was distributed through Internet advertisements in 2008 (Wolfe 2008). An increase in cyberattacks targeting new mobile technologies and Wi-Fi-enabled devices such as iPhones and iPods has been predicted by experts (Sophos 2009).

Vulnerabilities in mobile devices can be exploited to install malicious codes the way it is done in desktop computers. In 2010, a significant number of vulnerabilities in mobile devices were reported (Symantec Corporation 2011a). While it may be difficult to successfully exploit many of these vulnerabilities, two were identified that affected Apple's iPhone iOS operating platform. These allowed users to 'jailbreak' their devices. The process is not very different from using exploits to install malware. However, in this case, users would be exploiting their own devices.

The availability of toolkits for malicious codes for mobile devices makes it clear that cybercrime is a serious business and like all businesses, it is driven by a return on investment consideration. This explains the current state of cybercrime threats for mobiles (Symantec Corporation 2011a).

All the requirements of an active threat landscape currently exist in the mobile domain. The installed base of smartphones and other mobile devices has grown to an attractive size. The sophisticated operating systems that these devices run on come with inevitable vulnerabilities (Symantec Corporation 2011a). In addition, the Trojans hiding in legitimate applications, sold in application stores, provide a simple and effective propagation method. What was nevertheless missing till recently was the ability to turn all this into a profit-centre equivalent to that offered by personal computers.

The chances of installing malicious applications are increasing exponentially as more and more users download and install third-party applications on their mobile devices. Most malicious codes are designed to generate revenue these days. The threat potential increases as people increasingly use their mobile devices for sensitive transactions like online shopping and banking. While the increase in Android malware volumes alone has shocked the world mobile malware has taken the world by storm, catching users completely unawares. Mobile malware has invaded device users' privacy by stealing personal and other kinds of confidential information. 'RuFraud' and 'DroidDreamLight' are just two of the most notorious Android malware variants, which came into the limelight recently, causing millions of users a lot of grief from losing data and, at times, money. DroidDreamLight is a mobile malware variant concealed with battery-monitoring, task listing or installed application-identifying tools, among others. It steals all sorts of device and personal information, which is then sent to a remote uniform resource locator (URL). This URL secretly sends messages to the affected user's contacts. It also checks if infected devices have been rooted, and if so, installs and uninstalls certain packages (Trend Micro 2012a).

12.2.2. Mobile Platforms—Security Threats

Android

The open nature of the Android applications market and the design ethos of its operating system make the Android more exposed to attack than the locked-down iPhone. Some components are built-in parts of the operating system (OS), and therefore, require full OS upgrades to patch vulnerabilities. This has caused issues for some older devices that cannot run newer editions of the platform. Linux-based platforms are relatively more open and allow access to low-level components but they also attract research into possible flaws and ways to exploit them for profit. All said and done, Android phones are considerably more exposed but attackers have to rely heavily on social engineering to lure users into installing rogue or malicious applications to gain access to their devices. Being alert and well informed about the latest scams is one of the most important aspects of staying secure (Sophos 2011).

In terms of functionality, Google's Android has tried to keep pace with the iPhone, and as devices diversify, the Android user base is expected to continue to grow. About 51.9 million Android-based devices were active all across the globe in 2011. More than 350 million are active Facebook users who access the site via mobile devices. More than 475 mobile operators worldwide deploy and promote Facebook's mobile products (Trend Micro 2012a). Android malware types include data stealers, premium-service abusers, click fraudsters, malicious downloaders and spying tools.

Symbian

Mobile giant Nokia's Symbian operating system continues to hold a considerable share of the smartphone market, despite losing a part of it to more advanced models. A notable quantity of real working malware can be seen on the Symbian operating system due to the combination of a large pool of potential victims and a relatively insecure operating model (Kenney and Pom 2011).

12.2.3. Mobile Device Security Solutions

Some of the mobile device security solutions include:

1. Traditional access control: This protects devices by using techniques such as passwords and idle-time screen locking.
2. Encryption: This conceals data at rest on the device to address device loss or theft.
3. Isolation: This limits the application's ability to access sensitive data or systems on the device.
4. Permissions-based access control: This set of permissions is granted to each application and each application is limited to accessing device data or systems within the scope of permissions. (Ng 2011)

Mobile Security Solutions

Fortunately for users, quality security solutions capable of protecting against these threats are available in the market. It is likely that as newer and more sophisticated devices become more widespread, older and less secure platforms will slowly die out. Some of the solutions deployed are discussed in the following lines (Ng 2011):

Mobile Device Management: This does not specifically protect against any one threat category, but helps reduce the risk of attack from many categories. It enables administrators manage iOS and Android devices remotely. Administrators can set security policies such as password strength, virtual private network (VPN) settings and screen-lock duration. They can also disable specific device functions, wipe missing devices and use the device's global positioning system (GPS) to locate missing devices.

Enterprise Sandbox: Its main objective is to prevent malicious and unintentional data losses. Though it does not block other attack categories explicitly, it does limit their impact. This essentially divides the device's contents into two zones: one is the secure zone used for enterprise data, and the other is the insecure zone used for an employee's personal and private data. This solution aims to provide a secure environment where enterprise resources such as e-mail, calendar, contacts, corporate websites and sensitive documents can be accessed.

Mobile Antivirus: The mobile antivirus is an effective tool for detecting known threats, but provides little protection against unknown threats. It expects traditional scanners to be replaced by cloud-enabled, reputation-based protection. It addresses threats in the malware threat category and subsets of malware-based attacks in the resource abuse, data loss and data integrity categories.

Secure Browser: Secure browser applications for iOS and Android check the visited URLs against blacklist or reputation databases and block malicious pages. A user has to use a third-party secure web browser for surfing. Secure browsers address the problem of web-based and social engineering attacks. They can also potentially block malware downloaded through browsers.

12.3. CLOUD COMPUTING—SECURITY PERSPECTIVE

Cloud computing is an extension of virtualization, that is, it adds automation to a virtual environment. Advancements in virtualization technologies enable enterprises to obtain more computing power from the underutilized capacities of physical servers. Server consolidation has reduced the traditional data centre footprint, thereby saving costs and promoting 'greener' information technology (IT). Service providers have discovered that they can use virtualization to enable 'multi-tenant' uses of what used to be 'single-tenant' or 'single-purpose' physical servers earlier. Private clouds are also generally founded on a virtual infrastructure for better resource usage and ease of provisioning. The structure of these different cloud models—private, public and hybrid—allow different levels of control and influence over security (Trend Micro 2012b).

Although cloud computing is emerging on the scene in a significant manner it has brought to the forefront various complicated legal challenges and issues. The issue of distribution of content and data across computer resources located in different territorial jurisdictions, connected to the 'cloud', has gained substantial recognition. While more and more companies are seemingly impressed by the business relevance of cloud computing, they are also quite concerned about the various legal issues and challenges that may arise with time (Duggal 2009).

As organizations move towards cloud computing for the inherent agility and economic benefits the model entails, they are increasingly moving towards hybrid enterprise environments that consist of a mix of 'non-cloud', 'cloud', external and internal IT service delivery models. This is due to the fact that not all application workloads, whether they are business-as-usual, mission-critical or highly innovative, are suited to cloud deployments and therefore, they may need to remain within the traditional scheme for reasons such as regulatory compliance, architecture and location where the data is stored. The cybersecurity challenge for cloud computing is therefore not only to protect data within public clouds and hosted private clouds, but also to ensure that governance, risk and compliance are addressed across the end-to-end infrastructure where applications and data may be highly virtualized (Unisys 2011).

With cloud computing becoming increasingly popular, concerns are being voiced about associated security issues that have arisen due to adoption of this new model. Since the characteristics of this innovative deployment model differ drastically from those of traditional architecture, the effectiveness and efficiency of traditional protection mechanisms need to be reconsidered (Trend Micro 2012b). An alternative perspective on cloud security is that this is but another, although quite broad, case of 'applied security' and that similar security principles that apply in shared multi-user mainframe security models also apply to cloud security. Traditional boundaries and perimeters in networks have been eliminated by virtualization and cloud computing. These new data centre technologies must support consumerization with a widening array of devices to access data, including smartphones, tablet computers, netbooks, notebooks and traditional laptops. Cloud security must accommodate these shifting usage patterns while supporting the infrastructure benefits of flexibility and cost savings (Trend Micro 2012b).

Security issues have been categorized into privacy bug exploitation, data segregation, data access, recovery, malicious insiders, accountability, management console security, multi-tenancy issues and account control. The solutions available vary from cryptography, particularly public key infrastructure (PKI), to the use of multi-cloud providers, improving virtual machine support, legal support and standardization of application programming interfaces (APIs) (Cloud Trust http://www.cloudtrust.biz/article/cloud_standads.html).

12.3.1. Trends in Cloud-Computing Threats

The relative security of cloud-computing services is a contentious issue that may be delaying its adoption. It is more secure to have physical control of the private cloud equipment than have the equipment off-site and under someone else's control. In order to ensure that data links are not compromised, it is necessary to have physical control and the ability to visually inspect the data links. There is unease amongst private and public sectors regarding external management of security-based services and this largely contributes to the reasons that bar the adoption of cloud computing. The very nature of cloud-based computing is such that it promotes external management of provided services. This delivers great incentive to cloud-computing service providers to prioritize building and maintaining strong management of security (Messmer 2009).

Using an on-premise data centre or private cloud may give enterprises a greater feeling of control over their data, both in terms of security and availability. However, the enterprise may actually gain improved availability through a service provider who is dedicated to offering on-demand computing services through a public cloud. Such service providers can build their cloud infrastructure to provide high availability and performance, supported by their cloud-computing experts. Often this infrastructure and staff exceeds the in-house capabilities of an enterprise. However, all data centres—whether in-house or through a service provider—can suffer outages (Trend Micro 2012b).

Amazon Web Services' (AWS) Elastic Block Store (EBS), which stores Amazon Elastic Compute Cloud (EC2) instances, experienced an outage that lasted for four days in April 2011. Amazon stated that 0.07 per cent of the volumes in the eastern United States region was not fully recoverable. The length of the outage, the fact that some data was lost and the complexity of the outage, as subsequently explained in detail by AWS, caused much discussion in the industry about the incident. AWS has stated that it is treating this incident as an opportunity to improve its infrastructure, and other prominent Silicon Valley companies such as Netflix have published blogs on lessons learned from the outage (Trend Micro 2012b).

12.3.2. Threat to Cloud Computing-Classification

Since cloud computing is founded on a virtual environment, the threats that apply to virtualization also apply to the cloud-computing space. As cloud computing expands to cover data stored in private and public clouds and on numerous roaming mobile devices, new threat avenues are being introduced and new approaches to securing data wherever it is located must be implemented (Trend Micro 2012b).

As with privately-owned hardware, cybercriminals posing as customers can purchase the services of cloud computing for nefarious purposes. This includes launching malicious attacks and cracking passwords using purchased services. In 2009, the popular Amazon service was illegally used as a command and control channel by a banking Trojan to issue software updates and malicious instructions to infected PCs. Attackers may use cloud-computing resources to support their attacks. In a recent example, Bloomberg News reported that hackers used AWS's EC2 cloud computing unit to launch an attack against Sony's PlayStation Network and Qriocity entertainment networks. The attack reportedly compromised the personal accounts of more than 100 million Sony customers (Bloomberg 2011b) .

Attackers also create their own clouds to disseminate resources. Botnets themselves are a form of cloud computing, pooling resources for criminal activities. A growing number of tools are available through clouds to help attackers.

Some aspects on the challenges of cybersecurity and cloud computing are represented in Figure 12.1.

In a cloud infrastructure, data is often moved to make the best use of resources. This means that enterprises may not always know where their data is located. This may be true in any cloud model, but is particularly true in the public cloud model. Service providers are expected to optimize resource usage to offer best cost savings to businesses. But they generally do not provide any visibility into how resources are shifted to achieve this. Also, in case of moving of data from one place to another, residual data may be left behind, which can be accessed by unauthorized users. Any remaining data in the old location should be shredded, but depending on the security practice, remnants of data may be still be available. This can be a concern with confidential data in private clouds and any sensitive data in public clouds (Trend Micro 2012b).

A cloud infrastructure gives flexibility to include more departments and users in an organization. A cloud portal is extendible to external sources such as partners. With this increased access also comes an increased risk of data leakage. In addition, businesses are faced with managing and securing a diverse set of mobile devices, often acquired by the employee, not the business itself. The cloud is often utilized for consistent access to applications and data on roaming end points. It can also be used by businesses to implement security on its employees' mobile devices. Security must balance flexible access with data protection (Trend Micro 2012b).

Figure 12.1
The Cybersecurity Challenge

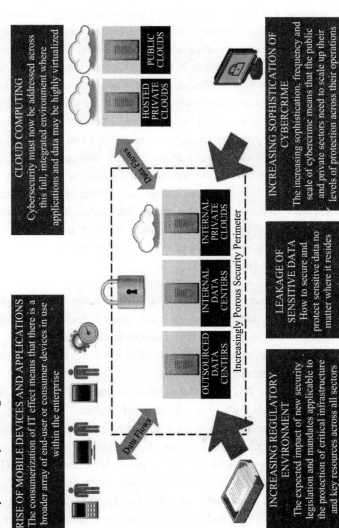

RISE OF MOBILE DEVICES AND APPLICATIONS
The consumerization of IT effect means that there is a broader array of end-user or consumer devices in use within the enterprise

CLOUD COMPUTING
Cybersecurity must now be addressed across this full, integrated environment where applications and data may be highly virtualized

PUBLIC CLOUDS

HOSTED PRIVATE CLOUDS

INCREASING SOPHISTICATION OF CYBERCRIME
The increasing sophistication, frequency and scale of cybercrime means that the public and private sectors need to scale up their levels of protection across their operations

Data Flows

INTERNAL PRIVATE CLOUDS

INTERNAL DATA CENTERS

OUTSOURCED DATA CENTERS

Increasingly Porous Security Perimeter

Data Flows

LEAKAGE OF SENSITIVE DATA
How to secure and protect sensitive data no matter where it resides

INCREASING REGULATORY ENVIRONMENT
The expected impact of new security legislation and mandates applicable to the protection of critical infrastructure and key resources across all sectors

SOURCE: Trend Micro (2012b).

12.3.3. Clouds—Practices to Stay Secure

As more and more organizations consider entrusting some or all of their IT functions to public cloud providers, the question arises as to how cloud-computing trends will impact cybercrime. Concentrating huge amounts of data at a centralized location provides criminals a bigger target. Whether it is a corporate data centre or a cloud provider's data centre, the fact remains that the bigger the target, the easier it is to hit it. Surveys have placed security concerns as one of the biggest challenges in the adoption of cloud computing, even though a plethora of security product vendors are doing their best to fill the gap. Encryption is a critical safeguard in a multi-tenant environment, ensuring that service provider employees and other customers of the service cannot view a business' data (Trend Micro 2012b). Encryption of all sensitive data is a must. In fact, it is the information, which is proprietary to any organization or that which the organization has collected from customers and business partners, that must be protected and the organization generally has a legal obligation to protect such information. Certain points that must be considered in a contract with the vendor of cloud-computing services include (National Institutes of Health 2012):

1. Privileged user access: This concerns who has access to data and their backgrounds. The contract should include signing non-disclosure agreements with the people having access.
2. Regulatory compliance: The vendor must be willing to undergo audits and security certifications.
3. Data location: It is important to know whether the business or organization controls the physical location of its data.
4. Data segregation: This deals with use of encryption to protect data. Also, it is essential to ensure deployment of firewalls, intrusion prevention systems (IPS) and intrusion detection systems (IDS) to protect each of the virtual machines separately.[3]
5. Recovery: It is essential to ask what happens to the business' or organization's data and applications in the event of a disaster.
6. Long-term viability: It is important to understand what happens to data and applications if the vendor's company goes out of business.

[3] IPS and IDS both are required for maximum protection against malicious traffic. In fact, vendors are increasingly combining the two technologies into a single box.

7. Investigative support: The business or organization must ask if the vendor will investigate illegal or inappropriate activity.
8. Security breach: To know what would happen in the event of a security breach is of paramount importance.

Finally, even though security implementation is a technical matter, responsibility is a legal one. No cloud vendor can offer a 100 per cent guarantee—the most trusted and reliable vendor can still fail. It is the responsibility of a customer to determine if it is comfortable with risk of putting service in the cloud. The cloud vendor may charge a premium based on the degree of accountability demanded. For instance, the vendor may replicate data and application availability at multiple sites to minimize the risk.

Just as cybercriminals exploit cloud technologies to their advantage, cloud-based fraud detection can also be used against them. Cloud services can detect patterns of criminal activity that would not otherwise be obvious, by collecting and sharing information about millions of devices across the world. With the right approach and security solutions, the public cloud can be just as secure as a typical traditional corporate data centre (Trend Micro 2010b).

12.4. CONCLUSION

It does not matter what kind of security systems you have installed in your organization, newer threats will continue to surprise you. It is difficult to evolve best practices in the area of cybersecurity. Individuals, organizations and nations have no choice but to match up to newer threats on a continuous basis.

SECTION III

IMPACT, TRENDS AND ROLE OF GOVERNMENT IN COMBATING CYBERCRIME

Laws and regulations continue to grow with the growth of cybercrime ... but are we more secure?

THIRTEEN

IMPACT OF CYBERCRIME

————•◦•————

13.1. INTRODUCTION

With time, the economy of the underworld has grown and flourished, and cybercriminals have developed new methods to trick their victims. Their business is amazingly lucrative, with profits aggregating to billions of dollars per year. Financial fraud has many aspects, be it swindling, debit- or credit-card frauds, real-estate frauds, drug trafficking, identity thefts, deceptive telemarketing or money laundering. The goal of cybercriminals is always the same—the intent is always to make as much money within as short a period of time as possible and to do so inconspicuously. Not only has the nature of cybercrime changed, the transformation has not spared the threats either. These have become more silent and more insidious in recent times. The threats are multi-pronged and geared to attack, infect and compromise data. The components of the threat always relate to one or more of the following vectors—e-mails, the Web and files.

The perpetrators of almost all threats are professional criminals. Botnets are managed and run while an organization of goons manages their networks. Again, making money is the primary aim. The Canadian pharmacy spam, the fake antivirus scam and others are all part of a well-organized business model based on the concept of affiliate networking. Cybercrime products sold via affiliate marketing, such as click fraud and selling credit card details may be highly profitable, but they are nevertheless illegal. Cybercrime is now rampant and considered usual business.

13.2. FINANCIAL IMPACT OF CYBERCRIME

Financial losses due to cybercriminal activities are on the rise today. What used to be insignificant and random in nature at one point of time has now evolved into serious business. The picture is radically different in the context of individual firms and when considering the economy as a whole. With money being the primary motive of cybercriminals and profitability running into billions, it is not surprising that cybercriminals resort to phishing, spam, malware and hacking to steal customer data, such as banking credentials, credit- or debit-card credentials and so on. Also, there exist virtual markets for credit card dumps, each market or country commanding separate rates, which may increase depending on the inclusion of the personal identification number (PIN).

Investigations reveal that operating an illegal 'free-of-charge' website, to download copyright-protected movies can generate millions of dollars, in less than a year, through advertisements (Gercke 2011b).

A study conducted by Suzanne Widup and the Digital Forensics Association (Widup 2010), in as many as 28 nations, for the period 2005–2009, has revealed the following financial losses:

- 2005—$9,460,667,694 lost or stolen due to malpractices
- 2006—$14,626,076,556 lost or stolen due to malpractices
- 2007—$32,455,634,361 lost or stolen due to malpractices
- 2008—$36,847,781,722 lost or stolen due to malpractices
- 2009—$45,621,167,528 lost or stolen due to malpractices

The above figures represent only the financial losses incurred through the theft of personal information (from Internet users) worldwide. It does not include the downstream or upstream costs or costs incurred by data owners trying to repair or retrieve the records. These figures clearly reflect that the world of cybercrime is no longer restricted to the petty thugs operating on a small scale but has extended itself to an array of high-profile criminals (Widup 2010).

The losses due to cybercriminal activities include financial losses as well as the losses in terms of productivity and time. A report by Javelin Strategy and Research (2010), estimates the total financial losses from identity frauds alone at 54 billion dollars in 2009, a marked increase from 48 billion dollars in 2008. The report pegs the overall financial losses, at 126.6 billion dollars, over a period of five years. This is very grim news indeed, since the world is turning to the Internet for everything these days. It is not possible to stop malicious hackers all the time but what can be done is to adopt tighter Internet security policies and other preventive and protective measures.

The international cybercriminal groups cost consumers billions of dollars every year and undermine their confidence in the international financial system. Transnational criminal organizations pose significant threats to financial and trust systems, such as banking, stock markets, e-currency, and value- and credit-card services, on which the global economy depend.

According to the United States government (National Security Council 2011):

> Today's criminal networks are fluid, striking new alliances with other networks around the world and engaging in a wide range of illicit activities, including cybercrime and providing support for terrorism. Virtually every transnational criminal organization and its enterprises are connected and enabled by information systems technologies, making cybercrime a substantially more important concern.

That cybercrimes can have a considerably serious impact on the economy than most conventional crimes is a widely accepted fact today. More than 43 per cent of the companies interviewed in the 2007 PricewaterhouseCoopers' biennial Global Economic Crime Survey said that they had been victims of one or more significant economic crimes. The report indicated that the average loss due to frauds per company increased from roughly 1.7 million dollars in 2005 to approximately 2.4 million dollars in 2007, a jump of nearly 40 per cent in two years (PricewaterhouseCoopers 2007).

The Norton Cybercrime Report (2011) indicates that the costs of resolving the impact of cyberattacks as well as their detection itself can be significantly high. Automated technologies enable offenders to generate high profits by committing various offences with rather small amounts each time. Victims who have lost insignificant amounts choose not to report the crime at all. Due to the high costs of resolution, many of these attacks remain undetected. The more developed the country and the more dependent it is on high-end technology, the higher the costs to resolve cyberattacks.

As noted in a report McAfee (2010b), the financial consequences of security incidents (including downtime, information and revenue loss) is an estimated average of two million dollars for all Web 2.0 technologies. According to OECD (2008b), Cybercrime is rapidly evolving from the domain of misguided pranksters, into more elaborate, profit-driven schemes involving organized-crime syndicates that may be based around the block, or halfway around the world. It is estimated that 85 per cent of malware today is created with profit in mind. As noted by Tim Weber (2009), online theft costs one trillion dollars a year. The number of attacks is rising sharply and too many people do not know how to protect themselves. Internet is becoming vulnerable day by day, it has now become part of society's central nervous system, and the attacks could threaten the whole economies.

Even though several studies have been conducted to identify and trace the financial impact of cyberattacks, much more needs to be done. Many cyberattacks go unreported due to missing mechanisms. Quantifying cybercrimes and their economic impact is vital for both governments as well as businesses, especially to adjust the legal and regulatory frameworks and institutional capacities.

13.2.1. Cost of Cybercrime

The costs related to cybercrime, which have a direct associated dollar value may be called 'quantifiable costs'. These may be costs due to either 'loss of money' or costs due to 'loss of revenue'. Loss of money implies the dollar amount stolen by cybercriminals while loss of revenue implies the dollar amount paid to wrong (cybercriminal) parties. It is important to understand the difference between the two economic aspects: revenue generated by cybercrime and losses caused by cybercrime. The full extent and impact of cybercrime is unknown. The following are some instances of losses due to cybercrimes in Germany (Gercke 2011b):

- Losses in Germany based on numbers provided by the Federal Police in 2010: 75 million dollars.
- Losses in Germany based on Symantec: 33 billion dollars.
- Number of 'data manipulation' cases in Germany in 2010, based on official statistics: 2,000
- Number of Germans affected by computer viruses in 2010: 12,000,000.

It is clear from the above that the losses are not only direct financial losses but also losses in terms of investments on cybersecurity and loss of reputation when such incidents occur. It is important therefore to provide some guidance to users on reporting obligations and establishment of reporting mechanisms (complaint centres) and so on.

Cybercrime costs the United States economy over 100 billion dollars per year (Kratchman et al. 2008; Mello 2007). Cybercrime costs publicly traded companies billions of dollars annually in terms of stolen assets, lost business and damaged reputations.

The United Kingdom lost up to 27 billion pounds a year to cyberattacks in 2010, according to a report from the Office of Cyber Security and Information Assurance (Detica and Office of Cyber Security and Information Assurance 2011). The risk is particularly severe for companies engaged in the pharmaceuticals, biotechnology, information technology (IT) and chemical sectors. A total of 9.2 billion pounds was lost through intellectual property theft, 7.6 billion pounds from industrial espionage and 2.2 billion pounds through extortion. The overall figures aggregated to 21 billion pounds of costs to businesses, 2.2 billion pounds to the government and 3.1 billion pounds to citizens. These figures are a mid range estimate and the actual losses could be much higher.

The final estimate of the cost of breaches, as reported by the Digital Forensics Association (Widup 2010), is over 139 billion dollars over the past five years. If we add the estimated records from previous calculations, the cost will rise to over 140 billion dollars. This however, does not include the costs suffered by others who are affected by the breaches—consumers whose data was disclosed, and other companies who must incur costs related to breaches in their downstream or upstream channels (Widup 2010).

13.2.2. State-Sponsored Cybercrime

According to a United States Government Accountability Office report (USGAO 2007), cybercrime has significant economic impacts and threatens national security interests. Various studies conducted by experts estimate the direct economic impact from cybercrime to be in billions of dollars annually. In addition, there is continued concern about the threat that those deemed adversaries, including nation states and terrorists, pose to national security. For example, intelligence officials have stated that nation states and terrorists could conduct a coordinated cyberattack to seriously disrupt electric power distribution, air traffic control and financial sectors. Also, according to testimony by the Federal Bureau of Investigation (FBI), terrorist organizations use cybercrime to raise money to fund their activities.

13.2.3. Nature of Losses

The Congressional Research Service (CRS) report for United States Congress (Cashell et al. 2004) identified that the types of attacks most frequently reported are not the ones that cause the greatest losses. Some findings of the study are diagrammatically represented in Figure 13.1.

Although precise data on online criminal activity and associated financial losses is difficult to collect, it is generally accepted that malware contributes significantly to these losses. Further, where data on cybercrime and its economic impact is available, businesses and governments are often reluctant

Figure 13.1
Types of Attacks Reported and the Dollar Value of Related Losses

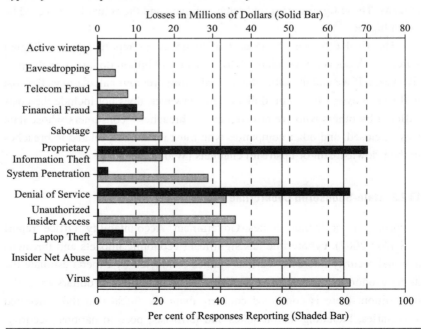

SOURCE: Cashell et al. (2004: CRS-7).

to share it publicly. It is important to note that these direct losses are not fully representative of the actual financial impact since they do not consider diminished customer trust in online transactions, loss of reputation, impact on the brand and other indirect and opportunity costs that are difficult to quantify (Cashell et al. 2004).

As per Andy Greenberg's (2009) report, the international retail hacking ring, which the United States Department of Justice says stole tens of millions of credit-card numbers, was no ordinary cybercrime operation. Commencing its nefarious activities in 2005, the widespread organization used a technique known as 'wardriving'—testing wireless networks for security vulnerabilities—to identify their targets. When the members found that retailer TJ Maxx, for instance, used an outmoded and easily hackable wireless standard, they broke into the store's network from a car in its parking lot and stole more than 45 million credit-card numbers from the company's account. The trick was repeated with other retailers and restaurants including Boston Market, Dave & Busters and Sports.

Internet companies, Amazon, eBay and Yahoo were affected the most by cybercrime news stories. Researchers have also addressed the question of whether cybercrime news stories negatively affect shareholder value. The study found that cybercrime and the resulting news stories did affect shareholder value, at least in the short term, in the form of significant decreases in stock prices. Since this was an event study, based on cybercrime news stories, it did not investigate the long-term impact. Such analysis would be problematic given other factors, beyond the event of the cybercrime, which would affect stock-market performance (Smith et al. 2011).

13.3. NON-FINANCIAL IMPACT OF CYBERCRIME

Cybercrimes can not only cause financial drain but also non-financial losses in terms of loss of productivity, loss of customer confidence, loss of reputation and the potential loss of accounts.

13.3.1. Social Impact

The adverse social implications of cybercrime are far-reaching. Estimates suggest that about 20–25 per cent of youth in the UK have at some point of time fallen prey to cyberbullying (nasuwt.org 2009). In Japan, for instance, cases of cyberbullying which affected children were as high as 20 per cent in 2009, as reported by the Japanese Education, Science and Technology Ministry. This was out of a total of 38,000 Internet bulletin boards operated by children in the country (Salaud 2009).

13.3.2. Political Impact

According to the United States Department of Homeland Security, when compared to the year 2006, the year 2007 saw a significant increase—152 per cent—in cyberattacks against the American Federal Agencies (United Press International 2009). The number of network intrusion attempts reported by the Pentagon in 2005 were more than 79,000 (Reid 2007). Within the next two years this number had gone up to more than 80,000 (Hamilton 2009). A classic instance of the impact that cybercrimes have on a nation's security is the series of attacks against the Department of Defense (DoD) networks. The information network of the DoD is spread over about 20 per cent of the entire Internet network (USGAO 2007). The DoD's networks faced as many as 22,144 attacks in 1999. This was a marked increase as compared to the number of 5,844 in 1998 (Wolf 2000). In 2008, the number of attacks on the DoD's networks annually was pegged at three million (Hess 2008; Shackelford 2012).

The cyberattacks against Estonia in April–May 2007 and those against Georgia in 2008 are significant with reference to the impact of the Internet on national security. A prime example of the consequences of cyberattacks, which are well coordinated with armed attacks by a military force, is the Georgia cyberattacks in 2008 (Claburn 2009). Again, the well-planned, distributed denial-of-service (DDoS) attack in 2007 against Estonian computer networks holds a place of significance in the history of cyberattacks. The attack by a botnet of as many as one million computers brought to a complete halt the functioning of the country's government ministries, the Parliament and major banks (Grant 2007).

These non-financial impacts are on account of the indirect expenses that accompany cyberattacks, such as loss of business hours, loss of customers' interest and trust and the resultant switching over to another services or goods provider of similar capacity. It is not a straightforward task to measure such kinds of impacts. Assigning a dollar value to such an impact is driven by multiple factors, such as the dimensions of the firm or country and its dependence on technology. These costs continue to accrue to the firm or country long after the immediate cyberattack has been repaired. Therefore, it is extremely important to pay attention to such types of costs. The economic impact of these costs is of such a magnitude that the victim has good enough reasons not to disclose the cyberattacks faced. Of late, analysts have begun to take interest in such types of costs.

A study conducted by the Information Security Media Group in 2010 (ISMG 2010) reveals that non-financial losses such as loss in productivity, loss in customer confidence and loss in customer accounts are major hassles that arise from cyberattacks. The same study also reports that fraudsters target not just automated teller machines (ATMs) or payment cards or checks but also aim at cross-channel frauds, that is, seeking to compromise customers in every way they interact with them.

According to Cashell et al. (2004), a firm going public with details of a cyberattack incurs additional costs such as impact on the financial market, effect on reputation, increase or decrease in liability and so on. It is these additional intangibles that create a negative incentive for organizations to hide any form of cyberattacks faced.

A study by McAfee in 2009 (McAfee 2009b) found that globally, the annual spam energy use aggregates 33 billion kilowatt hours (KWh), or 33 terawatt hours (TWh). This is equivalent to the electricity consumed in 2.4 million homes in the United States. The same study also proposes that spam filtering saves 135 TWh of electricity per year and filtering spam, though beneficial, fighting it at the source is even better. When McColo, a major source of online spam, was taken offline in late 2008, the energy saved in the ensuing lull—before spammers rebuilt their sending capacity—was equivalent to taking 2.2 million cars off the road. Much of the energy consumption associated with spam comes from end users deleting spam and searching for legitimate e-mails.

13.5. CYBERTHREAT TO ONLINE TRANSACTIONS

Faced with crime that is continually becoming more professional, banks and large online sales companies are strengthening their infrastructure to protect themselves better. Small and medium-sized businesses, for whom e-commerce is the key to a prosperous future, have a vital need for security solutions that will help them earn or retain the confidence of their customers. However, due to either lack of training or pure negligence, these companies sometimes find themselves helpless in the face of attacks that are becoming increasingly sophisticated and underhanded.

Payment through bank cards is still regarded as one of the best methods of making payments over the Internet. When the number of transactions was still low, the inherent risk could be deemed 'tolerable' by different parties. But today, with such high volumes, the brand image of some traders is deteriorating. This has also annoyed consumers who in turn have begun to complain. As a result banks have been saddled with losses they would rather avoid.

Security solutions from recognized vendors that implement tools and software for managing records and vulnerabilities help companies comply with security standards. At the other end of the chain, increasing awareness among users and the availability of more intuitive and transparent security tools for computers are key development areas for the future.

As transactions and payments go online, fraudsters come up with techniques to dip into these new financial flows. There is no doubt that highly organized types of frauds, such as phishing, will continue to develop. Direct attempts at defrauding or compromising bank computer systems also have a long history. Vladimir Levin and a group of St. Petersburg hackers attempted to remove 10.7 million dollars from Citibank in 1994 (Cisco 2001, quoted in OECD 2011). In 2004, key loggers were used against Sumitomo Mitsui Banking Corporation in London in an attempt to move 229 million pounds to 20 accounts in 10 different countries (Young 2009, quoted in OECD 2011). There were also many instances of runs on banks, though historically most of these were precipitated by bad lending or failure to anticipate changed eco-nomic conditions.

The issue here is the impact of these activities on a 'global shock' scale. A potential risk remains that more successful criminal activities will only tip these conditions into some sort of systemic consumer distrust of online banking and payment systems and result in unacceptable costs of fraud for businesses, while providing an increased funding stream for other criminal activities (OECD 2011).

13.6. FACTORS TO MEASURE THE IMPACT OF A SECURITY BREACH

The impact of a security failure on an organization's business may take into account the consequences of a loss of confidentiality, integrity and availability of assets. This would include unauthorized disclosure, modification, disruption, destruction, loss of information, denial of service and so on. It would also include realistically assessing the likelihood of security failures in the light of prevailing threats and vulnerabilities, and the impact associated with the threats and the safeguards currently implemented.

Some tangible impact can be measured quantitatively in terms of lost revenue, the cost of repairing the system or the level of effort required to correct problems caused by a successful threat action. Other impacts (such as loss of public confidence, loss of credibility, damage to an organization's interest) cannot be measured in specific units but can be qualified or described in terms of high, medium and low impact. System and data sensitivity can be determined based on the levels of protection required to maintain the system and the availability, integrity and confidentiality of data. An adverse impact on an information asset may be mapped in terms of one or more of the following:

1. Loss of image or reputation or goodwill (intangible)—stakeholder expectation and perception, loss of public confidence, loss of credibility, damage to an organization's interest—which result in negative consequences for goodwill and reputation.
2. Loss of revenue (impaired operations), business (opportunity cost), loss of recovery (due to integrity or availability loss), loss of system functionality and operational effectiveness.
3. Financial loss due to damaged asset.
4. Statutory or legal or contractual non-compliance and loss because of that (loss of public confidence, embarrassment, or legal action against the organization).
5. Impact to citizens in terms of loss of privacy, injury, death and so on.
6. Loss to other organizations depending on the interfaces.
7. National loss (terrorist activity, social impact and the like).

Therefore, the adverse impact of a security event can be described in terms of loss or degradation of any, or a combination of any, of the above impact factors.

13.7. ECONOMIC FACTORS AFFECTING CYBERCRIME

There has been a fundamental shift in the nature of cybercrimes from being random, experimental and opportunistic attacks to being more organized, targeted and direct, while having financial implications. This has been mainly due to perverse incentives, such as being able to earn huge sums of money in a short span of time with very little labour, which is an outcome of the IT market and global economic trends. Apart from money being involved directly in cybercrimes, there is also a rise in the degree of intangible losses, like loss of confidence and the shifting of customer accounts.

It is seen that economic quantification of cybercrime is not only a time-consuming activity, but is also equally difficult. The first and foremost major obstacle is the lack of availability of data on the frequency and severity of cyberattacks, although rules are now being created to plug this gap. Second, it is difficult to measure the intangible or non-financial impact of these cyberattacks.

In terms of country-specific observations, it has been seen that developed nations and big economies are major sources as well as lucrative destinations for cyberattacks. This is due to the high volumes of e-business transactions that are conducted in these economies, which make them soft and easy targets for cybercriminals. The recent global recession also added more incentives for the cybercrime industry. The United States is seen to be both an attractive source as well as destination of financial cybercrime. In India, even though technology and computer skills are fairly advanced, the level of employment is equally high and this has kept cyberattacks random and mischievous in nature, although occasionally there have been instances of financial elements being involved.

13.7.1. Factors That Make Commission of Crime Tempting

Attractiveness of the Target

The attractiveness of a target is measured in terms of monetary or symbolic value, and portability (Clarke 1995). Accessibility, visibility, ease of physical access and lack of surveillance are some factors which make the target attractive (Bottoms and Wiles 2002; Clarke 1995).

Weak Defence Mechanisms

Poor informal surveillance (for example, not keeping a watch on activities that may otherwise raise suspicions in the neighbourhood) is another reason for a high crime rate (Taylor et al. 1995). This is what makes sparsely populated neighbourhoods vulnerable to violent crimes (Browning et al. 2004; Wilson 1987).

13.7.2. Economic Processes Motivating a Cybercriminal's Behaviour

High levels of unemployment among the youth cause frustration and can lead them to cybercrime. It has been observed that a fairly large number of cyberattacks originate from eastern Europe and Russia. The students here are good at mathematics, physics and computer skills, but tend to use their knowledge for the wrong purposes (Blau 2004). The United States-based Internet Fraud Complaint Center noted that, 'frustrated with the employment possibilities offered in Romania, some of the world's most talented computer students are exploiting their talents online' (Sofia News Agency 2003). The 1998 financial crash in Russia left many programmers unemployed (Serio and Gorkin 2003). A self-described hacker from Moscow noted: 'Hacking is one of the few good jobs left here' (Walker 2004).

India's low cybercrime profile is attributed to the development of a legitimate IT industry in the country. Nandkumar Saravade, director of cybersecurity for India's National Association of Software and Service Companies (NASSOM) notes: 'Today ... any person in India with marketable computer skills has a few job offers in hand' (Greenberg 2007).

'Cyber offences are most imminent if their technological viability coincides with a high level of economic temptation to break the rules' (Hirschauer and Musshoff 2007: 248). The significant financial benefits arising from cybercrimes provide positive incentives to cybercriminals. Poor probability of cybercriminals being caught and prosecuted (Kshetri 2006) and the leniency of punishments give hackers an economic boost (Becker 1995).

'Low earnings are a factor behind crime and teenagers have lower earnings and fewer opportunities' (Hirschauer and Musshoff 2007). Law enforcement agencies throughout the world have made efforts to prosecute cybercriminals. For example, the Computer Crime & Intellectual Property

Section of the United States Department of Justice reported the prosecution of 118 computer crime cases from 1998 to 2006 (OECD 2009).

13.8. PROBLEMS IN ESTIMATING LOSS

The threat of cybercrimes is rising in direct proportion to the Internet usage throughout the world today. However, not all cybercrimes are of a serious nature. Some may be harmless too. It is nevertheless a challenging task to correctly gauge the size of the global cybercrime industry. Again, measuring with a reasonable level of accuracy, the economic, social and political consequences of cybercrimes and web attacks is difficult and this is true in the case of any underworld economy (Naylor 2005).

Reliable statistics hardly exist to assist in this endeavour. Even empirical findings relating to the various indicators of cybercrime lack consistency.

It is a challenge for law-enforcement officials around the world to catch and punish the guilty parties since the people involved are scattered across many different geographical areas. The different estimates for cybercrime have received widespread criticism. It is believed that the vested interests of the organization may create difficulties in arriving at unbiased estimates of the levels of cybercrime. There is a possibility that the true levels may not be reflected due to over- or underestimation (Rush et al. 2009). It is true that many web attacks go unreported and therefore the impact may always be underestimated. On the other hand, one may argue that security companies have vested interests in exaggerating cybercrime statistics. Data collated from diverse sources however indicates that the losses from cyberattacks can be quite substantial.

Although estimates are published regularly by many associations, groups and companies, it is difficult to meaningfully compare and evaluate the consequences (Rush et al. 2009). There is no standard formula for arriving at the projected loss from cybercrimes. Different combinations of direct, indirect and opportunity costs exist. For instance, actual money lost, intellectual property theft, costs of repairing or replacing infected networks and equipment, man hours lost, and intangible losses such as loss of customer confidence in the victimized company, may be included in the loss estimates (USGAO 2007).

Measuring cybercrime-related indicators in an economy and comparing them across jurisdictions is not an easy task and several logical issues arise.

It is not easy to clearly identify the country in which a cyberattack originates. While cybercrimes may originate in one country, the criminals masterminding them may be sitting in a totally different location. In 1999 for instance, two employees of a company based in the United States, 'Phonemasters', were caught for attacking the networks of United States telecom companies. The racket involved downloading thousands of Sprint calling-card numbers and selling them to intermediaries in Canada and Switzerland. Investigators tracked the perpetrators to an organized crime group headquartered in Italy (Williams 2001).

Lack of uniformity in preferences, institutional differences and constraints across jurisdictions make estimates of cybercrimes different. For instance, while on the one hand the United States Constitution protects free speech, on the other hand British, French and German laws prohibit content related to racism or Holocaust denial on the Internet (Kshetri 2010).

The probabilities of reporting of different types of cybercrimes also differ. For instance, it is less likely that a 'synthetic identity fraud', which victimizes only businesses, will be reported to authorities than most other types of identity thefts (Cheney 2005; Roberds and Schreft 2009).

Very few of the cost estimates for cyber hazards, cyber incidents, cyberattacks or cyberwarfare explain key assumptions. Since there is rarely much in terms of physical losses, the immediate direct losses are often very low. But how far does one include remedial costs, particularly, if parts of those go into the installation of detective, preventive and mitigating technologies that should have been there in the first place? Looking more generally at the consequential losses, what are the criteria for inclusion? For example, an insurer might be prepared to pay out for a genuine loss of revenue (based on a previous year's business records), but not for a lost business opportunity. For businesses, there may also be a loss of reputation to consider. In a wider event, there is also the problem of looking at losses from the perspective of who pays for them. For example, if one has a valid insurance policy and incurs a covered loss, one will be compensated for most of that loss, while it could be said that paying out on claims is a normal part of an insurer's business. Estimates of annual global losses attributable to cyber events or cybercrimes are even more problematic as there is no guarantee that all possible victims have been included, or that they have provided detailed responses (OECD 2011). The report by Cashell et al. (2004) raises further issues about how a loss can be measured.

Barriers for committing more serious acts of espionage and sabotage are however declining all the time. In November 2011, four people were arrested in the Philippines in connection with the hacking of several United States telecommunications companies that resulted in losses of two million dollars for one company, AT&T, alone, and these funds were diverted from the phone companies to accounts of known terrorism financiers. While many experts downplay concerns about a 'cyberwar' between geopolitical powers, others point to several states that are known to be devoting significant resources to develop cyber weapons and defences. In 10 years, Stuxnet and GhostNet could look as crude and primitive as websites during the dot-com bubble (WEF 2012b).

Reliable indicators of the financial impact of cyberattacks are hard to come by. Cyber risks definitely constitute a significant threat to businesses. However, more information is needed to allow businesses to gauge the extent of the risk since many remain unreported or under-reported. It is possible that the impact of cybercrimes on companies goes unreported, with victims preferring not to disclose that their systems have been compromised.

However, the fact that cybercrime is more frequently in the news suggests that this trend is changing. There is a growing market for cyber risk insurance, covering risks ranging from computer security liability to business interruption, cybercrime and cyber extortion. The market for cyber risk-related insurance is expected to grow over the next decade, especially due to recent regulatory and legal changes. For example, the United States Securities and Exchange Commission (SEC) guidance released in October 2011 indicates that a computer breach should be viewed as a potential material event requiring disclosure, regardless of whether the breach involved release of confidential data or not. The European Union and Asia have begun to adopt similar breach notice laws (WEF 2012b).

13.9. CONCLUSION

Security of information—safeguarding computer systems and the integrity, confidentiality and availability of data on them—is a critical policy issue for any organization and has grown in importance due to the continual integration of computers into different aspects of modern human life. Of late, there has been a continual increase in cyberattacks, with a high probability that future attacks may impact much more severely than those experienced in the present. The financial services and payment-card industry pose a serious risk to other lines of business as well. Institutions therefore need to diversify and build up their prevention and detection approaches to minimize losses. In addition to financial loss, a cybercrime results in non-financial losses such as loss of productivity, loss of customer confidence and the potential loss of accounts. Awareness programmes for users, employees and customers and the deployment of cybercrime detection and apt prevention tools is the only way forward. The challenge is to find the right tools and take the right approach to awareness.

FOURTEEN

TRENDS IN CYBERCRIME

---◆---

14.1. INTRODUCTION AND GROWTH IN CYBERCRIME OVER THE LAST FEW YEARS

Cybercrime started off as a result of professional jealousy and was committed essentially by people who were proficient in computer and network skills or were politically motivated. Moreover, cybercrime was an experiment being performed by those who were curious to know more about emergent technology. In most cases, it was simple hacking acts that caused few losses. As seen with the 1986 Cuckoo's Egg and the 1988 Morris worm, the intentions were either politically motivated or simple attempts to assuage curiosity.

It was not until the 1980s that actual tangible damage to computer systems became a prominent possibility. Cybercriminals resorted to using access via authorization to break through security systems and alter data for financial gains or destroy data as an act of revenge. Given the way the telecommunications technology took giant steps in the world of information technology (IT), technocrats with crime on their minds devised new ways to penetrate systems and networks. Coders in the 1980s began to script software that could damage and destroy, including self-replicate, to interfere with the ways personal computers worked.

In 1982, the first virus was written by a high-school student for Apple II computers, hidden in a floppy disk and ready to be loaded on to an operational system, it was an awful poem which used to appear on the screen on every 50th boot. A mischievous act in the 1980s became a prominent crime tool subsequently. In a similar manner, a curious graduate student wrote software in 1988, which replicated itself on to computers hooked up to the ARPAnet. This was a wishful attempt to measure the size of the Internet but the student was unaware that he was giving this world a crime tool which would be known as 'worm' in the times to come.

Most of such cybercriminal acts evolved in the Western world because of the ample availability of requisite resources in terms of political and financial motivations. Russia, which was believed to have developed various techniques to steal data during the Cold War also contributed significantly to the evolution of cybercrime.

As the Internet increased its span to include many diverse systems worldwide, cybercriminals resorted to accessing inadequately protected systems, completely unauthorized, for nefarious activities, political actions and economic rewards. In 1989, the Trojan came into notice. A diskette, which contained the Trojan virus and claimed to be a database of information about Acquired Immune Deficiency Syndrome (AIDS), was mailed to AIDS researchers and subscribers of the British magazine *PCWorld Business*. It rendered computers useless and money for AIDS research.

As the 1990s progressed, financial crime increased, credit-card fraud found a place in the category of identity theft. In 1994, the first financially motivated incident occurred and a hacker stole 10 million dollars from Citibank (Chawki and Abdel Wahab 2006).

In July 1995, one of the most notable events in the realm of malware development was the release of the world's first widely distributed macro-language virus. This appeared in Microsoft Word for Windows documents. It displayed how a macro-programming language that was common to many Microsoft products could generate self-reproducing macros, which could spread from one document to another. Within a few months, there were many clearly destructive versions of this demonstration virus floating in cyberspace.

Over time, the world of cybercrime became more organized. Cyber-criminals started using newer techniques and the degree of sophistication increased as well. In short, criminal gangs introduced a professional element to the world of cybercrime. Mischief was slowly replaced by malicious intent and the lure of financial gains.

In addition to becoming technologically adept, criminals have also been advancing in terms of techniques, precision and sophistication, with regard to both targets and motivations. It would not be wrong to posit that cybercrime techniques are evolving in parallel to new technology trends.

After the release of 'Back Orifice' in 1998, cybercriminals began to demonstrate a smarter series of cyberattacks. In the twenty-first century, it was time for the world to see the arsenal of advanced threats so carefully developed by these gangs of virtual marauders.

One popular method was sending spam e-mails that invited recipients to click on a link or attachment, causing them to accidentally install the malware. This is what happened in 2000 with the infamous 'I Love You' worm, which travelled as a spam e-mail with 'I Love You' in the subject line and an attachment that purported to be a 'love letter for you'. This proved enticing enough for tens of millions of Windows users who fell for it (McAfee 2010a). These attacks gave cybercrooks the attention and the financial gains they sought.

In February 2000, the first and one of the biggest distributed denial-of-service (DDoS) attacks occurred. It was a Canadian hacker who launched the DDoS attack, taking down high-profile websites such as Yahoo, Amazon and CNN. In 2003, the first organized attempt to create a botnet came to light. The same year also witnessed the SQL Slammer worm, which targeted the Microsoft structured query language (SQL) server. It became the fastest spreading worm and is recognized as one of the most sophisticated tools of cybercriminals today.

In 2004–05, lured by monetary gains and aided by professionals, cyber scammers decided it was time to go beyond doing damage and make real money.

The biggest advances in cybercrime happened in this period when cybercriminals created malware that could gain unauthorized access to computers while simultaneously remaining concealed. Cybercriminals used software called root kits to conceal malware, preventing its detection by security checks. This trick yielded passwords and credit-card information and spread viruses. Other technological advances made by cybercrime impacted overall Internet security. Cybercrooks could in one attempt affect and lay low hundreds or even thousands of machines simultaneously through remote control and without the computer users' knowledge. Enabling this bunch of zombie computers that blindly followed their commands empowered cybercriminals significantly enough to be able to launch attacks on other computers or websites, or even distribute spam.

By 2006–08, the cybercrime industry became more organized. Several gangs were formed and the span of cybercrime increased way beyond what it was a decade previously. With a growing amount of money at stake, cyber-criminals began organizing raids under different names for a common cause.

To protect their growing business empires, attackers also became more discrete in their methods, while still showing off their technological brilliance. For example, cybercrooks would use their skills to find unknown vulnerabilities in applications and then try to exploit these before they could be patched. The span of attacks increased and in 2007 it was Pentagon which was under attack.

Between 2009 and 2010, social networking and engineering became the preferred tools for cybercriminals. As social networking sites such as Facebook and Twitter started widening their coverage, so did the cybercrooks. Towards the latter half of the period between 2001 and 2010, cybercrooks realized that they could get personal information of millions of users through social networking websites—where this information was easily available—by using simple applications that could be used to trick users. With users posting everything about where they lived and worked to their current location, all cybercrooks had to do was virtually interact with users to gain access to their information. They did this by employing social engineering, that is, finding out which topics interested Internet users and then, designing attacks using these popular subjects as a lure. For instance, a cybercriminal could track hot topics on Twitter and then post a message mentioning the topic, with a link to a dangerous website that stole credit-card and other personal information. In one recent social-engineering scam, cybercrooks took advantage of Facebook users' curiosity about who was viewing their profiles and had them download a fake application that allowed them to know who was looking at their page. Instead of the desired application, the victims downloaded a malicious pro-gram that hit their Facebook message centre and sent spam, including mes-sages advertising the scam they had fallen for. Another ongoing Facebook scam involves gaining wrongful access to accounts and sending messages to everyone in the user's contact list saying that the user had been robbed while abroad and needed money to be wired to get home. This 'I've been robbed!' scam is yet another instance of social engineering that has cost many people their hard-earned money (McAfee 2010a).

Cybercrooks are also known to distribute scareware. This remains one of the most common Internet threats today, representative of the considerable leap in technological innovation with regard to cybercrime, because it demonstrates how easily the best scammers can overwhelm and manipulate an individual. By playing to the fears of Internet users that almost everything in the virtual world is unsafe, these cybercrooks gain the upper hand and get away. Just as the attacks target individuals, likewise, concerted attacks are also made against corporations, governments and organizations, as a form of social protest and rebellion. The case of the WikiLeaks hacktivists, who launched DDoS attacks against websites such as MasterCard and Visa after they distanced themselves from the news leak site, is but one instance. The Stuxnet worm, which could potentially damage utility companies and their control systems, and even nuclear facilities, is another example. Over time, cybercrime has evolved from being a single act to overcome a personal challenge and gain notoriety to a carefully deliberated and coldly lucrative enterprise, while also playing the part of a political weapon (McAfee 2010a).

14.1.1. Some Other Incidents of 2010

On 29 January, the home page of the Oklahoma Tax Commission's website was compromised with a malicious script code. After the page was loaded, the browser executed the injected script in the background. The injected script code would go through a series of unclear techniques that ultimately took the victim computer to an attack website, without her consent or knowledge (Websense 2010).

The earthquakes in Haiti also illustrate this criminal behaviour. Shortly after the first terrible trembles struck the poor island nation, relief efforts started pouring in and the scams started pouring out. E-mails sent to unsuspecting victims asked for donations to fraudulent causes (McAfee Labs 2010a).

News of targeted Chinese-based attacks at numerous companies came out during the period between December 2009 and January 2010. The targets included Adobe, Google, Rackspace, Northrop Grumman, Dow Chemical and governments in Germany and France (Websense 2010).

In June, a cybercriminal organization named 'Goatse' was able to exploit a security flaw through an AT&T web application. The breach exposed e-mail addresses of iPad 3G users, many of whom were high-ranking media persons, as well as government and military members of Apple's early adopter pro-gramme. Numerous members of the United States Department of Defence's advanced research team had their information exposed (Websense 2010).

In July 2010, Massachusetts-based South Shore hospital publicly announced the loss of 800,000 files that included 15-year records of health and financial information of patients, business partners, vendors, staff and volunteers. The variety of information lost varied from person to person but included the following common facts: full name, address, phone number, date of birth, social security number, driving licence number, medical record number, patient number, bank account information, credit-card number, and medical diagnoses and treatment details (Websense 2010).

In February 2010, a new malicious spam campaign began which spoofed Google's job application responses. The messages looked very well written and were probably excerpts from actual Google job application responses which made them so believable (Websense 2010).

On 5 January 2011, Hamilton Breach Brands Inc. experienced a data security breach on their e-commerce servers and it was believed that the personal information of their customers was being compromised.

By the end of 2010, WikiLeaks caused a global furore. The site published private, secret and classified media submissions from anonymous news sources and news leaks, leading to sustained and sophisticated 'tit-for-tat' cyberattacks. This underlines the importance of data security and cyber caution for large-scale businesses and governments, and at the personal level as well (Sophos 2011).

Although cybercrime can take place anywhere and at anytime, it has been observed that certain geographical locations are more vulnerable to specific types of cybercrimes due to existing economic, sociocultural and geopolitical situations around the globe. Frequent incidents of cybercrime have made the Internet a breeding ground for nefarious activity. Unsuspecting users can have their computers infected and used for committing cybercrime within minutes of connecting to the Internet. The true geographical origin of an attack is however difficult to ascertain.

According to a new study by McAfee (2012), data theft and breaches from cybercrime may have cost businesses as much as one trillion dollars globally in the form of lost intellectual property and expenditures for repairing the damage in 2011. Symantec has been conducting a study to examine malicious activity by country since 2006. The findings from 2010 report indicate that the United States, China, Germany and Brazil are amongst countries ranked high in malicious activity.

14.2. CYBERCRIME IN DEVELOPING COUNTRIES

With the rapid growth of the Internet and many economic activities coming under its purview, cybercrime has picked up momentum in developing countries; they have become top sources of such activities. Cybercrimes in the domestic as well as international spheres have victimized businesses and consumers alike. Developing countries are likely to contribute to most of the growth in the global personal computer (PC) market (Miller 2008) and special attention needs to be paid to such countries. There is a rapid growth of broadband networks in many developing countries. This is likely to make them a fertile ground for hackers.

According to Business Daily Update (2006), rapid increase in the number of broadband users was the reason for the rise of cybercrime in Asia. Forty-one per cent of the world's total Internet users are located in Asia. China alone accounts for one-fifth of global Internet users with a national Internet-user population of 300 million. This coupled with the rapid year-on-year growth in the Chinese use of the Internet (1200 per cent increase from 2000 to 2008) more than accounts for the rise in instances of malware originating from China.

Latin America experienced an increase of 41 per cent in the number of broadband connections in 2007 and the average broadband penetration is expected to reach 30 per cent in 2013 (Screen digest 2008). During the period from 2001 to 2006, Peru's broadband subscriber base increased by more than 80 per cent annually reaching the half-a-million mark in 2006 (ITU 2006). Today more and more cyberattacks are being reported by developing countries. Cybercriminals from Japan, Malaysia, Korea, the United States and China have been targeting computers in Philippines (Conti 2007). In a well-publicized case, Canada-based hackers took advantage of slack cybersecurity measures and eventually stole 44 million dollars by intruding into a network of about 100,000 'zombie' computers in developing countries like Brazil, Poland and Mexico (Harwood 2008).

Cybercrime laws are not well developed in most developing countries. This is a hindrance to the prosecution of cybercrime. One example of this is the 'Love Bug' computer worm developed by a suspect in the Philippines in 2000, which infected millions of computers worldwide. Local investigations were hindered by the fact that the development and spreading of malicious software was not at that time adequately criminalized in the Philippines.

Another example is Nigeria, which has come under pressure to take action over financial scams distributed by e-mail.

The Israeli attacks against the Gaza Flotilla stirred various political hacktivist groups into action. Some hackers, claiming to be Turkish, defaced Israeli domain sites such as that of the Tel Aviv Municipality and posted protest messages with videos shot by the Al Jazeera news service. Turkish hackers also defaced several Facebook accounts owned by Israelis. They sometimes replaced the original profiles with the same message before posting their protest to a group page on Facebook (McAfee Labs 2010b).

Developing economies are a potential source of cybercrime and are known to use highly sophisticated techniques such as SQL injection, phishing and Trojans for financial gains. Growing economies such as India are being made a medium, using the vast pool of computers as botnets.

A relative study has shown that the African subcontinent which has a very low broadband penetration is not conducive, from a cybercriminal's standpoint, to carry out cyberattacks (Reilly 2007) bringing us to the conclusion that infrastructure development is one of the key factors leading to the rise in cybercrime rates.

14.2.1. Some Insights on Brazil

Brazil is a growing economy and constitutes the vast majority of all cybercriminal activity in Latin America. Findings show that Brazilian cybercriminals are constantly dealing with collaborators outside the country for financial gains from cybercrimes, indicating the financially motivated and organized nature of cybercrime activity. The significant increase in cybercrime could be attributed to Brazil's growing infrastructure and increase in broadband usage. Incidents such as a cyberattack resulting in a power grid blackout, exposure of valuable data from a government website and a ransom request related to that have been reported. As a result of the increasing levels of malicious code activities and high-profile attacks in Brazil, a new cybercrime bill has been proposed.

Two broad classes of trends characterized the Latin American threat environment in 2009: first, an intensification of activity by both criminals and authorities and second, deeper levels of integration with cybercrime environments in other parts of the world. While cybercrime in Brazil and the rest of Latin America will continue to increase marginally in frequency and severity, the rapid improvement of law enforcement's capacity to respond to cyber-threats will prove to be the more consequential development in future (iDefense 2008).

The report by Rush et al. (2009: 33) states that Brazil has emerged as a significant player on the global cybercrime stage and can be best described as a 'cesspool of fraud'. This is attributed to the fact that the country lacked any form of effective legislative framework to combat cybercrime.

Brazil reflects wider Internet penetration and increasing number of online banking customers, which provides a permissive environment for different types of cybercrimes. A small but active community of fraudsters, who prefer the use of card skimmers and other physical means of data theft, are very active. Banks in Latin America, particularly those in Brazil, have also been developing their ability to counter cyber fraud.

14.2.2. The Case of Russia

In recent years Russia has been accused many a time of conducting cyber-attacks against its political opponents. The Russian government however has denied any involvement, stating that even though these attacks can be traced back to Russia, they cannot be traced to government computers or agents. The Russian government has labelled these attacks as incidents of hacktivism by anonymous citizens, perpetrated out of patriotism (iDefense 2008). A number of these attacks were denial-of-service (DoS) attacks that used a vast bot net-work. Russian consumers and financial institutions will begin to suffer from cybercrime and need more effective protection in the days to come.

The cyberattacks on Georgia in August 2008 were found to originate from Russia and were much publicized and widely debated. Although public aware-ness of such attacks is fairly recent, professional attention on cyberattacks has been around for much longer. For instance, Estonia was victimized by a series of DoS attacks in 2007. The attacks on the government and commercial web-sites lasted for weeks, hampering much of Estonian e-commerce activity. Technical analysis traced these attacks to Russia but the Russian government denied any involvement.

The Russian Business Network (RBN) has been linked by security firms to child pornography, corporate blackmails, spam attacks and online identity thefts, although most Russian cybercrime has been known to be directed towards financial frauds, particularly through botnets and phishing. It has not been possible so far to track down RBN since it has no legal identity, is not registered as a company and persons heading it are anonymous, known only by their nicknames. Its websites are registered at anonymous addresses with dummy e-mails. It does not advertise for customers. Those who want to use its services contact it using Internet messaging services and pay with anonymous electronic cash. VeriSign estimates that a single scam, called 'Rock Phish' (where Internet users were defrauded into entering personal financial information such as bank account details) made 150 million dollars in a year (Knowledge Globalization Institute 2010).

14.2.3. The Indian Story

Like Brazil, India too is a developing country with high growth in technology, growing exposure to the Internet and increasing Internet-based activities. Cases of cyber fraud have been reported in India as well. The sudden spurt in call centres and poor awareness about technology and legislations among individuals and employees are major causes behind such frauds. As per the United Press International Asia.com (July 2011), the constructive use of information technology can be credited for the enormous rise in India's stature and economy in the world. With rising technology and Internet usage, India is also becoming a prime target for cyberattacks.

Cities such as Mumbai have registered more cybercrime cases than conventional crimes such as burglary, arson and murder in recent years. With the massive growth curve of the outsourcing business in India come mounting challenges. To manage such growth in a way that ensures security of data is the main challenge. Events of data breach due to human errors, social media-based spamming and unorganized cybercrimes are the major issues in India. Major crimes reported in India are defacement of websites, denial of service, spamming and so on.

India is also facing cyber espionage from one or more neighbouring countries. In March 2009, a spy network from China hacked into government and private systems in 103 countries. The targets included many Indian embassies and the headquarters of the Dalai Lama. The website of India's Ministry of External Affairs was hacked by Chinese hackers in May 2008. Despite official denial, identities and passwords of several Indian diplomats were reported to have been stolen by at least one website. Many hacking incidents were reported after a massive troop standoff between India and Pakistan following the terror attacks on the Indian Parliament in December 2001. The website www.armyinkashmir.com was also targeted by Pakistani hackers in 1999 as it provided factual information about daily events in the Kashmir valley. Pakistani hackers posted photographs of Indian security officials allegedly killing Kashmiri people and blamed the government of India for the atrocities being committed there. This obviously had a disturbing impact in the valley.

The National Informatics Centre Case, 2008

In May 2008 senior Indian government officials in New Delhi were said to have confirmed that Chinese hackers targeted the Ministry of External Affairs (MEA) and the National Informatics Centre (NIC), which provides network support to the central and state governments, as well as other administrative bodies in India. The unnamed officials were quoted as saying that this was China's way of gaining 'an asymmetrical advantage' over a potential adversary. The MEA's secure servers were intruded upon in 2008. A routine security check performed by intelligence agencies detected the security breach. A team of auditors with the help of the NIC tracked down the Internet protocol (IP) addresses and the media access control (MAC) addresses of hackers and confirmed that China was behind the intrusions.

Security loopholes in the firewalls of the MEA triggered such an audacious attempt. Sources also said that it was an attempt to sniff at data related to the Tibet policy in the MEA systems. Getting such information would put China one step ahead in political matters related to Tibet, which was crucial at the time. China used traditional hacking methods such as computer viruses and worms, but in sophisticated ways, to intrude into the servers. Spyware (software that allows snooping on browsing activity and invades privacy) was also used.

Fortunately the hackers could not gain any data because important security information was not stored on computers with Internet connections. Alarmed by the breach, the government sent a team of intelligence officials to audit the security standards of systems and computers in key Indian missions around the world, starting with the embassy in Beijing. It was confirmed by the MEA that there was no loss or damage in any form, whether tangible or intangible.

A study by Norton (2011) showed that the Indian population surveyed spent an average of 30 hours per week online, as compared to the global average of 24 hours per week. The time spent online clearly points to the fact that most people in India are now using the Internet to fulfil all their needs, from professional to personal. The report by Rush et al. (2009) indicates that there has been a leap in cybercrime in recent years. Reported cases of spam, hacking and fraud have multiplied fifty-fold between 2004 and 2007. The report voices real concerns about the security of companies from Europe and the United States that are increasingly outsourcing IT functions and software development tasks to India, Brazil, Russia and eastern Europe in order to take advantage of good IT skills and lower wage costs. This phenomenon, offshore outsourcing, has raised new concerns about the security risks involved, where access to valuable financial information can provide an opportunity for different criminals to enter the cybercrime business (Rush et al. 2009: 35).

India is fast emerging as a soft target for organized cybercrime, with four in every five online adults confessing to having become victims of identity thefts in 2010. Indians are also more prone to phishing attacks. This is not due to the rise in the number of people using the Internet, but due to lack of awareness. That India is among the world's top 15 countries hosting phishing sites that steal confidential information such as passwords and credit-card details may help put the lurking danger in perspective (Shivakumar 2009).

14.2.4. Cybercrime and China

China has seen an increase in the number of cybercrimes in recent years. It has an estimated 500 million Internet users as compared to the United States (which holds the second place) with only 200 million (CINIC 2011). According to a report by the People's Daily Online, many domestic computers were controlled via overseas-based IP addresses in 2010. A report by China's primary computer security monitoring network, the National Computer Network Emergency Response Coordination Center of China (CNCERT/CC), stated that 47,000 overseas IP addresses were involved in attacks against 8.9 million Chinese computers in 2011. The existing Chinese legal infrastructure, which is largely modelled on a system of reactive legislation, is insufficient to address the magnitude of the problem (Qi et al. 2009).

The report by Rush et al. (2009) likewise identifies China as a major player in the cybercrime network. Corporate identity theft is common in China. The types of brand abuse that everyone already knows about are

'Oh Canada' (Canadian pharmacy spam), Western Union, Pfizer spam and so on. Brand abuse related to pharmacy spam is very popular in China as proved by the Canadian pharmacy and Pfizer spam. These are well organized and politically motivated attacks targeted at big brands and are of a transnational nature.

Chinese phishers mostly use free and low-priced domain registrars outside the country to attack users and companies inside China. Indigenous phishers attacking Chinese institutions such as banks, securities firms and CCTV, the major state television broadcaster. A majority (70 per cent) of all malicious domain name registrations made worldwide in 2010 were registered to phish Chinese targets. Most of the phishing attacks were targeted against Taobao. com, which is similar to eBay and Amazon. Taobao.com is the China's most popular e-commerce site and is the world's second most phished target after PayPal (APWG 2011a).

In recent years, there has been a substantial rise in the number of high-level hacking incidents reported, allegedly by Chinese hackers. Attackers originating from China have been accused of infiltrating government computer systems in the United States, the United Kingdom, Germany, South Korea, France and Taiwan. Chinese hackers have also been accused of data theft from foreign commercial and financial institutions as well as non-government organizations in regions where China has a national interest. These include Tibetan groups active in India, organizations advocating on the conflict in the Darfur region of Sudan and the Falun Gang. Patriotic cyber activity has been reported to intensify during crises such as Sino-American or Sino-Taiwanese tensions (Information Warfare Monitor 2009).

The United States Department of Defense has reported cyberattacks by other countries. Most notable in the series of attacks since 2003 were the 'Titan Rain' attacks that targeted numerous defence companies as well as the Department of Defense.

Titan Rain, 2004

Titan Rain is thought to rank high among the most pervasive cyber espionage threats that United States computer networks have ever faced. Titan Rain was first discovered in March 2004, though the attacks are believed to have been initiated in 2003. The United States gave the codename 'Titan Rain' to the growing number of Chinese attacks since 2003, notably directed at the

Pentagon but also hitting other United States government departments, including Sandia National Laboratories, Redstone Arsenal, National Aeronautics and Space Administration (NASA) and Lockheed Martin—the world's largest weapons maker (Palmer 2011). Titan Rain first caught the eye of Shawn Carpenter, a computer-network security analyst at Sandia National Laboratories, when he helped investigate a network break-in at Lockheed Martin in September 2003. Methodical and voracious, the hackers wanted all the files they could find, and were able to get them by penetrating secure computer networks at the country's most sensitive military bases, and offices of defence contractors and aerospace companies. Eventually Carpenter followed the trail to its apparent end, in the southern Chinese province of Guangdong. He found that the attacks emanated from just three Chinese routers that acted as the first connection point from a local network to the Internet. Hundreds of Defense Department computer systems had been penetrated by an insidious program known as a Trojan. According to an alert issued by the government, these compromises allow an unknown adversary to not only get controls over the Department of Defense (DOD) hosts, but also have the capability to use the DOD hosts in malicious activity. The potential also exists for the perpetrator to shut down each host. The hackers could commandeer a hidden section of a hard drive, zip up as many files as possible and immediately transmit the data to South Korea, Hong Kong or Taiwan before sending them to mainland China. They always made a silent escape, wiping their electronic fingerprints clean and leaving behind an almost undetectable beacon which allowed them to re-enter the machine at will. An entire attack took 10 to 30 minutes. The hacking not only gained access to very sensitive material, it also left behind many back doors and 'zombified' machines, meaning that any future hacking could be now achieved more easily. Known to be one of the biggest hacks of all time, it is believed that the hacking originated from China (Thornburgh 2005).

The Information Warfare Monitor carried out an investigation in 2009 for studying a cyber espionage network based on allegations of Chinese cyber espionage against the Tibetan community. The investigation started with Tibetan computer systems, which were found to be conclusively compromised by multiple infections that gave attackers access to sensitive information. This investigation uncovered a network of 1,295 infected hosts in 103 countries with four command and control servers in China (named GhostNet control servers). It also revealed that the GhostNet was capable of taking full control of infected computers, including searching and downloading files and covertly operating attached devices like microphones and web cameras. Of the compromised systems, at least 30 per cent were found to be high-value diplomatic, economic, political and military targets. These included embassies, ministries of foreign affairs, the Association of Southeast Asian Nations (ASEAN) Secretariat, South Asian Association for Regional Cooperation (SAARC) and the Asian Development Bank, among others. An analysis of the data stolen from politically sensitive targets was also recovered during the course of the investigation. Cyberspace can be a strategic domain for a country as it can help redress the military imbalance. Chinese cyber espionage is definitely a cause of global concern (Information Warfare Monitor 2009).

Pentagon under Cyberattack, 2007

In June 2007, Chinese military hackers working for the People's Liberation Army (PLA) penetrated the United States Defense Department's computer networks. The Pentagon acknowledged the attack and said it resulted in the affected network—an unclassified e-mail system used by policy aides working for the Defense Secretary, Robert Gates—going down for more than a week as the attacks proceeded. China denied any role in the attacks (Bloomberg Businessweek 2010).

China Attacks Google and Others, 2009

On 12 January 2010, Google revealed that it had detected a 'highly sophisticated' attack on its corporate network that had originated from China. The targets were the Gmail accounts of a few human-rights activists. Google said its investigation revealed that at least 20 other large companies, which it did not identify, were targets too. Later, chip maker Intel disclosed it had been attacked at about the same time as Google (Bloomberg Businessweek 2010).

The Cyberattacks on South Korea, 2011

In a massive cyberattack, Chinese hackers managed to decimate South Korea by targeting a popular social networking site. The attacks, which compromised a total of 35 million users, were directed at the Cyworld website, as well as the Nate Web portal run by SK Communications. The hackers appeared to have stolen phone numbers, e-mail addresses, names and encrypted information of millions of site users. The source of the breach, first revealed by the Korean Communications Commission, was traced back to computer IP addresses based in China (Hoffman 2011). The massive hack followed after a series of attacks directed at South Korea's government and financial organizations, including a government-backed bank, 1.8 million customers data at Hyundai Capital, as well as the Korean Government ministries, the National Assembly, the country's military headquarters and networks of United States forces based in the country (Hoffman 2011).

14.3. CYBERCRIME IN DEVELOPED COUNTRIES

That cybercrime is prevalent across the globe since it is an easy source of making money is well known. Cases of financial fraud are known in almost all countries but high financial traffic makes developed countries, such as the United States and United Kingdom, highly targeted for the majority of credit-card and banking frauds. Developed countries with the highest-speed Internet connections rank high in cybercrime incidents since constantly connected systems tend to be more attractive to cybercriminals.

14.3.1. The United States and Cybercrime

The United States reports a high incidence of cybercrime, both as a source of and as a destination for cyberattacks. A high number of broadband connections with high online availability is the major reason behind this. Cybercrime costs the United States economy over 100 billion dollars per year (Kratchman et al. 2008; Mello 2007). The United States military and intelligence agencies planned a cyberattack on Iraqi financial systems before the invasion of Iraq in 2003. This would have resulted in the freezing of billions of dollars in Saddam Hussein's personal bank accounts, stopped payments to Iraqi soldiers and stifled war supplies (McAfee 2009d).

Many cybercrimes in the United States are motivated by revenge and malicious intent. The Americans indulge in crimes like crashing a company's database (perpetrated by sacked workers); sending hate mails; holding a network administrator hostage by stealing passwords and so on. These crimes might be annoying but they are comparatively less threatening (Global Internet Security Threat Trends, Symantec, 2009).

Many a time, cybercrimes are well organized with financial motivations since financial traffic is high in the United States and other European countries. As per reports by Lunev (2001) and Walker (2004), hackers have attacked computer networks of the White House, the Pentagon, North Atlantic Treaty Organization (NATO)'s military websites and the Interpol. Secret source codes have been stolen from Microsoft and credit-card information stolen from a number of American banks. As per Grow and Bush (2005) and Hahn and Layne-Farrar (2006), many of the cyberattacks targeting businesses and consumers in the United States come from perpetrators operating from outside the United States.

The White House issued a plan to fight internationally funded organized cybercrime. The primary target would be transnational cybercrime. 'During the past 15 years, technological innovation and globalization have proven to be an overwhelming force for good,' President Obama said during his announcement of the strategy. 'However, transnational criminal organizations have taken advantage of our increasingly interconnected world to expand their illicit enterprises.' The 56 priorities of the strategy include enhancing intelligence and information sharing, as well as protection of the nation's financial system and strategic market against transnational organized crime (National Security Council 2011).

Cybercrime rings from central and eastern Europe were pointed out by Obama to be the most damaging. It has cost citizens and businesses in the United States one billion dollars in online fraud alone. As per the Secret Service, anonymous online fraudsters cost the nation's financial infrastructure billions of dollars every year (National Security Council 2011).

In the United States, over the course of one year, the amount of money lost to cybercrime has nearly doubled, from 265 million dollars in 2008 to 560 million dollars in 2009, according to reports by the Internet Crime Complaint Center (2008, 2009), which is supported by the Federal Bureau of Investigation (FBI). In 2009, computer hackers broke into the Pentagon's 300-billion-dollar Joint Strike Fighter project, F-35 Lightning II. The F-35 programme is the costliest weapons program ever. As hackers carefully encrypted the stolen data, investigators were unable to determine the amount or nature of the lost data (KPMG International 2011).

In most countries, the private sector accounts for the majority of cyber-security spending. The United States is a notable exception where government spending is almost equal to spending by the private sector. The strong technology industry in the United States, combined with the fact that its defence and intelligence budgets are significantly larger than those of any other country are key market drivers (PricewaterhouseCoopers 2011).

Albert Gonzalez is said to be the single most prolific identity thief in the history of the United States. Gonzalez was involved in a large number of cases, the most prominent among them being the Shadowcrew case (1.5 million data items stolen), the TJX Companies case (46 million data items stolen) and the Heartland Payment Systems case (130 million data items stolen—the single largest case ever in the United States). Gonzalez not only used the stolen data to withdraw cash from automated teller machines (ATMs), but also sold it conspirators sitting in eastern Europe. Although his net gains from these exploits are still unclear, the forfeiture of 1.6 million dollars, one condominium, a luxury car and some personal items were included in his guilty plea. It is quite possible that Gonzalez has additional wealth stacked away in secret accounts overseas, because these assets seem rather modest considering the extent of his activity (United Nations Office on Drugs and Crime 2010).

14.3.2. Status of Cybercrime in the United Kingdom

The United Kingdom remains amongst the world's most highly targeted information security environments in the world. Even if it is presently suffering from a relatively intense economic contraction, the United Kingdom is a wealthy and highly internationalized country with an extensively digitized economy, standing as a hub of global financial and commerce systems. Cybersecurity in the United Kingdom is becoming a problem for both government and business houses. The government's shortcomings and dangers to banking customers are the main cybercrime concerns among the public. As observed by Tim Weber (2009) cybercrime is predominantly affecting individuals in the United Kingdom through financial frauds, identity thefts and identity frauds, sexual offences and computer misuse.

Cybercrimes in the United Kingdom are seen to be well organized. Just like in the US, it is seen mostly in verticals such as banking and financial services, central and local government offices and the police department (Aguilar-Millan et al. 2008).

A recent development has been the compromise of chip and pin devices at the time of manufacturing itself. This has led to massive compromises of financial data as well as hacking of data belonging to the Ministry of Defence and intelligence services. The financial system is not the only victim since the threat of a politically motivated cybercrime also exists. Throughout 2008, at least five public statements made by high-level policymakers hit the press. It was said that the United Kingdom was presently under persistent cyber espionage attacks by foreign entities, though the full extent of these was left unelaborated (iDefense 2008).

The annual cost of cybercrime in 2010 in United Kingdom has been estimated at 27 billion pounds (approximately 43 billion dollars) (BBC News 2011). A major portion of that comprises intellectual property theft and cyber espionage activities. Government spending on cybersecurity has increased significantly in efforts to combat digital crime. In February 2011, the government allocated 63 million pounds (approximately 100 million dollars) to build upon existing expertise in the Serious Organised Crime Agency (SOCA) and the Metropolitan Police Central e-Crime Unit. In the United Kingdom, the cost of identity fraud in 2010 was said to be 1.2 billion pounds (just under two billion dollars) (KPMG International 2011). Losses may not only be financial, but may also include damage to reputations. In reality, many victims do not report such crimes, while financial institutions often do not wish to publicize customers' bad experiences. The actual incidence of identity theft is likely to far exceed the number of reported losses (ITU 2009b).

14.3.3. Cybercrime across Some Other Developed Countries

Canada's cybercrime landscape has undergone dramatic changes in the past year. Canada has also been a victim of cyberattacks. Canada not only ranked second in the world for hosting phishing sites from January to May 2011, but it also suffered a 319-per cent jump in the number of servers hosting those phishing sites . In January 2011, hackers infected computers in two Canadian government departments, leaving many officials without Internet access for nearly two months (KPMG International 2011). In Germany, phishing activity is estimated to have increased 70 per cent year on year in 2010, resulting in a loss of 17 million euros (approximately 22 million dollars), according to a joint report by the German information technology trade group Bitkom and the German Federal Criminal Police Office (KPMG International 2011).

14.4. CONCLUSION

There is a lot of diversity in global cybercrime. The types of digital threats users face differ depending upon where they are and what they use. The nature of cybercrime activity is such that the criminal may be in one corner of the world and the impact felt in another. The boundaries have gradually ceased to exist, considering the anonymity of cyberspace. And this has made cybercrime a complex and dangerous threat in our times.

FIFTEEN

ROLE OF GOVERNMENT AND REGULATORY MECHANISMS

———————•◆•———————

15.1. INTRODUCTION

In the world of computers, materials and properties have different meanings. In spite of the classical shape of tangible property, in cyberspace, many properties are not of a material nature. In this situation, we have assets, which need protection, but the problem is that they may not be categorized as per the classical penal laws. Another problem in most legal systems is that the theft must be committed against tangible property. Where the object of crime is information or data, the property in question may be intangible. There are many ways in which to commit fraud using the computer. It may be perpetrated by altering information stored in a system or by altering the outputs. In most legal systems, computer fraud does not need a new law. It can be covered by the existing legal rules.

The government and regulatory mechanisms have a critical role to play in containing cybercrime. It will be extremely difficult for companies to win business in international markets if the government as well as local and international law agencies do not crack down on illegal Internet activities. A lack of collaboration between the industry and the government has also hampered the ability of law-enforcement agencies to solve cybercrimes. Most businesses do not report cybercrimes because they are scared to face the consequences. They think doing so would undermine their credibility; lead to bad public relations; damage reputation; and adversely affect their stock prices.

Security breaches can have a far-reaching impact not only on a company's finances but on its reputation as well. Companies are required to prove their compliance with certain regulations. There is an expectation from customers, employees, and partners—anyone who entrusts a company with their sensitive information—that this information will be safe in the hands of the company.

In most incidents of cybercrime, the offenders and victims live in different jurisdictions. Industrialized countries have adequate resources to set up anti-cybercrime institutions. However, it's the developing countries that lack these facilities. Inter-jurisdictional collaborations are a necessity but not all companies are geared up to the challenge. According to Walden (2005), cooperation among law-enforcement agencies is 'notoriously slow and bureaucratic'.

A further slack in the law-enforcement system is caused by the unavailability of a database of cybercriminals. The profiles of most of the new breed of criminals differ from those of the conventional ones. In Russia, for instance, most hackers are young, educated and work independently, and this does not fit conventional criminal profiles. The innovations in cybercrimes also present challenges to the judicial systems. For petty cybercrime cases, it is difficult to find an attorney (Katz 2005). Experts also say that explaining cybercrimes to judges is difficult.

Securing a financial services network environment is another major challenge. The issue lies in not only meeting the basic business requirement of ensuring that a customer's financial information remains private and secure, but also in doing so in accordance with the variety of industry and government regulations. Financial organizations must consider all the potential damage that can occur to their business if sensitive data is lost or stolen, which may include lawsuits, negative publicity, loss of sales and customer confidence, and permanently tarnished reputations. By implementing a strong authentication system, banks and other financial organizations can secure their digital communication and transaction systems, and increase profitability by lowering operational costs. With the rise in the number of electronic transactions, such as credit- and debit-card purchases, online banking and investments, it is increasingly important for financial service providers to institute strict controls over how customer information is protected on their networks, both during and after transactions. Having a strong authentication platform is imperative to ensuring trust and preserving the financial service brand.

According to the Government Information Security (28 July 2011), concerns over cybercrimes in the financial space are in the spotlight. The Federal Financial Institutions Examination Council of the United States has issued its latest authentication guidance, a supplement to its 2005 online authentication guidance, which specifically addresses online banking frauds. It says 'layered security and customer education are critical to the fight against financial cybercrimes. But so is regulatory oversight.'

15.2. GOVERNMENT AND REGULATIONS

Any violation in information security can cause international embarrassment, breaches in national security, financial losses and non-delivery of essential citizen services. The government has a critical role to play. In today's well-connected world, security initiatives by governments collectively help strengthen national security. Every government department caters to a heterogeneous group of users who differ in their awareness and skills relating to information technology (IT). Since governments address diverse groups, its processes and information systems are also more complicated.

Most nations have legislated to give legal effect to electronic transactions and also to prevent the misuse of IT resources. India's Information Technology Act, 2000, the United Kingdom's Computer Misuse Act, 1990, Malaysia's Computer Crimes Act, 1997, the United States Electronic Signatures in Global and National Commerce Act, 2000, Australia's Electronic Transactions Act, 1999 and Mexico's E-Commerce Act, 2000 are some notable legislations in this context. Although there is no reliable data on the criminal convictions under these statutes, there is a general consensus about the fact that the deterrent effect of these legislations on prospective hackers has not been very significant. Again, not many civil matters relating to electronic signatures have been heard in courts. Laws on these issues need to mature with time.

Organizations are faced with a number of regulations related to IT security one way or another. These include, in the United States, the Sarbanes–Oxley Act, 2002, Health Insurance Portability and Accountability Act (HIPAA), 1996, Gramm–Leach–Bliley Act, 1999, Federal Information Security Management Act (FISMA), 2002; in Canada, the Personal Information Protection and Electronic Documents Act (PIPEDA), 2000; and in the European Union, the Data Protection Directive, 1995, amongst others.

The Sarbanes–Oxley Act, 2002, is of particular interest because it mandates stronger internal controls and institutes personal liability for executives of companies that are publicly traded in the United States.

Since the legal systems in different countries are different, cybercriminals take advantage of the regulatory arbitrage (Levi 2002). Economies worldwide vary greatly in terms of the legal systems relating to cybercrimes. Not surprisingly, many organized cybercrimes are initiated from countries that have few or no laws directed against cybercrimes and little capacity and willingness to enforce existing laws (Grow and Bush 2005; Williams 2001).

Malicious actors make the most of the fact that many countries do not have adequate legal frameworks or cybercrime laws and cyber investigation capabilities. They also take advantage of the complex challenges faced by law-enforcement agencies and the fact that responses to incidents are constrained by geographical boundaries when working outside their jurisdictions. Cross-border information sharing among law-enforcement entities is a critical element of investigating and prosecuting cybercriminals. While mechanisms such as the G8 24/7 Network provide for points of contact among such law-enforcement entities, it is unclear how such networks cooperate among themselves (OECD 2008b).

It is apparent that cybercrimes differ from other crimes in terms of permissiveness of regulatory regimes (Mittelman and Johnston 1999), regulatory arbitrage (Levi 2002), and culture and ethical attitudes that influence external and internal stigma (Aguilar-Millan et al. 2008; Donaldson 1996; Kwong et al. 2003).

Regulatory institutions consist of bodies (such as the Department of Justice and Department of Homeland Security in the United States) and existing laws and rules (for example, the Gramm–Leach–Bliley Act, 1999 in the United States) that influence individuals and organizations to behave in certain ways (Eltringham 1995).

15.3. INTERNATIONAL APPROACHES TO COMBAT CYBERCRIME

Cyberattacks are global problems and for this reason, global-level institutions are likely to be more effective in dealing with such problems.

National-level institutions provide a number of mechanisms to influence the cybercrime landscape. The lack of strong rule of law is responsible for the rise in the number of cyberattacks. The effectiveness of regulations depends upon the administrative capacity of the state and the citizens' willingness to accept the established institution. This means that even if governments in some developing countries want to fight against cybercrimes, the lack of regulatory framework implies that they lack the formal authority to do so.

A large number of anti-cybercrime institutions are being established and strengthened due to the increasing cybercrime rate. There is tremendous pressure on governments to improve regulatory institutions and infrastructure to counter cybercrimes. For instance, the Business Software Alliance in the United States persuaded the Congress to pass legislation to 'treat cybercrime as organized crime' and hike the related penalties (Natividad 2008).

In 2009, a series of cyberattacks were launched against popular government websites in many countries, effectively shutting them down for several hours. Claims that are most disturbing relate to the possibility that this limited success may embolden future hackers to attack critical infrastructure, such as power generators or air-traffic control systems—with devastating consequences on a country's economy and national security.

Many governments have instituted Computer Emergency Response Teams (CERTs) for their countries and many of them have either developed or are in the process of developing security measures tailored for their requirements. A special mention may be made here of the Federal Information Security Act (FISMA), 2002, a United States federal law that explicitly requires federal agencies to develop and implement information security programmes, with the heads of agencies being made responsible for these programmes. In addition, Section 303 of the FISMA stipulates that the National Institute of Standards and Technology would be the nodal agency for the development of security-related standards, guidelines, associated methods and procedures and minimum requirements for federal agencies.

In Brazil, for example, in August 2009, the federal government established the Critical Infrastructure Protection Information Security Working Group, under its Department of Information and Communications Security. The group has been working on information security and incident response plans. Again, in Australia, a 2009 defence white paper announced the establishment of a national Cyber Security Operations Centre, within the military's Defence Signals Directorate (McAfee 2009a).

Cybersecurity plays an important role in the ongoing development of information technology, as well as Internet services. Making the Internet safer (and protecting Internet users) has become integrated with the development of new services as well as government policies. Cybersecurity strategies—for example, the development of technical protection systems or the education of users to prevent them from becoming victims of cybercrime—can help to reduce the risk of cybercrime.

An anti-cybercrime strategy should be an integral element of a cybersecurity strategy. The ITU Global Cybersecurity Agenda is a global framework for dialogue and international cooperation. It coordinates international responses to the growing challenges to cybersecurity to enhance confidence and security in the information society, and builds on existing work, initiatives and partnerships with the objective of proposing global strategies to address these related challenges (ITU 2009).

15.3.1. Collaboration

Collaboration, which may be in the form of cross-border, or even government–industry collaboration, is important for organized action against cybercrime and for initiating activities such as increasing the shutdown of affected domains, freezing payment accounts that are suspected of fraud, isolating bad networks and so on. The McColo spam and Avalanche phishing incidents are examples where this kind of collaboration has been effective. Collaboration is also required to build a knowledge repository on the best practices followed and security assurance, a common vulnerability database, and common criteria for information security products. It is all the more important for countries to collaborate at the time of a cyberattack as was seen in the case of Estonia, discussed earlier.

The United States and India signed a Memorandum of Understanding in July 2011 to promote closer cooperation and timely exchange of information between the organizations of their respective governments responsible for cybersecurity.

In 1997, the Group of Eight (G8) countries established a 'Subcommittee on High-tech Crimes' to deal with the fight against cybercrime. During its meeting in Washington, D.C., in the United States, the G8 Justice and Interior Ministers adopted ten principles and a ten-point action plan to fight high-tech crimes. The heads of the G8 countries endorsed these principles later, which include the following:

1. There must be no safe havens for those who abuse information technologies.
2. Investigation and prosecution of international high-tech crimes must be coordinated among all concerned States, regardless of where harm has occurred.
3. Law-enforcement personnel must be trained and equipped to address high-tech crimes.

In 1999, the G8 emphasized on crimes (such as child pornography), as well as traceability of transactions along with transborder access to stored data. This has translated into some laws which are being seen now. In 2007, the G8 agreed to criminalize misuse of the Internet by terrorist groups.

United Nations

The 8th United Nations Congress on the Prevention of Crime and the Treatment of Offenders was held in Cuba in August 1990. Based on the resolution passed here, the United Nations (UN) published a manual in 1994 on the prevention and control of computer-related crime. In 2000, the General Assembly adopted a resolution on combating the criminal misuse of information technologies similar to the ten-point action plan laid down by the G8 in 1997. In 2004, the UN created a working group to deal with spam, cybercrime and other Internet-related topics, emphasizing the interest of the UN to participate in ongoing international discussions on cybercrime threats (Schjolberg and Ghernaouti-Helie 2011).

A number of United Nations System decisions, resolutions and recommendations address issues related to cybercrime. The most important ones are:

1. In 2004, the United Nations Economic and Social Council adopted a resolution on international cooperation in the prevention, investigation, prosecution and punishment of fraud, the criminal misuse and falsification of identity and related crimes.
2. In 2004, the Council adopted a resolution on the sale of illicit drugs via the Internet.

3. In 2007, the Council adopted a resolution on international cooperation in the prevention, investigation, prosecution and punishment of
economic fraud and identity-related crime.

International Telecommunication Union

The International Telecommunication Union (ITU) is the lead agency of the
World Summit on Information Society that took place in two phases in
Geneva, Switzerland (in 2003) and in Tunis, Tunisia (in 2005). Governments,
policymakers and experts from around the world shared ideas and experiences
about how best to address emerging issues associated with the development of
a global information society, including the development of compatible standards and laws. The outputs of the Summit are contained in the Geneva
Declaration of Principles, the Geneva Plan of Action, the Tunis Commitment
and the Tunis Agenda for the Information Society. The Geneva Plan of Action
highlights the importance of measures in the fight against cybercrime
(ITU 2009).

European Union

In 1999, the European Union launched the initiative 'eEurope', by adopting
the European Commission's communication eEurope–An Information Society
for All. In 2000, the European Council adopted a comprehensive eEurope
Action Plan and called for its implementation before the end of 2002. In 2001,
the European Commission published a communication titled 'Creating a Safer
Information Society by Improving the Security of Information Infrastructures
and Combating Computer-related Crime'. In this communication, the Commission analysed and addressed the problem of cybercrime and pointed out the
need for effective action to deal with threats to the integrity, availability and
dependability of information systems and networks. In 2002, the Commission
presented a proposal for a 'Framework Decision on Attacks against Information
Systems'. With partial modification it was finally adopted by the Council in
the same year.

The European Network and Information Security Agency (ENISA) has
been actively working with the European Commission ministers and departments and European Union (EU) member states on policy and operational

issues around cybersecurity. Through these discussions, it has emerged that private-public partnerships are the most promising approach for tackling issues such as information sharing, cross-country collaboration, cloud computing and identity management. ENISA also heads the European Public Private Partnership for Resilience (EP3R). The EP3R is the flexible governance framework applicable all across Europe in the context of information and communication technology infrastructure. It works to foster cooperation between the public and private sectors on security and resilience objectives, baseline requirements, policy practices and measures. In the EU, private-public partnerships have been successful in handling many policy and operational issues concerning cybersecurity (Cisco 2010).

Organisation for Economic Co-operation and Development

In 1983, the Organisation for Economic Co-operation and Development (OECD) initiated a study on the possibility of international harmonization of criminal law in order to address the problem of computer crime. After receiving a request (from the Strategic Planning Unit of the Executive Office of the Secretary General of the UN) to produce a comparative outline of domestic legislative solutions regarding the use of the Internet for terrorist purposes, the OECD published a report on the legislative treatment of cyberterror in the domestic laws of individual states in 2007.

In 2008, the OECD report suggested that there is a need for a strategy of global partnership against malware, to avoid it from becoming a serious threat to the Internet economy and to national security in the coming years. Today, however, communities involved in fighting malware offer essentially a fragmented local response to a global threat (OECD 2008b).

15.3.2. National Policies to Combat Cybercrime

United States of America

Cyberterrorism and cybercrime incidents in the past two decades have led to a push for stricter control and regulation on cyber activity. More and more countries are now joining the United States in this effort.

On 25 June 2010, the United States government released to the public a draft version of an upcoming policy against Cybercrime, titled 'National

Strategy for Trusted Identities in Cyberspace: Creating Options for Enhanced Online Security and Privacy' (Department of Homeland Security 2010). It says:

> One key step in reducing online fraud and identity theft is to increase the level of trust associated with identities in cyberspace. While this Strategy recognizes the value of anonymity for many online transactions (e.g., blog postings), for other types of transactions (e.g., online banking or accessing electronic health records) it is important that the parties to that transaction have a high degree of trust that they are interacting with known entities.

Fundamentally, this policy should enable the United States government to create verified online identities for its citizens in a closed identity ecosystem, backed by private corporations such as Verizon, Google, PayPal, Symantec and AT&T (Hopkins 2011). Users will then be able to use one login to sign in to many websites that implement this functionality and their personal details will be retrieved from a central location maintained by the government. This proposed policy has created controversy over its effect on issues of privacy and anonymity on the web (Hopkins 2011; McCullagh 2011). The security of data is also crucial, since the personal information of all the participating citizens could be subject to a hacking attack. A similar attempt has been made by China with its China Wide Web, a countrywide intranet that is closed to outsiders (Macavinta and Wingfield 1997).

If the framework proposed by the United States, regarding having a single identification and single e-mail linked to personal details, is agreed upon by other countries in a feasible manner, it will be considered as a major breakthrough to check cybercrimes.

Until recently, it was understood that when an organization or government body wanted to take action against a website that facilitated illegal activity, they would have to move legally against the owner(s) of the website, its (Internet service provider) ISP or its users. Recently, the Department of Homeland Security in the United States, in an unprecedented move, took back ownership of many '.com' domain names that were used to host sites facilitating illegal activity. Domain names ending in '.com' are regulated by the United States-based Internet Corporation for Assigned Names and Numbers (ICANN).

The year 2010 saw a continued focus on cybersecurity legislations by the United States government, with increasing momentum towards creating a comprehensive bill that would cover law enforcement, critical infrastructure protection, research and development, and global norms for cybersecurity. Another notable development for the government in 2010 was the Obama administration, which made strengthening national cybersecurity one of its top priorities. It reached a significant milestone in November 2010 when the new United States Cyber Command (also known as CYBERCOM) finally achieved full operating status. CYBERCOM works along with the National Security Agency and has the authority to defend the nation's military networks from cyberattacks.

Growing concerns about foreign entities hacking into networks to gather intelligence information; the effects of theft, by domestic and international cybercriminals of intellectual property from businesses, on the competitive edge of the United States; and a focus on ensuring supply chain integrity for software and hardware, are just some of the key factors behind the recent push by United States lawmakers for more substantial cybersecurity legislation. However, while obviously well intended, the several new legislative proposals now being considered by the United States Congress may have a conflict of interest with private industry. There is also concern within private industry that the new regulatory demands that may evolve from proposed cybersecurity legislation could prevent enterprises from responding effectively to emerging and changing threats.

The Central Intelligence Agency (CIA) in the United States is ramping up cybersecurity efforts with increased investments in technology, a move that the CIA claims will also boost efficiency. The CIA has released its five-year strategy, known as 'CIA 2015'. Technology is one of three key initiatives in the plan, which aims to help the CIA act quickly and effectively to address terrorism, cyberthreats and 'dangerous technology'. In particular, the CIA will be investing in human-enabled technical collection and advanced software tools to manage large amounts of data (Long 2010a).

New cybersecurity legislations have made the private sector more concerned about increased government regulations, but lawmakers are working to assure industry that they are an important part of a team effort, not a target. The bill, approved by the Senate Commerce Committee in March 2010, includes provisions for auditing company security plans and incentives for adopting good cybersecurity practices. The private sector is worried that the government will be able to control their security protocols (Long 2010b).

United Kingdom

The United Kingdom will continue to remain among the world's most heavily targeted information security environments. Even if it is suffering a relatively intense economic contraction currently, it is a wealthy and highly internationalized country with an extensively digitized economy, standing as a hub of global financial and commerce systems. Moreover, it wields the best military forces and intelligence apparatus in the EU, and remains a first-order politico-diplomatic power on the world stage. As such, it remains a salient, accessible and high-value target of cybercrime and cyber espionage, despite the fact that its IT networks are as advanced, and well protected as much of the rest of the developed world. Cybersecurity in the United Kingdom is fast becoming among the most recognized problems in business and government. The British press has been increasingly attentive to such issues, especially the government's shortcomings and the dangers to banking customers. A stream of surveys repeatedly highlights this growing concern among the public (iDefense 2008).

China

The Chinese government has in the past taken some initiatives to control the growing spam originating from Chinese domains. On 11 December 2009, the China Internet Network Information Center (CNNIC), a state body, released an update on its auditing of domain name registrations. As of today, domain name applicants must submit a formal paper-based application when making an online application to the registrar. This includes the original application form with the business seal, company business licence and a photocopy of identification. This occurred when China was taking steps to improve the connotation of the 'made in China' label. These registration changes will make the '.cn' domain very unattractive for criminals and fraudsters who are always on the lookout for domains that they can register anonymously, preferably paying with stolen credit cards. This appears to be a great step in making the domain name space of '.cn' a safer place.

Like many developing economies, China's growth has far outpaced its ability to create and enforce legislation or—even more importantly—change cultural attitudes towards protecting digital privacy and sensitive data. For example, the China Compulsory Certification process has been identified as one technique used by the Chinese government to appropriate intellectual property. The certification requires companies wishing to sell electronic components in China to submit drawings, schematics and the finished product to the Chinese governmental body overseeing the certification. This is, however, a concern for many companies as their designs or technology might be used for piracy (McAfee 2009c).

India

The report by Rush et al. (2009) on cybercrime raised fears about the security of business process outsourcing operations in India, which has become one of the hubs for operations outsourced by countries like the United States, United Kingdome and other European countries. However, the Indian government, as well as the industry, has been taking proper care to handle these fears and to tighten security guidelines and frameworks to be followed by companies that handle outsourced operations. There have been continuous amendments in Indian cyberlaws.

In India cybercrime is dealt with by both the Indian Penal Code (IPC) and the Information Technology Act, 2000, which was amended in 2008. Since policing is a matter under the jurisdiction of the state, and complaints have to be lodged with the local police, most cybercrimes are registered under the IPC. The police at the local level therefore need to be conversant with the Information Technology Act or it will be difficult to prove cybercrimes. India also needs to build up its cyber forensic capabilities.

The Information Technology Act, 2000 and Amendment in 2008
The Information Technology Act, 2000, a legal framework for transactions carried out electronically, was enacted to facilitate e-commerce, e-governance and to deal with computer-related offences. Over the years, with several new forms of computer crime, misuse and fraud taking place, a need was felt to strengthen the legislation pertaining to information security. The government had enacted the IT Act to focus on the evidential value of electronic transactions and provide legal recognition to electronic documents. Leveraging the experience gained, amendments to the IT Act were approved by Parliament on 22 December 2008 to strengthen provisions in respect of data protection, e-governance, technological utility in respect of signatures, new computer

offences such as phishing, identity theft, e-commerce frauds, impersonation, video voyeurism and data retention. The amendments also provide for liabilities of service providers and intermediaries in the event of deficient services.

The Information Technology (Amendment) Act, 2008, has been published in the Official Gazette. The amendment upgrades the existing legal framework to instil users' and investors' confidence in the area of information technology in the country.

Latin America

Cybercrime in Brazil constitutes the vast majority of all cybercrime that occurs in Latin America. The rate of cybercrime has remained on a steady upward trajectory, essentially reflecting the wide Internet penetration and increasing numbers of online banking transactions. Brazilian cybercriminals have long operated in a relatively permissive environment. Nevertheless, a small but active community of fraudsters, who prefer the use of card skimmers and other physical means of data theft, are equally active. Most Brazilian hackers and cybercriminals are proficient enough in English and Spanish so that they encounter little difficulty when they liaison with their counterparts in the rest of Latin America and the rest of the world to find new tools and techniques. Law-enforcement organs in most parts of Latin America, and especially those in Brazil, have lacked backing by the force of legislation, to deter and combat cybercrime. However, recently there have been changes; Brazil, Argentina, Chile and Mexico have all initiated cyber legislation where none existed or drastically increased the resources necessary to properly prosecute cybercrimes.

In June 2008, Argentina approved an extensive update to its criminal code to cover cybercrimes, including malicious code distribution and system breaches. The Chilean government is also currently building upon earlier efforts, by requiring banks to implement two-factor authentication technologies to secure transactions (iDefense 2008).

Brazil has also approved a new set of cybercrime laws. The Brazilian government has established a body that will oversee the country's cybersecurity. The organization, dubbed the cyber security technical group, functions under the government ICT security department and includes Brazil's ministers of justice, foreign relations and defence, as well as officials from the army, navy and aeronautical agencies. This group is in charge of protecting government communications systems and databases, as well as safeguarding critical infrastructure (Business News Americas 2009).

Law enforcement is also likely to show marked progress in the other most important aspect of fighting cybercrime: inter-departmental and international cooperation. The Brazilian police assumed that a key cause of their difficulties was the lack of cooperation among different police units throughout the country. Officials also noted that Brazilian cybercriminals were dealing more with collaborators in other countries, and demanding that other police forces do so. Indeed, by mid-2008, a few instances of cooperation between the Brazilian Federal Police and their counterparts in Spain and the United States had led to the dismantling of major, interconnected cyber fraud cartels (iDefense 2008). By all accounts, this is only the beginning; international cooperation is a key part of the new strategy to fight cybercrime. Banks in Latin America, particularly those in Brazil, have also been progressing rapidly in their abilities to counter cyber fraud. Most have instituted two-factor authentication for all online banking customers and are currently expanding their internal security capabilities. This is already beginning to decrease the success rate of certain types of longstanding phishing attacks, combined with banking Trojans.

15.4. WHAT IS AN INFORMATION SECURITY INCIDENT?

An information security incident is any violation of the information governance or information security policy. The term information security incident and suspected incidents is very broad and includes, but is not limited to, incidents that relate to the loss, disclosure, denial of access to, destruction or modification of the Practice's information, or information systems.

An information security incident can be defined as any event that has resulted or could result in:

- The disclosure of confidential information to an unauthorized individual.
- The integrity of a system or data being put at risk.
- The availability of the system or information being put at risk.

An adverse impact can be defined, for example, as:

- Threat to personal safety or privacy.
- Legal obligation or penalty.
- Financial loss.
- Disruption of Practice business.
- An embarrassment to the Practice.

The following are examples of security incidents:

- Using another user's login id or swipe card.
- Unauthorized disclosure of information.
- Leaving confidential or sensitive files out.
- Theft or loss of IT equipment.
- Theft or loss of computer media, such as a floppy disk or memory stick.
- Accessing a person's record inappropriately, for example, viewing one's your own record or a family member's, neighbour's or friend's.
- Writing passwords down and not locking them away.
- Identifying that a fax has been sent to the wrong recipient.
- Sending or receiving sensitive e-mail to or from 'all staff' by mistake.
- Giving out or overhearing personally identifiable information over the telephone.
- Positioning of computer screens where information could be viewed by the public.
- Software malfunction.
- Inadequate disposal of confidential material.

It is important that information security incident reports give as much detail as possible, including a description of activities leading up to the security incident, information about circumstances prevailing at the time, how the incident came about, how the incident was detected.

The information security incident or suspected incident report should include full details of the incident in as much details as possible to enable a full investigation to be carried out if necessary. However, when logging incidents, personal details should, wherever possible, be omitted.

Whenever possible, when reporting information security incidents, any protocol or procedure which may have been compromised should be referenced in the report. All information security incidents must be prioritized in accordance with the severity of the incident by the person logging these on the incident reporting system.

The policy requires that information security incidents be reported as soon as possible after they occur, or have been identified. Reports sent immediately after the incident are likely to be the most valuable; if there is a delay between an incident occurring and the discovery of said incident, the incident should still be reported.

15.5. REPORTING OF CYBERCRIME

In the United States, the United States Computer Emergency Response Team (US-CERT) was established in 2003 to protect the nation's Internet infrastructure. US-CERT coordinates defence against and responses to cyberattacks, across the nation. It is the operational arm of the National Cyber Security Division of the Department of Homeland Security. It is a public-private partnership body. It interacts with federal agencies, industry, the research community, state and local governments and others, to disseminate reasoned and actionable cybersecurity information to the public. US-CERT also provides a way for citizens, businesses, and other institutions to communicate and coordinate directly with the United States government about cybersecurity.

In India, the Indian Computer Emergency Response Team (CERT-In) is the national nodal agency for responding to computer security incidents as and when they occur, similar to US-CERT. This body has been operational since January 2004. The Indian cyber community constitutes CERT-In. According to the Information Technology (Amendment) Act, 2008, CERT-In has been designated to serve as the national agency to perform the following functions in the area of cybersecurity:

- Collection, analysis and dissemination of information on cyber incidents.
- Forecast and alerts on cybersecurity incidents.
- Emergency measures for handling cybersecurity incidents.
- Coordination of cyber incident response activities.

- Issue guidelines, advisories, vulnerability notes and white papers relating to information security practices, procedures, prevention, response and reporting of cyber incidents.
- Such other functions related to cybersecurity as may be prescribed.

The CERT-In website, www.cert-in.org.in, has forms for reporting incidents and vulnerabilities that are supposed to be filled by any organization or corporate entity when confronted with security breaches or computer security incidents. By reporting such computer security incidents to CERT-In, system administrators and users can receive technical assistance in resolving these incidents. This also helps CERT-In to correlate the incidents reported and analyse them, draw inferences, disseminate up-to-date information and develop effective security guidelines to prevent occurrence of such incidents in future. Table 15.1 shows the number and categories of incidents handled by CERT-In between 2004 and 2010.

Table 15.1
Year-wise Summary of Security Incidents Handled by CERT-In

Security Incidents	2004	2005	2006	2007	2008	2009	2010
Phishing	3	101	339	392	604	374	508
Network Scanning/Probing	11	40	177	223	265	303	477
Virus/Malicious Code	5	95	19	358	408	596	1,817
Spam	–	–	–	–	305	285	981
Website Compromise and Malware Propagation	–	–	–	–	835	6,548	6,344
Others	4	18	17	264	148	160	188
Total	23	254	552	1,237	2,565	8,266	10,315

SOURCE: CERT-In (2011: 7).

CERT-In also proactively tracks website defacements suggesting suitable measures to protect the web servers of concerned organizations, tracks the open proxy servers existing in India and proactively alerts concerned system administrators to properly configure the same in order to reduce spamming and other malicious activities originating from India, as well as tracking bots and botnets involving Indian systems. After tracking the IP addresses of command and control servers and bots operating within India, actions are taken to clean the systems and prevent malicious activities.

To meet the challenges posed by the new kinds of crime made possible by computer technology including telecommunication, many countries have reviewed their respective domestic criminal laws so as to include computer-related crimes. Governments are also making legislations to ensure that every company, from large to midsized and even small ones, has Internet policies and security solutions. However, legislations enacted by different countries cover only a few of the classified computer-related offences, while owing to dynamic and fast-changing technology, new types of offences may occur frequently.

15.6. CONCLUSION

International cooperation is a necessity to combat cybercrime. This requires building of appropriate regulations and anti-cybercrime institutions in each country. Preventing 'safe havens' for cybercrimes is one of the key challenges in the fight against cybercrime. While 'safe havens' exist, offenders will use them to hamper investigation. Developing countries that have not yet implemented cybercrime legislation may become vulnerable, as criminals may choose to base themselves in these countries to avoid prosecution. In such cases, international pressure on these countries will eventually make them pass appropriate regulations.

SECTION IV

BEING SAFE, BEING CYBER SECURE

Absolute security is a myth ... but we still have to plan.

SIXTEEN

SAILING SAFE

———————◆•◆•◆———————

This chapter proposes recommendations for safe computing in view of the threats discussed in the previous chapters. It covers aspects such as handling of e-mails, use of firewalls, password management, precautions with USB memory sticks, wireless technology, Bluetooth technology, online presence, etc. The chapter tries to cover everyday tips for safe computing.

16.1. SECURE E-MAIL ACCESS

E-mail is valuable business information and needs protection from a range of threats. Some of the characteristics that make e-mail and e-mail attachments convenient and popular are also the ones that make them a common tool for attackers: e-mail is easily circulated—forwarding e-mail is so simple that viruses can quickly infect many machines. Most viruses don't even require users to forward the e-mail—they scan a user's computer for e-mail addresses and automatically send the infected message to all the addresses they find. Attackers take advantage of the reality that most users will automatically trust and open any message that comes from someone they know. E-mail programs try to address all users' needs—almost any type of file can be attached to an e-mail message, so attackers have more freedom with the types of viruses they can send. E-mail programs offer many 'user-friendly' features—some e-mail programs have the option to automatically download e-mail attachments, which immediately exposes your computer to any viruses within the attachments.

It is important to take some basic precautions when handling e-mails. For instance, the official address must be used for business purposes only and not for personal use. Also, do not leave the e-mail account open and unattended— it is better to shut it down before leaving the workstation. Do not open links in an e-mail to connect to a website. Instead, it is advisable to open a new browser window and type the uniform resource locator (URL) directly into the address bar. Do not give confidential information through forms embedded in e-mails. Sending unsolicited e-mail messages, including 'chain letters', 'junk mail' or other advertising material should be strictly avoided.

Common e-mail security solutions include spam filters, antivirus protection and data encryption.

16.2. HANDLING E-MAIL ATTACHMENTS

Do not open e-mail or attachments from unknown sources. Be suspicious of any unexpected e-mail attachment, even if it appears to be from someone you know. A simple rule of thumb is that if you do not know the person who is sending you e-mail, be very careful about opening that e-mail and any file attached to it. This includes e-mail messages that appear to be from your Internet service provider (ISP) or software vendor and claim to include patches or antivirus software. ISPs and software vendors do not send patches or software in e-mails. Should you receive a suspicious e-mail, the best thing to do is to delete the entire message, including any attachment. If you are determined to open a file from an unknown source, save it first and run your antivirus checker on that file, but also understand that there is still a risk. If the mail appears to be from someone you know, still treat it with caution if it has a suspicious subject line (for example, 'Iloveyou' or 'Anna Kournikova') or if it otherwise seems suspicious (for instance, it was sent in the middle of the night). Also be careful if you receive many copies of the same message from either known or unknown sources. Finally, remember that even friends and family may accidentally send you a virus or the e-mail may have been sent from their machines without their knowledge. Such was the case with the 'I Love You' virus that spread to millions of people in 2001. When in doubt, delete! If you receive an e-mail from a trusted vendor or organization, be careful of phishing, a high-tech scam used to deceive consumers into providing personal data, including credit-card numbers, and so on. The best way to make sure you are dealing with a website you trust, and not a fraudster, is to initiate the contact yourself.

Save and scan any attachments before opening it. If you have to open an attachment before you can verify the source, take the following steps:

- Be sure the signatures in your antivirus software are up to date.
- Save the file to your computer or a disk.
- Manually scan the file using your antivirus software.
- Open the file.

Turn off the option to automatically download attachments. To simplify the process of reading e-mail, many e-mail programs offer the feature to automatically download attachments. Check your settings to see if your software offers the option, and make sure to disable it.

16.3. APPLICATIONS FOR SECURE E-MAIL ACCESS

Secure e-mail is a server-based application that protects sensitive data sent by e-mail when it leaves the corporate boundary. Secure encryption allows you to access, store and send your mail in a secure, private environment that keeps your confidential information from being accessed by outside parties. Secure e-mail software is available, and there are many advantages to using it. The most important advantage of secure e-mail is its inaccessibility to third parties of any kind. Messages sent using secure e-mail are not passed through public servers but are passed via private servers. When the recipient replies, his e-mail is also sent via the secure server, so the e-mail is never left open to public access via exposed servers. When you share information with business associates, secure e-mail ensures that the information you send is protected. Messages sent through secure e-mail are encrypted, which means the information in the e-mail is scrambled and coded, and only the person to whom the mail is addressed can break the code by entering her approved login information. This ensures that even if a third party somehow gains access to your e-mail files, she will not be able to read them. This protects your e-mails from identity theft and business secrets trading. You will not receive spam e-mails when you use a secure e-mail service. Unlike most e-mail services, where the only e-mails you do not receive are ones you have blocked, secure e-mail works the other way around—the only e-mails you receive are from pre-approved e-mail address you have given permission to contact you. Most secure e-mail programs come with built-in virus protection that will warn you of a suspicious e-mail and scan all attachments for threats before you open them. This protects your computer from harmful viruses that can destroy your files or transmit sensitive information.

16.4. USE OF FIREWALLS FOR SAFETY

Equip your computer with a firewall. It creates a protective wall between your computer and the outside world. Firewalls come in two forms, software firewalls that run on your personal computer and hardware firewalls that protect a number of computers at the same time. They work by filtering out unauthorized or potentially dangerous types of data from the Internet, while still allowing other data to reach your computer. Firewalls also ensure that unauthorized persons cannot gain access to your computer while you are connected to the Internet. You can find firewall hardware and software at most computer stores and in some operating systems.

16.5. DOWNLOAD OF SECURITY UPDATES AND PATCHES

Most major software companies today release updates and patches to close newly discovered vulnerabilities in their software. Sometimes bugs are discovered in a program that may allow a criminal hacker to attack your computer. Before most of these attacks occur, software companies or vendors create free patches that they post on their websites to close the vulnerabilities. You must be sure you download and install the patches. Check your software vendors' website regularly for new security patches or use the automated patching features that some companies offer. This is possible only if you are using licensed version of the software. Ensure that you are getting patches from the correct patch update site. Your system may be compromised by installing patches obtained from bogus update sites or e-mails that appear to be from a vendor that provides links to those bogus sites. If you do not have the time to do the work yourself, download and install a utility program to do it for you. There are available software programs that can perform this task for you.

16.6. PASSWORD MANAGEMENT

Your password should be as unique as you are. Therefore, use hard-to-guess passwords. Mix upper case, lower case, numbers or other characters not easy to find in a dictionary, and make sure they are at least eight characters long. Passwords will only keep outsiders out if they are difficult to guess. Do not share your password, and do not use the same password in more than one place. If someone should happen to guess one of your passwords, you would not want them to be able to use it in other places. The golden rules of passwords are:

- A password should be as meaningless as possible, for example, ym5#HX62.
- Passwords should be changed regularly, at least every 90 days.
- For enhanced security, some form of two-factor authentication should be used. Two-factor authentication is a way to gain access by combining something you know (personal identification number, PIN) with something you have (token or smart card). Automatic screen locking facility should be used whenever the system is kept idle.
- The 'remember password' feature of applications such as Microsoft Outlook should not be used.

16.7. BACK UP OF COMPUTER DATA

Backing up data on your computer may not be fun or exciting. But if you get a virus or other electronic infection and your system crashes or has to be wiped clean, you will be so glad you did. Make copies of essential documents, photos, music files—anything you would be troubled to lose. You can use a variety of media—compact disks (CDs), digital video disks (DVDs), USB drives, external hard-disk drives, a server or Internet site that allows you to store documents. Experienced computer users know that there are two types of people: those who have already lost data and those who are going to experience the pain of losing data in future—which means everyone is vulnerable to data loss and you need to take precautions. Back up small amounts of data on CDs, USB drives and larger amounts on external hard disks. If you have access to a network, you may save a copy of important data on another computer in the network. Hard disk fails—and if you use it long enough, eventually it will—and you will need those backups. Many people make weekly backups of all their important data.

16.8. HANDLING FILE-SHARING RISKS

Your computer operating system may allow other computers on a network, including the Internet, to access the hard drive of your computer in order to 'share files'. This ability to share files can be used to infect your computer with a virus or look at the files on your computer if you do not pay close attention. So, unless you really need this ability, make sure you turn off file sharing. Check your operating system and 'help' files in your other programs to learn how to disable file sharing. Do not share access to your computer with strangers.

16.9. DISCONNECTING FROM THE INTERNET

The digital highway is a two-way road. You send and receive information on it. Disconnecting your computer from the Internet when you are not online lessens the chance that someone will be able to access your computer. And if you have not kept your antivirus software up to date, or do not have a firewall in place, someone could infect your computer or use it to harm someone else on the Internet. Therefore, help protect others: disconnect when not in use.

16.10. READING THE END-USER LICENCE AGREEMENT

Read through the end-user licence agreement (EULA) before clicking 'I Accept' and installing unfamiliar software. Yes, it is a pain to read all that fine print. But if you do not, you may be sorry. By law, the EULA is where companies disclose what they will do with your private information (if they share it, you may start receiving a lot of spam, for example); what other software they may be packaging with your download (beware—many times what is packaged with it is essentially spyware); and any hidden fees or costs. If you cannot find or understand the EULA, think twice before proceeding: the program's creator may be trying to hide something from you.

16.11. WEB BROWSING SOFTWARE SELECTION

Most computers come bundled with the Internet Explorer browser—to browse the Web. However, there are other Internet browser options that may be more secure. While more secure versions of Microsoft's Internet Explorer have been released in recent years, criminals and hackers are still likely to target users of this browser for frauds and scams for a long time to come, since it is still most predominantly used. You are less likely to be targeted for phishing scams and spyware and adware if you use some other browser to surf the Web. For example, Mozilla's Firefox is a free, more secure Internet browser.

16.12. PRINCIPLE OF LEAST PRIVILEGE

Everyone should have computer accounts with as few privileges as necessary for them to work productively. Most operating system allows you to set 'user' and 'administrator' accounts—which have varying levels of privileges and access. In case of a virus or other malicious software attack, the damage may be less severe if being operated by a limited user account. Setting up user and administrator accounts is quite straightforward.

16.13. ANTI-SPYWARE AND ADWARE PROGRAMS

When you download and install software on to your computer, other applications may enter into your system as add-ons, without your knowledge. Like viruses, these adware and spyware programs can sneak into the computer's hard drive with little or no warning, and hide their tracks in ways that make it difficult for even the most sophisticated computer users to find and delete permanently. If you have a few of these unwanted add-ons , they will slow down your computer significantly. These intrusive applications can also invade your privacy by sending information about you to strangers. They can even render your computer vulnerable to attack. It is therefore important to use antivirus solutions and malware removal tools regularly.

16.14. USING USB DRIVES

A USB flash drive is a data storage device that includes flash memory with an integrated universal serial bus (USB). USB pen drives have become one of the very handy types of media using which large volumes of data can be copied and moved from place to place with ease. A USB flash drive allows up to 100,000 write–erase cycles, depending on the exact type of memory chip used, and a 10-year shelf storage time. The USB flash drive is now the preferred method for sharing files between people at the same physical location. This ease of use also comes with certain degrees of danger. And of course, it has become a prime target for malware authors. Modern malware—including high-profile examples such as Conficker and Stuxnet—exploit USB drives to automatically run when inserted into a target computer. The most common feature exploited by attackers is the Windows 'autorun' feature. You may have noticed that when a USB pen drive is inserted into a computer the Windows operating system, an 'autorun' feature pops up and asks for the user's input. By clicking the 'OK' button, it is enabled. Many attackers place a file, which typically has a name like 'autorun.exe'. For an average user, this file looks legitimate and during the antivirus scans if detected; the user may treat it as a false positive and retain the file. Once this file (which actually has a malicious code inside) is run, the virus automatically propagates into the computer and infects the targeted files of the operating system, user data, or both. Attackers use this way to silently extract information about passwords, sensitive data, encryption keys, intellectual property and the like. The user of the computer may not even know that data is being stolen from her computer. Stuxnet took it one step further and exploited an unpatched security vulnerability to bypass even the need for 'autorun' to be enabled (Sophos 2011).

A USB flash drive should not be used in a computer you cannot trust; even putting the drive in such a computer can infect it with malware. It is better not to use it as a backup device also because it is too easy to lose it. If, due to any reason, data is backed up is on a USB device, then it is important to store it safely and separately. Some USB flash drives have a write-protect mechanism, consisting of a switch on the housing of the drive itself, which prevents the host computer from writing or modifying data on the drive.

Using personal equipment or media in an organization's premises and connecting them is not permitted by most organizations. In some organizations, computers are configured to disable the mounting of USB mass storage devices by users other than administrators. Some organizations disconnect USB ports inside the computer or fill the USB sockets with epoxy. The portability, ease of use, capability and large volume for storage make them any attacker's easy choice.

Targeted attacks also frequently use the social engineering trick of planting USB drives at frequently visited places so that curious employees will pick them up and insert them into company systems, breaching the corporate network boundary. Flash drives are commonly given away as freebies at trade shows, a practice which could bring about major embarrassment if inadequate security procedures are used. IBM learnt this lesson in 2010 when the complimentary USB drives it handed out at the AusCERT security conference in Queensland, Australia, were infected by not one, but two pieces of malware (Sophos 2011).

16.14.1. What if the Company Authorizes the Use of USB Pen Drives?

If a company allows use of USB pen drives, it is a very good sign that the company is technology savvy. Use of pen drives for information transfer for intra- and inter-firm functions can be very speedy and the media can be reused. But this again poses the threat of data loss, data theft and data leakage.

It is preferable to encrypt the data in the pen drive in transit so that only the intended recipient of the information is able to receive, understand and see the information. Nowadays, several manufacturers are providing built-in tools to encrypt the data being copied on to a pen drive. It is always good practice to use organization-owned pen drives and portable storage devices for business purposes. It would be wise to keep separate pen drives for business and personal use.

As we have already discussed, always use a genuine, updated antivirus to clean the pen drive if any infection exists. It is always preferable not to use 'unknown' pen drives or portable media. Inserting them into organization computers can be dangerous, resulting in impairing critical functions and causing damage to the firm's reputation, business and capital.

16.14.2. How to Physically Secure USB Pen Drives and Portable Devices

So far, we have discussed USB pen drives. There are many other devices that need attention, like laptops, personal digital assistants (PDAs), mobile phones with enhanced capabilities and so on.

Sensitive data may reside on a company's laptop. If the laptop gets stolen, there are chances that all the sensitive information in the laptop could easily be compromised.

There are some measures which can protect the theft or loss of the devices. These are as follows:

- Always keep the user-account password enabled. Never divulge it to anyone. Writing the password down defeats the purpose of using a password.
- Never leave your laptop unattended. Always keep it with you in and keep a close watch.
- Enable the Internet connection firewall (through the control panel).
- Use software restriction policies.
- It is good practice to fasten the laptop using a lock. These locks will not prevent theft. But they are at least a hindrance to the thief. Because if she forcibly tries to remove the lock, the laptop may get damaged. So there are less chances that such secured devices will be chosen by a thief.
- As prevention is always better than cure, regularly taking a backup of the important contents of the laptop and keeping them in a secure place is good practice.
- Be careful when putting your laptop bag down. Never leave it behind you or in a place where a thief could snatch it without you noticing. If you have to put the bag down, hook a chair leg or your foot through the loop of the strap to stop someone running off with it.
- When carrying your laptop bag, try to keep it in front of you rather than behind you.
- Take a note of any identifying information on your laptop: the serial number, make, model and any other identifying features.

It cannot be guaranteed that even after all the above said measures are followed, the laptop will be safe. It is precisely here that the notion of physical security of data comes in.

Certain measures can be taken so as to prevent loss of data. Here are some of them:

- As discussed earlier, use strong passwords. Do not use your name or your company's name or the laptop model number as the password for your user account. Never write or paste the password on the laptop or the carry case.
- Encryption is another method to protect data. It may seem a bit technical in nature. But there are many packages available in the market for a reasonable price. Use one.

- Make sure your insurance covers your laptop for use outside the home or office or business (including travel).
- Following good safety practices such as backing up important data can be helpful in retrieving files in case a laptop has to be changed.

When your laptop is stolen, you not only lose the hardware, you lose the data on the hard drive. There is also a psychological cost that is often not thought of until it happens to you. In such cases:

- Notify the police, vendor or supplier of your laptop, and the Internet service provider.
- Protect yourself by changing all e-mail, messenger, credit-card, Wi-Fi access keys at office or home, as well as bank and other passwords which might have been stored in the laptop.
- Learn more about identity theft, now that the likelihood of you becoming a victim has increased.
- Notify clients, if affected. If you had stored any personal information for clients, access to their sites, passwords, or the like, notify them immediately so that they can change them.
- If your computer had company-confidential information, government-related information, or personal information of other people, notify your employer immediately.
- You can also request your Internet service provider, through the investigating agency, to track the laptop if it was used to access the Internet through your account or through some other account but using the same network interface card.

16.15. BLUETOOTH TECHNOLOGY

Bluetooth technology is a wireless technology used for short-range communications. Bluetooth capability is present in almost all the modern communication equipment including mobile phones, PDAs, laptops, handheld devices and so on.

It has been widely accepted as a standard for short-range communications such as sending images, music, small files and the like. The devices which have Bluetooth technology can search for other devices in a particular vicinity and connect to each other. The limitation of this technology is the range and the speed of communication. This technology works on short-range radio waves. Other technical details are not so relevant from a normal user prospective. This technology can be very useful for communication between devices, provided some safe methods are used. For this, let us first understand how connecting to other Bluetooth devices work.

For example, let us take two mobile phones that are Bluetooth-enabled. When the Bluetooth connection is turned on in both the devices, a device can be made to search for other Bluetooth devices in the vicinity. Once it is detected, it can try to connect to the other via a PIN, which is typically a number, four to five characters long.

There are usually two modes available for Bluetooth devices. One is a 'discoverable' mode. The other is a normal mode in which the devices are not discoverable. There are many methods by which Bluetooth technology can be exploited. Common effects of exploitation are corruption of data, theft of contact details and corruption of system data. Other forms include reception of data via Bluetooth from unknown persons. Such requests should never be encouraged and should be actively denied.

16.15.1. What More Can I Do to Protect against Attack via Bluetooth?

Here are some steps that may be followed to minimize the chances of attack via Bluetooth.

- Use the Bluetooth connection sparingly. Use it only when required. Turn it off when not in use.
- Disable the 'discoverable' mode on the device.
- Go through the device manual for some quick tips which can make you use the device safe and better. Understanding the usage will prevent half the security problems from occurring.
- Avoid using the device where there are a lot of people or where there are high chances of 'sniffing'. Sniffing is overhearing an electronic transmission.

16.16. WIRELESS INTERNET SAFETY

Wireless technology is the transfer of information over a distance without the use of enhanced electrical conductors or 'wires'. The distances involved may be short or long. In recent years, wireless networking has become more available, affordable and easy to use. Wi-Fi gives you the freedom to go anywhere and still be connected to your office, your family and other important aspects of your life. In fact, hotspots are an everyday connection method for travellers and remote workers to browse the Internet, check their e-mail, and even work on their corporate networks while away from the office.

Wireless hotspots are changing the way people work. These wireless local area networks (WLANs) provide high-speed Internet connection in public locations—as well as at home—and need nothing more than a laptop or notebook computer equipped with a wireless card. Home users are adopting wireless technology in great numbers. Most WLAN hardware has gotten easy enough to set up that many users simply plug it in and start using the network without giving much thought to security. If you do not think twice about jumping onto whatever inexpensive or free wireless network is available—for instance, a neighbour's network at home—consider this: if it is an 'unsecured wireless network', it is just as easy for a criminal to get on it as it is for you! Unsecured wireless is not encrypted, so sniffers could easily be logging the sensitive information you send over the network, such as logins, passwords or credit card numbers. Additionally, in a public place, someone could also 'shoulder surf', watching over your shoulder as you type. So, you should avoid conducting your private business on public wireless.

Hotspots range from paid services to public, free connections. Hotspots are everywhere, including: coffee shops, restaurants, libraries, bookstores, airports and hotel lobbies. Many of these places will inform you that they have a hotspot for wireless Internet use and may provide you with a password, if required. You can also use a directory to find a hotspot near you.

But they all have one thing in common—they are all open networks that are vulnerable to security breaches. And that means it is up to you to protect the data on your computer. Therefore, when accessing the Internet from public locations, try to choose more secure connections. It is not always possible to choose your connection type—but when you can, opt for wireless networks that require a network security key or have some other form of security, such as a certificate. The information sent over these networks is encrypted, which can help protect your computer from unauthorized access.

Taking a few extra minutes to configure the security features of your wireless router or access point at home is time well spent. The following paragraphs outline some of the things you can do to protect your wireless network.

Do not auto-connect to open Wi-Fi networks. Connecting to an open Wi-Fi network such as a free wireless hotspot or your neighbour's router exposes your computer to security risks. Although not normally enabled, most computers have a setting available allowing these connections to occur automatically without notifying you. This setting should not be enabled except in temporary situations.

Monitor the access points you are connecting into. There may be multiple wireless networks where you are trying to connect. These connections are all access points, because they link into the wired system that gives you Internet access. So how do you make sure you are connecting to the right one? Simple—by configuring the laptop to let you approve access points before you connect.

Wi-Fi signals normally reach to the exterior of a home. A small amount of signal leakage outdoors is not a problem, but the further this signal reaches, the easier it is for others to detect and exploit. Wi-Fi signals often reach through neighbouring homes and into streets, for example. When installing a wireless home network, the position of the access point or router determines its reach. Try to position these devices near the centre of the home rather than near windows to minimize leakage.

Enable firewalls on each computer and the router. Modern network routers contain built-in firewall capability, but the option also exists to disable them. Ensure that your router's firewall is turned on. For extra protection, consider installing and running personal firewall software on each computer connected to the router.

Make sure your firewall is activated. A firewall helps protect the laptop by preventing unauthorized users from gaining access to the system through the Internet or a network. It acts as a barrier that checks all incoming information, and then either blocks the information or allows it to come through. Also, it is important to keep strong passwords for the Wi-Fi access point or router.

Turn off the network during extended periods of non-use. The ultimate in wireless security measures, shutting down your network will most certainly prevent outside hackers from breaking in. While impractical to turn off and on the devices frequently, consider doing so during travel or extended periods offline. While computer disk drives have been known to suffer from power cycle wear-and-tear, but this is a secondary concern for broadband modems and routers.

16.17. WORKING SECURELY FROM WIRELESS HOTSPOTS

To make network access easier for their users, public hotspots typically leave all security turned off. This means that any information you send from a hotspot is most likely unencrypted, and anyone within range of the WLAN, whether at a next table or in the parking lot, can access and use your Internet connection, and look at your unprotected information.

Disable file and printer sharing. File and printer sharing is a feature that enables other computers on a network to access resources on your computer. When you are using your laptop in a hotspot, it is best to disable file and printer sharing—since when it is enabled, it leaves your computer vulnerable to hackers. You can turn this feature back on when you return to the office.

Encrypt important files on the laptop, which requires a password to open or modify them. Because you must perform this procedure on one file at a time, consider password-protecting only the files that you plan to use while working in a public place.

Consider removing sensitive data from the laptop completely.

If you are working with extremely sensitive data, it might be worth taking it off your laptop altogether. Instead, save it on a corporate network share and access it only when necessary or carry it separately on a hard disk and unplug the hard disk when you have finished the work.

16.18. ONLINE SHOPPING—BEING SECURE

Online shopping is the process of buying goods and services from merchants who sell on the Internet. Shoppers can visit web stores from the comfort of their homes and shop as they sit in front of the computer. Consumers buy a variety of items from online stores. In fact, people can purchase just about anything from companies that sell their products online. Books, clothing, household appliances, toys, hardware, software and health insurance are just some of the hundreds of products consumers can buy from an online store.

With online shopping, a person logs on to the Internet, visits the store's website, and chooses the items they desire. The items are held in a virtual shopping cart until they are ready to make their purchase. Online stores never close—they are open 24 hours a day.

16.18.1. Know What to Look for When Shopping Online

Online shopping is great. But ensure that the site you are buying from is a secure site. There are a number of ways to identify a secure site:

- Before you make a purchase, check for the letters 'https' in front of the web address—the 's' stands for secure—and this indicates that you are using a secure connection.
- Look out for the security icon (a locked padlock or an unbroken key symbol) in the web browser frame. You can double click on this symbol to look at the security certificate.
- Check the web address generally. If the URL changes from what you would expect in the course of your transaction, log out immediately and shop elsewhere. Check that the website displays a full postal address and phone number.
- Holders of a valid credit card have the authorization to purchase goods and services up to a predetermined amount, called a credit limit. Use a trusted money transfer system.
- Avoid online shopping from public or shared computers or virus-infected computer.
- Use virtual keypad to key in passwords, which protects your passwords from malicious spyware and Trojan programs designed to capture keystrokes.
- Web browsers are capable of storing browsed information during the session. To prevent that, always close browser window after the session.

16.19. SECURE SOCKETS LAYER AND ITS USE

Secure sockets layer (SSL) is a global standard security technology developed by Netscape in 1994. SSL establishes an encrypted link between a web server and a browser. This link ensures that all data passed between the web server and browsers remain private and integral. SSL is an industry standard and is used by millions of websites to protect online transactions with their customers.

To be able to create an SSL connection a web server requires an SSL certificate. When a company or business chooses to activate SSL on your web server it will be prompted to complete a number of questions about the identity of its website and company. Its web server then creates two cryptographic keys—a private key and a public key.

The public key does not need to be secret and is placed into a certificate signing request (CSR)—a data file also containing your details. The CSR should then be submitted. During the SSL certificate application process, the certification authority will validate the company's details and issue an SSL certificate containing such details and allowing it to use SSL. The company's web server will match the SSL certificate issued to it to its private key. The web server will then be able to establish an encrypted link between the website and a customer's web browser.

The complexities of the SSL protocol remain invisible to customers. Instead their browsers provide them with a key indicator to let them know they are currently protected by an SSL encrypted session—the lock icon in the lower right-hand corner, clicking on which displays your SSL certificate and the details about it. All SSL certificates are issued to either companies or legally accountable individuals.

Typically an SSL certificate will contain a company's domain name, its company name, address, city, state and country. It will also contain the expiration date of the certificate and details of the certification authority responsible for the issuance of the certificate. When a browser connects to a secure site it will retrieve the site's SSL certificate and check that it has not expired, it has been issued by a certification authority the browser trusts, and that it is being used by the website for which it has been issued. If it fails on any one of these checks the browser will display a warning to the end user letting them know that the site is not secured by SSL.

Here are some of the main benefits that come with SSL protection on an e-commerce website:

16.19.1. Server Authentication

When a website has SSL, it is protected as well as its customers. The server—which is basically another name for a computer that stores information about a website for viewing by customers and others—must have a digital certificate. SSL provides these certificates, and is able to read them. Certificates come from a trusted third party that can guarantee encryption. The certificate is proof that the server is what it says it is. SSL makes it harder for fraudsters to pretend to be another server. Customers feel safe, knowing that a website really are legitimate, and they are more willing to do business with the company. The company is protected as well when it engages in business-to-business transactions with other companies and websites that have valid SSL certificates.

16.19.2. Private Communication Capability

Another advantage of SSL protection is that it makes conversations private. The encryption used by SSL turns useful data, such as credit-card numbers, addresses and other payment information, into useless bits of information. Random characters appear. Only the right recipient—the one with the encryption key—can decode the messages. This means that a private communication channel is established. If someone else tries to intercept the information, it will appear to be useless.

16.19.3. Customer Confidence

This is an extremely important benefit of having SSL certification. It assures customers that a company is taking the proper steps to protect their personal and payment information and that such information is not going to intercepted and stolen for unapproved purposes. A well-informed and seasoned Internet shopper knows that SSL protection is a necessity. Many savvy online shoppers will not buy from e-commerce merchants who do not encrypt transactions using SSL. If a company wants loyal customers, it is a good idea to purchase some sort of SSL certificate so that buyers feel confident in engaging in business with it.

16.19.4. Benefits for Web Hosts

For web hosts, having SSL provides another layer of benefit. SSL will protect private information and do what is expected of it. It can encrypt payments from clients. The web host can provide more services for its client, and charge money for retailers to use its shared SSL certificate. The online business gets SSL certification for less money, and the web host is able to make a little more income.

16.20. CRYPTOGRAPHY AND ITS APPLICATIONS

Cryptography is the science of secret writing. It is the art of protecting information by transforming it into an unreadable format concealed from the casual reader and only the intended recipient will be able to convert it into original text. The original message is known as plain or clear text. The way of encoding the message contents to hide it from outsiders is called encryption. The encrypted message is called cipher text. The process of retrieving the plain text from the cipher text is called decryption. Encryption and decryption usually make use of a key, and the coding method is such that decryption can be performed only by knowing the proper key.

Cryptography is necessary when communicating over any un-trusted medium over any network, particularly the Internet. There are some specific security requirements in the context of any application-to-application communication, including:

1. Authentication: The process of proving one's identity.
2. Privacy or confidentiality: Ensuring that no one can read the message except the intended recipient.
3. Integrity: Assuring the recipient that the message received has not been altered in any way from the original.
4. Non-repudiation: A mechanism to prove that the sender really sent this message.

Cryptography not only protects data from theft or alteration, but can also be used for user authentication. There are, in general, three types of cryptographic schemes: secret key (or symmetric) cryptography, public-key (or asymmetric) cryptography and hash functions. In all cases, the initial unencrypted data is referred to as plain text. It is encrypted into cipher text, which will in turn (usually) be decrypted into usable plain text.

The types of cryptography algorithms are:

1. Secret Key Cryptography (SKC): Uses a single key for both encryption and decryption such as data encryption standard and advanced encryption standard. These methods focus on the encryption and decryption of the information.

2. Public Key Cryptography (PKC): Uses one key for encryption and another for decryption such as RSA and elliptic curve cryptosystem. PKC focuses on the public exchange of the key.

3. Hash Functions: Uses a mathematical transformation to irreversibly 'encrypt' information. It is a function, mathematical or otherwise, that takes a variable-length input string and converts it to a fixed-length output string.

16.21. USING A DIGITAL CERTIFICATE

Digital certificates are the electronic counterparts to an electronic message used for security purposes. You can present a digital certificate electronically to prove your identity or your right to access information or services online.

Digital certificates bind an identity to a pair of electronic keys that can be used to encrypt and sign digital information. A digital certificate makes it possible to verify someone's claim that they have the right to use a given key, helping prevent people from using false keys to impersonate other users. Used in conjunction with encryption, digital certificates provide a more complete security solution, assuring the identity of all parties involved in a transaction.

A digital certificate is issued by a certification authority (CA) and signed with the CA's private key.

A digital certificate typically contains the following:

1. Owner's public key.
2. Owner's name.
3. Expiration date of the public key.
4. Name of the issuer (the CA that issued the digital certificate).
5. Serial number of the digital certificate.
6. Digital signature of the issuer.

The most widely accepted format for digital certificates is defined by the CCITT X.509 international standard; thus certificates can be read or written by any application complying with X.509.

Digital certificates can be used for a variety of electronic transactions including e-mail, e-commerce, groupware and electronic funds transfers. Netscape's popular Enterprise Server requires a digital certificate for each secure server. For example, a customer shopping at an electronic mall requests the digital certificate of the server to authenticate the identity of the mall operator and the content provided by the merchant. Without authenticating the server, the shopper should not trust the operator or merchant with sensitive information like a credit-card number. The digital certificate is instrumental in establishing a secure channel for communicating any sensitive information back to the mall operator.

There are two main types of digital certificates that are important to building a secure website, and these are server certificates and personal certificates.

16.21.1. Server Certificates

Server certificates allow website visitors to safely transfer their personal information like credit-card and bank account information without worrying about theft or tampering. Server certificates are also responsible for validating the website owner's identity so that the visitors can feel as though they are dealing with a legitimate source when creating or inputting passwords, bank account details, or credit-card numbers into the website.

For any business or website that requires such information, server certificates are an important part of the website-building process, one that cannot be skipped or overlooked for any reason. Having a server certificate can be to the website owner's advantage because it gives the business an air of professionalism that is often not found when dealing with an e-commerce business where customers have little assurance as to the legitimacy or professionalism of the people that they are dealing with.

16.21.2. Personal Certificates

Personal certificates are a slightly different in that they allow a website to validate a visitor's identity and even restrict their access to certain portions of the website. You might want to set your website up so that web pages are only available to certain people, and personal certificates can help you to do this. Personal certificates can be used for things such as sending and receiving e-mail for private account information like forgotten passwords or username information. Personal certificates are ideal for communications such as providing partners and suppliers controlled access to websites for shipping dates, product availability and even inventory management.

16.21.3. Where to Get One

Digital certificates are issued by certificate authorities, just as state govern-ments issue driver's licences. There are several public companies in the busi-ness of issuing certificates. Certificate authorities are responsible for managing the life cycle of certificates, including their revocation.

An individual wishing to send an encrypted message applies for a digital certificate from a CA. The CA issues an encrypted digital certificate contain-ing the applicant's public key and a variety of other identification information. The CA makes its own public key readily available through print publicity or perhaps on the Internet.

The recipient of an encrypted message uses the CA's public key to decode the digital certificate attached to the message, verifies it as issued by the CA and then obtains the sender's public key and identification information held within the certificate. With this information, the recipient can send an encrypted reply.

16.22. COOKIES—SETTINGS FOR SAFETY

A cookie is a small text file stored on a user's web browser. The cookie is set by sending a piece of information from a web server to a web browser (such as Internet Explorer or Google Chrome). A cookie is entirely 'passive' and does not contain any software program, a virus or spyware. A cookie is com-posed of two parts, its name and its content or value of the cookie. Moreover, the lifetime of the cookie is determined. Technically, only the web server that sent the cookie can access it again when a user returns to a website associated with that web server.

16.22.1. Advantages of Cookies

A cookie contains information linked from a user's web browser to a specific web server of a website. If a web browser accesses that web server again, the web server can read from and react to that information. Cookies store useful information and ensure a user-friendly experience and support safety efforts for many online offers and services, for example, language preferences, pri-vacy settings, shopping baskets of online shops or relevant advertisements.

Cookies allow a web server to recognize the web browser until a cookie expires or is deleted. Cookies store useful information that improve the user's Internet experience, such as storing language settings in order for a user to see the website in her language; allowing a user to remain logged-in her webmail; banking securely online; 'remember'ing the items taken last time, and so on.

Cookies are not active programs. As a result, they cannot be spyware (that illegally intercepts data) and cannot carry a virus. They do not have access to the information on a user's hard drive. They are not 'active', executable software. Usually cookies contain only generic browser recognition or are associated with anonymous data. When cookies are set, the user is informed about it (typically in the privacy section of a website or in the terms of use or other user contract). If websites use cookies to collect personal data, data protection laws require those websites to inform users about the collection of personal data and the purpose of such collection.

Here is some key information to deal with a browser's cookies management setting tools:

16.22.2. Google Chrome

Open the browser. Click on the icon representing 'Tools' at the right of the window and choose 'Options'. Click the 'Under the Hood' tab and click 'Content Settings' in the 'Privacy' section. Choose the preferred settings in the 'Cookies' tab.

16.22.3. Internet Explorer

Open the browser. Click on 'Tools' at the right of the window and choose 'Internet Options'. Click on the 'Privacy' tab. The user can choose between different levels of automatic cookies management or choose to do it manually by clicking on 'Advanced'.

16.22.4. Mozilla Firefox

Open the browser. Click on 'Tools' and choose 'Options'. Click on the 'Privacy' tab. In the 'History' section the user can choose between different scenarios ('Remember history'/'Never remember history'/'Use custom settings for history') and define exceptions.

16.23. HOW TO IDENTIFY A TRUSTED WEBSITE

There are several aspects to identify before a website can be characterized as 'trusted'. A trusted website must do the following:

1. Get links from seed sites or from websites that are linked from seed sites. Seed sites are websites that are manually marked as trustworthy by search-engine owners. For example, if Airtel.in has been chosen as a seed website by Google then a link from Airtel.in will have a positive effect on the TrustRank of a website.
2. Not link to spam websites. If a website contains links to websites of a dubious quality then that website is not considered trustworthy and must be avoided.
3. Have technology to protect data sent by a customer during a transaction, that is, SSL or secure electronic transmission (SET), to protect data.
4. Have a privacy policy for its consumers, which must be read carefully by the user. If the user has some objection to the privacy policy, she should not buy anything on that website, but if she makes a decision to buy on that website, she should give out only a minimum amount of information.

16.24. INSTANT MESSAGING AND CHAT ROOM SAFETY

The risk of using instant messaging (IM) and chat rooms is that identities can be elusive or ambiguous: people may lie about their identity, accounts may be compromised, users may forget to log out, or an account may be shared by multiple people. All of these things make it difficult to know who you are really talking to during a conversation.

Trying to convince someone to run a program or click on a link is a common attack method, but it can be especially effective through IM and chat rooms. In a setting where a user feels comfortable with the 'person' she is talking to, an attacker has a better chance of making someone use the malicious software. Online interactions can be easily saved at the other end. If you are using a free commercial service the exchanges may be archived on a server. You have no control over what happens to those logs. You also do not know if someone looking over the shoulder of the person you are talking to, or if an attacker might be 'sniffing' your conversation. Add to it the fact that the default security settings in chat software tend to be relatively permissive to make it more open and usable and this can make it more susceptible to attacks.

16.24.1. Using Instant Messaging and Chat Rooms Safely

Check the default settings in the chat software and adjust them if they are too permissive. Make sure to disable automatic downloads. Some chat software offers the ability to limit interactions to only certain users, and you may want to take advantage of these restrictions. Beware of revealing personal information unless you know who you are really talking to. You should also be careful about discussing anything you or your employer might consider sensitive business information over public IM or chat services.

In some situations, the identity of the 'person' you are talking to may not matter. However, if you need to have a degree of trust in that person, either because you are sharing certain types of information or being asked to take some action like following a link or running a program, you must try to verify the identity of the person you are talking to.

Do not believe all the information that is exchanged. The information or advice you receive in a chat room or by IM may be false or, worse malicious. Try to verify the information or instructions from outside sources before taking any action. Keep software up to date. This includes the chat software, browser, operating system, the mail client and, especially the antivirus software.

16.25. SAFE BROWSING

16.25.1. Erasing Tracks after Browsing

Internet browsers make surfing the Web easy and convenient by remembering users search tracks, histories, forms and website histories. Many Internet browsers even fill passwords for you automatically. All Internet browsers provide ways for users to edit privacy settings. So, periodically clear your track and history to ensure your web browsing privacy.

16.25.2. Deleting Browsing History

Your Internet browser uses a 'cache' to speed up your web browsing. When you visit a URL it first checks the cache to see if you have been there before and it checks if any of the information has been downloaded before. For example, if the website has lots of images the same image may appear on multiple pages. The image gets downloaded to your cache and when you visit the next page that same image does not need to be downloaded again, instead it is displayed from your cache.

16.25.3. Erasing Internet History List

As you surf the Internet, your browser remembers every website and every URL that you have visited within the past few days. You can delete this list of URLs and web addresses in your browser using the functions provided. This will delete the entire list of websites you have visited.

16.25.4. Deleting Internet Cookies

Cookies typically store user-specific information such as usernames and passwords used to access web pages. They are also frequently used to store web page customization information. Although they provide you with the convenience of not having to re-enter your credentials every time you visit a web page, the private data they may store can represent a security risk.

You may delete cookies in browsers by clicking on the 'delete cookies' button. This will delete all the cookies stored on your computer.

16.25.5. Erasing Typed URLs List

Every time you manually type a website address in your browser's address bar, your computer remembers the addresses you have typed. If you click the drop-down on your address bar you will see all the addresses that you have previously typed. Deleting your browser's typed URL list manually can be done by editing your Windows registry.

16.26. HANDLING PRIVACY ISSUES

Privacy actually involves the exercise of control over the type and amount of information a person reveals about herself on the Internet and who may access such information. Specifically, Internet users may achieve an adequate level of privacy through controlled disclosure of personal information. Personal information is generally defined as any information relating to an identified or identifiable natural person. With the growth of the digital age, more and more personal information of consumers and citizens is finding its way into massive databases owned and controlled by the private sector and governments. This raises concerns on how such information is used or shared, how it is protected and who is accountable. The challenge with respect to data privacy is to share data while protecting personally identifiable information.

In order to keep their information private, people must be careful about what they store online and what they look for while browsing. When filling forms or buying items over the Internet, activity and behaviour patterns of users are logged and these can be tracked. This is because all user information was not private (as was meant to be) and companies use it to send users spam and advertisements on similar products.

In today's world, millions of people experience loss of privacy. It is a normal practice that we shop online and give our bank details and credit-card information to various websites. The advent of e-commerce has greatly simplified our lives. But inherent risks from sharing the sensitive information such as banking details and card details exist.

Privacy measures are provided on several social networking sites to try to provide users protection for their personal information. On social networking websites such as Facebook, privacy settings are available for all registered users. The settings available on Facebook include the ability to block certain individuals from seeing your profile, the ability to choose your 'friends', and the ability to limit who has access to your pictures and videos. It is the user's choice to apply such settings when providing and storing personal information on the Internet.

Another way of keeping track of online behaviour and then using it for gains is by getting information from cookies. Most of the time, specific user-related or computer-related data is stored in cookies and they are used to track behaviour. Cookies are one of the most common concerns in the field of privacy. Some organizations engage in profiling people's web browsing habits and collecting the URLs of sites visited. The resulting profiles can potentially link to information that personally identifies the individual who did the browsing. Some web-oriented marketing research organizations may use this practice legitimately to improve their understanding of particular markets and also to profile users.

Many programs and operating systems are set up to perform logging of user data. This may include recording times when the computer is in use, or which websites are visited. If a third party has sufficient access to the computer, the user's privacy may be compromised. This can be avoided by disabling usage logging, or by clearing usage logs regularly. Online activities are increasing at a rapid pace and keeping one's identity anonymous is a difficult task to achieve.

SEVENTEEN

SUGGESTIONS FOR BUILDING A SECURITY PROGRAMME AND CONCLUDING REMARKS

———•◦•———

Based on the discussions thus far, we may conclude that cybercrime is a real, fast-growing phenomenon, which is becoming a cause of concern, globally. Cybercrime will continue to rise in the days to come; therefore, better preparedness is what will make a difference. The worst-case cost of a successful security attack can be calculated by the total cost to the organization and to those around it. There is a growing potential for misuse and abuse of information systems. Most security breaches can be avoided if reasonable security practices are put in place at all times rather than after the incident has taken place. In this context, I shall discuss some important issues and critical success factors for the management of information security.

IMPORTANT ISSUES IN MANAGEMENT OF INFORMATION SECURITY

Information, like any other element, is an asset to an organization and needs to be protected. An organization should plan for reasonable security depending upon the value of the information. Information security relates to the protection of information recorded, processed, stored and transmitted. Information must be protected from any kind of harm, mainly from threats leading to its loss, non-availability, alteration and wrongful disclosure. The objective of information security is to protect the interests of those relying on information and systems, from the harm resulting from failure of availability, confidentiality and integrity. The four important issues in information technology (IT) security that need to be addressed are:

1. Confidentiality: It means ensuring that information is available only to those who are authorized to have access. Appropriate controls need to be exercised depending on the sensitivity of the data.
2. Integrity: It means safeguarding the accuracy and completeness of information and processing methods. Information has integrity only when it is whole, complete and uncorrupted. Any unauthorized alterations to data could be potentially disastrous.
3. Availability: It means ensuring that information and vital services are available to authorized users when required. It also means that the authorized user is able to access information without interference or obstruction.
4. Non-repudiation: With the world shifting gradually to a paperless mode of transacting, suitable mechanisms and legislations are required to give legal validity to electronic transactions and ensure that no party can repudiate its involvement in the transaction.

Any implementation of measures regarding information security should begin with an understanding of the scope and context, the critical information handled by the organization, an analysis of the IT environment, the legal and regulatory requirements and the vendor arrangements. It should also include defining roles and responsibilities within the organization. This would help to define the critical information security requirements in the organization.

An organization should establish the scope and boundaries in terms of characterization of the organization, its location, assets and technology and include details of and justification for any exclusion of departments and processes from the scope. The management should recognize the importance of information security and define roles and responsibilities to manage the risk.

Identifying risk for an IT system requires a thorough understanding of the system's processing environment, which includes information related to hardware, software, data and information, network, storage and so on. The system's complexity depends, to some extent, on the functional structure and operating environment of the organization. The practices followed for authentication, patch deployment, change management, configuration management, updates, database planning and the like depend partly on the organizational objectives, the roles and responsibilities in the organization, and an analysis of the IT environment.

It is important to protect the organization's information resources against internal and external threats. Some important issues which should be taken care of when designing security at the organizational level include:

- Implementing a company-wide information security policy, in line with current industry benchmarks.
- Providing secure e-mail access to employees.
- Providing secure access for business partners to access web-enabled applications over the Internet.
- Protecting critical IT applications from malicious users.
- Ensuring a functional information security architecture that can scale up with the growing business.

Cybercrime is becoming more organized as shown by recent incidents. Therefore, the response to them must also take on a new structure and focus. Individuals, organizations, law enforcement agencies and IT solutions providers must all work hand in hand to take on the evolving challenge of cybercrimes. New strategies and solutions are needed specifically in three key areas—people, policies and technology. Organized crime is successful where laws are confusing or lax, or where the law enforcement body is not prepared or structured enough to fight back. Therefore, adequate attention needs to be paid to the preparation of laws and their enforcement.

A large part of essential processes in manufacturing, utilities, banking and communications industries are on networked computers. As a result, incidents of online fraud have drastically increased. Lack of security eventually causes lack of public trust in online services. Cybercrime makes people reluctant to enter the electronic world. This hinders interchange between people, businesses and governments, impacting everything from education to commerce (Horn 2006).

Vulnerability exploits are key tools used by cybercriminals. They buy and sell information on system vulnerability, exploit codes, and deal in other types of malware. Proactive methods like employing system testing can be used to identify system vulnerabilities efficiently, depending on the criticality of the IT system and available resources (for example, allocated funds, available technology, persons with the expertise to conduct the tests).

Critical infrastructure is a term used by governments to describe assets that are essential for the functioning of a society and economy. The series of incidents discussed in earlier chapters highlights that the threat to critical infrastructure is real and governments need to take adequate steps to protect against it.

MAKING INFORMATION TECHNOLOGY A BUSINESS ISSUE

Security is not only an IT issue. An organization may have the best security programme in terms of policies, standards, firewalls and other technology devices, but the security programme will be ineffective without the management's involvement. At the heart of any system is the data and the owner of that data is the business. It is not about managing some IT devices. It is important that the management be truly involved in managing security as well.

INVOLVEMENT OF THE TOP MANAGEMENT

The management should initiate and provide formal approval to the process of implementing a security programme within the organization. The management may be represented by a steering committee comprising senior management personnel and group heads. The steering committee should have the approval of the top management, which includes approval of the information security policy, establishing roles and responsibilities in the organization, and communicating to the organization the importance of meeting the information security objectives. An acceptable level of risk for the organization needs to be worked out with the management's approval. Apart from the above, the management should ensure that periodic reviews of information security are conducted and corrective actions are taken as and when required to improve the effectiveness of the security plan.

The management should ensure that information security procedures support the business requirements. It should help maintain adequate security by correct application of safeguards and controls. It should carry out reviews when necessary and react appropriately to the results of these reviews. This will help ensure continuing suitability, adequacy and effectiveness of the security programme. The input to a management review may include the results of auditing and reviewing the security plan, a study of the latest threats, feedback from interested parties, and techniques, products or procedures, which could be used in the organization to improve the security plan's performance and effectiveness.

The management's involvement is most important in deciding on the questions of security requirements, regulatory or legal requirements, contractual obligations and levels of risk or criteria for accepting risks.

DEPLOYMENT OF ADEQUATE DEDICATED RESOURCES TO THE SECURITY PROGRAMME

Organizations need to dedicate sufficient resources for the management of cybercrime, which also includes awareness building and investment in new security technology to align with the changing threat landscape. Apart from budget and fund allocation, this means that there should be dedicated staff for detecting and preventing cybercrime.

BETTER INFORMATION SECURITY GOVERNANCE

Governance is the set of responsibilities and practices exercised by those responsible for an organization (for example, the board of directors and executive management in a corporation, the head of a government organization) with the express goals of (a) providing strategic direction; (b) ensuring that organizational mission and business objectives are achieved; (c) ascertaining that risks are managed appropriately; and (d) verifying that the organization's resources are used responsibly.

Organizations must ensure that governance structures for risk management and cybersecurity are in place prior to focusing on the specific details at the information-system level (networks, communications, data and applications). The issue of IT security must deserve a place of priority in corporate governance. Information security governance is a coherent system of integrated security components such as products or technology, personnel, training, processes, policies, and so on. It also includes clearer allocation of resources, roles and responsibilities on security issues, naming the persons who have decision-making rights, having a formal department to manage and deliver on information security and minimize the risk to the organization and stakeholders. It is important to avoid any disconnect between policies, processes and technology.

Apart from a steering committee with representation from senior management and group heads, a chief information security officer's position should be established to oversee the implementation of the security programme. Further, it is important to link information security governance to IT governance and corporate governance issues in an organization.

STRONG FOCUS ON ENTERPRISE ARCHITECTURE AS THE STARTING POINT

A strong focus on enterprise architecture and information security architecture is the foundation for securing networks, communication, data and applications. The review of enterprise architecture and information technology infrastructure should be the starting point for incorporating security into the organization. Standardization, consolidation and optimization of IT infrastructure reduce complexity and are effective approaches to effectively deploy security. The risks to an enterprise are increasing in variety and intensity. There can be no uniform information security set-ups suitable for all organizations. The set-up varies depending on enterprise architectures. The structure is right for a specific enterprise at a specific time. It also depends on the extent of outsourcing, complexity of the site, service providers and other factors.

STAKEHOLDER INVOLVEMENT AND AWARENESS BUILDING

The challenge is not only to secure networks, communications, data and applications but also to create awareness of the best practices on what is to be done and how it is to be integrated with the organization's operating environment and enterprise architecture.

In many cases, implementing best practices, having sufficient policies in place and a programme of user education can prevent or expose a targeted attack. For example, restricting the use of USB devices limits exposure to threats designed to propagate through removable media. Educating users not to open e-mail attachments and not to click on links in e-mails or instant messages can also help prevent breaches. If a breach occurs, strong password policies that require the use of different passwords across multiple systems can prevent the attack from expanding further into the network. Limiting user privileges can help to reduce the number of network resources that can be accessed from a compromised computer.

At the other end of the chain, increasing awareness among users and the availability of more intuitive and transparent security tools for computers are key development areas for the future.

ALIGNING THE SECURITY EFFORT CONTINUOUSLY WITH NEWER THREATS

No matter the kind of security systems put in place in an organization, newer threats will continue to come up. It is difficult to evolve best practices in the area of cybersecurity. Individuals, organizations and nations have no choice but to match up to newer threats on a continuous basis.

An understanding of the scope and context of the organization, operating environment, legal and contractual requirements and business risks is important to define information security priorities and align them with a security programme on an ongoing basis. Organizations must understand the environment in which information systems operate so that their information security programmes can address actual and potential problems.

The primary aim of an information security exercise is to protect the organization's ability to function and achieve its mission and objectives. For this, a high-level overview of the risk-management process and the role that risk plays in that process is important. When assessing business risks, one generally looks for organization-wide risks to operations and assets. The assessment of business risks can be used as an input to the detailed risk-assessment process to decide criticality of assets. The safeguards and protective measures implemented should cover business risks across the organization.

COMPLIANCE

An organization must ensure that it caters to the legal and regulatory requirements of information security. The ISO 27005 document on risk assessment states:

The regulatory requirements applicable to the organization should be identi-fied. These may be laws, decrees, specific regulations in the organization's field or internal/external Security Assurance Framework and Best Practices for Government Sector 2011 Page 18 of 108 regulations. This also concerns contracts and agreements and more generally any obligations of a legal or regulatory nature.

A security audit needs to be undertaken from time to time (at least once in a year) to ensure compliance with the security policy and legal and regula-tory requirements.

COLLABORATION

Collaboration, which may be in the form of cross-border, or even government–industry, is important for organized action against cybercrime and for initiat-ing activities such as increasing the shutdown of affected domains, freezing payment accounts that are suspected of fraud, isolating bad networks and so on. Collaboration is also required to build a knowledge repository on best practices and security assurance, building a common vulnerability database, building common criteria for information security products and so on. It is all the more important for countries to collaborate at the time of a cyber-attack, as against Estonia (discussed in earlier chapters).

International cooperation is needed to develop policies on cybercrime-related issues. The security policy may deal with different laws and regula-tions with which organizations must comply. Security policies help protect one of the most valuable assets of a company—its data, whether they are corporate secrets or private data of its employees and customers.

Just like other international issues are resolved at the global level through common governing bodies, there is a need to recognize cybercrime through an international body with the intention to make common laws to handle the crimes and criminals behind it. Cybercrime can no longer be handled in silos by each country and collective efforts are the need of the hour since cyber-criminals are also spreading their bases to many countries. However, the true intentions of several countries' governments behind forming such an interna-tional consortium may be in doubt, since some countries already consider their cyber advancement as a strategic tool, to take advantage of, in case of war.

BALANCING ACCESS AND CONTROL

Balancing access and control is important. On one hand, there is a pressure to provide stakeholders access to information, while on the other, one must adequately protect sensitive information. It is important to facilitate business with secure access to information and information systems. All information is not of similar value to an organization. Highly valuable information needs to be protected more carefully than that which is less valuable. Therefore, a balanced approach to security is required. A minimum level of security should be provided to each information asset so that risk is at an acceptable level. At the same time, it must be realized that putting in place any sort of protection mechanism and safeguard entails hard and soft costs. Therefore, any extra effort on securing an information asset should be commensurate with the risk.

There is a delicate balance between access and control. Too much access to information assets can increase the exposure to risk. However, excessive controls in an effort to enhance security may affect the productivity of employees. Therefore, a balanced approach to information security is important so that risk is at an acceptable level. This acceptable level of risk needs to be reviewed periodically in light of the changing threat scenario and the past experience of the organization. Risk to information systems is a function of the likelihood that some threat will attack or exploit some vulnerability in the system and a calculation of the potential impact resulting from these attacks or exploitations.

PRINCIPLES OF 'LEAST PRIVILEGE' AND 'NEED-TO-KNOW'

The principle of 'least privilege' requires that in a particular computing environment, a user, a program or a process should access only the information and resources that are necessary for its operational requirement and not beyond that. 'need-to-know' means only legitimate users should be able to access the information for official purposes. As with most security mechanisms, the main aim is to make it difficult for unauthorized persons to access information. 'need-to-know' also aims at discouraging 'browsing' of sensitive material by limiting access to the smallest possible number of people.

REASONABLE RETURN ON INVESTMENT AND COST OF SECURITY

As the cost of information security continues to go up, organizations must strive for 'reasonable security practices'. A reasonable and balanced approach means that there is an optimum level of investment on information security safeguards and counter measures (controls). Every additional safeguard introduced on the information assets by way of technology, processes or management interventions entails tangible and intangible costs and needs to be suitably justified. Due to these reasons, the management of risk becomes the most critical part of the entire security management effort. It ensures that the organization has a reasonable level of safeguards on all critical information assets and that it is not over-protecting or under-protecting an information asset.

FIRST 'ESSENTIAL' THEN 'EXCELLENT'

Mitigation efforts should ensure that the 'essential' requirements of security are met and only then should the planning for additional security be done to achieve excellence. The 'essential' requirements would depend on the scope and context of the organization. Some of these requirements could include securing business partner connections, creating a data retention plan, monitoring event logs, creating an incident response plan, increasing awareness, engaging in mock drills and so on.

This also means defining a 'baseline security' for government and industry. All organizations, irrespective of their mission and business objectives, require some basic security practices. These security practices may be decided at the level of the steering committee as part of the information governance structure. These practices help prepare the organization for implementing the security programme.

SECURITY WITH THIRD-PARTY SERVICE PROVIDERS

External service providers include joint ventures, business partnerships, outsourcing arrangements and/or supply chain procurement exchanges. An organization should define the type of external services it uses. As a next step, it should identify the type of information exchanged under those services and do a risk assessment. This information should be used to identify the additional controls required for use of services offered by external service providers. The growing dependence on external service providers presents new challenges for organizations. Proper screening and background checks of service providers, who will work on the organization's premises, should be carried out. Depending upon the information exchanged, non-disclosure agreements and indemnity against intellectual property rights' violations should be built into the contract with third-party service providers. The receipt of a signed non-disclosure agreement must always precede the disclosure of sensitive information to consultants, contractors and temporaries. Service level agreements with external service providers should clearly address the issue of security breach. They should also consider back-end subcontracting agreements since any lapse may have the potential to cause damage to the organization.

HAVING THE RIGHT KIND OF KEY PERFORMANCE INDICATORS

It is also important to have effective key performance indicators (KPIs) and metrics to avoid disconnect between policies, processes and technology. These KPIs must be reviewed and updated on an ongoing basis, keeping in view the changing nature of threats and newer risks associated with them. Equally important is security benchmarking and the integration of operational indicators with strategic indicators.

CONDUCTING MOCK DRILLS

To test organizational preparedness, cybersecurity mock drills should be carried out from time to time. This can help the organization assess the effectiveness of the security programme in terms of response and recovery. The Computer Emergency Response Team (CERT) in each country can carry out such mock drills at the country level and internationally to check on the preparedness of different organizations and readiness to other critical infrastructure requirements.

BUILDING A KNOWLEDGE REPOSITORY ON BEST PRACTICES ON INFORMATION SECURITY

It is important to systematically capture, organize and share best practices in the area of information security. Awareness of these best practices can make a difference in aligning the security effort. Industry, academia and government need to collaborate in building such a repository of best practices on information security and use it for awareness building.

FINALLY, ABSOLUTE SECURITY IS A MYTH ... BUT YOU STILL HAVE TO PLAN

Security of information—safeguarding computer systems and the integrity, confidentiality and availability of data on them—is a critical policy issue for any organization and has grown in importance due to the continual integration of computers in different aspects of modern human life. Users need to understand cybercrime in greater detail and take adequate protection measures so that they feel safe online. Individuals, organizations, law enforcement bodies and IT solutions providers must all join hands to study and meet the evolving challenge posed by cybercrime, specifically in the design of new strategies and solutions, which will become necessary in key areas—people, processes, policies and technology. International cooperation is a necessity to combat cybercrime. This requires building of appropriate regulations and anti-cybercrime institutions.

Recent law enforcement actions and continued takedown efforts by industry do seem to have had an effect on the operations and activities of cybercriminals. Nevertheless, one must not think that cybercriminals are sitting idly by while their industry gets dismantled. This book is a wake-up call for all. The discussions and examples presented demonstrate the magnitude of the problem of cybercrime. Users, professionals, the information security community, as well as policymakers, need to come to terms with the new reality rapidly. Keeping alert and being well informed on the latest threat components remain the most important aspects of staying secure.

BIBLIOGRAPHY

———————————

Abreu, E. 2000. 'Kevin Mitnick Bares All', 28 September 2000, *Network World Fusion*. Available online at http://www.networkworld.com/news/2000/0928mitnick.html (accessed on 18 April 2013).

Africa News. 2007. 'Internet Banking Fraud on the Increase', October.

Aguilar-Millan, S., J. E. Foltz, J. Jackson and A. Oberg. 2008. 'The Globalization of Crime', *The Futurist*, 42 (6): 41–50.

Akner, P. 2010. 'How to Protect Against Spam, Norton, Your Security Resource'. Available online at http://us.norton.com/yoursecurityresource/detail.jsp?aid= protect-against-spam (accessed 17 February 2012).

Antonopoulos, A. 2009. 'ATM Hack: Organized Crime or Market Forces?', *Network World*, 26 (8): 20.

APWG. 2010. 'Global Phishing Survey: Trends and Domain Name Use in 2H2009', Spring edition, May. Available online at http://www.antiphishing.org/reports/ APWG_GlobalPhishingSurvey_2H2009.pdf (accessed on 25 July 2011).

APWG. 2011a. 'Global Phishing Survey: Trends and Domain Name Use in 1H2011, January–June 2011', November 2011. Available online at http://www.antiphishing. org/reports/APWG_GlobalPhishingSurvey_1H2011.pdf (accessed on January 2012).

APWG. 2011b. 'Phishing Activity Trends Report 1H2011, January–June 2011'. Available online at www.inteco.es/file/T3JGP0L_6Tts6FaJU6Kqtg (accessed on 12 January 2012).

Arbor Networks. 2010. 'Worldwide Infrastructure Security Report'. Available online at http://www.arbornetworks.com/worldwide-infrastructure-security-report.html (accessed on 12 February 2012).

Arbor Networks. 2011. 'World Wide Infrastructure Security Report, 2010, Vol.- VI', *Arbor Network*. Available online at www.arbornetworks.com/.../485-worldwide-infrastructure-security-report (accessed on 16 February 2012).

Aspan, M. and K. Soh. 2011. 'Citi Says 360,000 Accounts Hacked in May Cyber Attack', 17 June 2011, Reuters. Available online on http://in.reuters.com/ article/2011/06/16/us-citigroup-hacking-idUSTRE75F17620110616 (accessed on 12 January 2012).

Backer, G. 1968. 'Crime and Punishment: An Economic Approach', *Journal of Political Economy*, 76 (2): 169–217.

BBC News. 2011. 'UK Cyber Crime Costs £27bn a Year', 17 February. Available online at http://www.bbc.co.uk/news/uk-politics-12492309 (accessed on 8 January 2012).

Becker, G. S. 1995. 'The Economics of Crime', *Cross Sections*, Fall: 8–15.

Bednarz, A. 2004. 'Profiling Cybercriminals: A Promising but Immature Science', *Network World*. Available online at http://www.networkworld.com/supp/2004/cybercrime/112904profile.html (accessed on 12 July 2011).

Beer, M. 1999. 'Suspected creator of Melissa virus arrested, Written by Matt Beer, Examiner Technology Writer', *SFGate, San Francisco Chronicle*. Available online at http://www.sfgate.com/news/article/Suspected-creator-of-Melissa-virus-arrested-3090073.php (accessed on 16 February 2012).

Bell, R. E. 2002. 'The Prosecution of Computer Crime', *Journal of Financial Crime*, 9 (4): 308–25.

Blau, J. 2004. 'Russia—A Happy Haven for Hackers'. Available online at http://www.computerweekly.com/feature/Russia-a-happy-haven-for-hackers (accessed on 12 July 2011).

Bloomberg. 2011a. 'IMF State-Backed Cyber-Attack Follows Hacks of Lab, G-20'. Available online at http://www.bloomberg.com/news/2011-06-11/imf-computer-system-infiltrated-by-hackers-said-to-work-for-foreign-state.html (accessed on 12 February 2012).

Bloomberg. 2011b. 'Sony Network Said to Have Been Invaded by Hackers Using Amazon.com Servers'. Available online at http://www.bloomberg.com/news/2011-05-13/sony-network-said-to-have-been-invaded-by-hackers-using-amazon-com-server.html (accessed on 12 February 2012).

Bloomberg Businessweek. 2010. 'Cyber Crime and Information Warfare: A 30-Year History', 14 October. Available online at http://images.businessweek.com/ss/10/10/1014_cyber_attacks/index.htm (accessed on 12 February 2012).

Bottoms, A. E. and P. Wiles. 2002. 'Environmental Criminology', in M. Maguire, R. Morgan and R. Reiner (eds), *Oxford Handbook of Criminology*, pp. 620–56. Oxford, UK: Oxford University Press.

Bradley, T. 2011. 'Lessons Learned from the Epsilon Data Breach', *PCWorld*. Available online at http://www.pcworld.com/businesscenter/article/224615/lessons_learned_from_the_epsilon_data_breach.html (accessed on 6 February 2012).

Bridis, T. 2006. 'Computer Research Warns of Net Attacks', *Yahoo!Finance*, 16 March. Available online at http://biz.yahoo.com/ap/060316 (accessed on 6 February 2012).

Browning, C. R., S. L. Feinberg and R. D. Dietz. 2004. 'The Paradox of Social Organization: Networks, Collective Efficacy, and Violent Crime in Urban Neighbourhoods', *Social Forces*, 83 (2): 503–34.

Bryan-Low, C. 2005. 'As Identity Theft Moves Online, Crime Rings Mimic Big Business: Russian-led Carderplanet Steals Account Numbers; Mr Harvard Hits

ATMs, "Common Punk" to "Capo"', 13 July 2005, *Wall Street Journal*: A.1. Available online at http://online.wsj.com/article/0,,SB112121800278184116,00. html (accessed on 10 January 2012).

Business News. 2009. 'Microsoft sues', 137, 9.

Business News Americas. 2009. 'Government Creates Cyber Security Body—Brazil', 9 September. Available online at http://www.bnamericas.com/news/technology/ Government_creates_cyber_security_body

Business Week. 2006. 'It's time to arrest cybercrime'.

Cantor, D. and K. C. Land. 1985. 'Unemployment and Crime Rates in the Post-World War II United States: A Theoretical and Empirical Analysis', *American Sociological Review*, 50 (June): 317–32.

Cashell, B., W. D. Jackson, M. Jickling and B. Webel. 2004. 'The Economic Impact of Cyber-Attacks', *CRS Report for Congress*, 1 April. Available online at http:// www.fas.org/sgp/crs/misc/RL32331.pdf and http://www.docstoc.com/docs/ 22081360/The-Economic-Impact-of-Cyber-Attacks---PDF

CBS News. 2010. 'Iran Confirms Stuxnet Worm Halted Centrifuges', CBS News. Available online at http://www.cbsnews.com/stories/2010/11/29/world/ main7100197.shtml (accessed on 16 February 2012).

CERT-In. 2011. 'Indian Computer Emergency Response Team (CERT-In): Annual Report (2010)'. Available online at http://www.cert-in.org.in/s2cMainServlet?pa geid=PUBANULREPRT (accessed on 12 January 2012).

Chabrow, E. 2010. 'Which Nation is Most Feared in Cyberspace?' *Govinfo Security*, 28 January. Available online at http://www.govinfosecurity.com/articles.php?art_ id=2129 (accessed on 12 June 2012).

Chawki, J. M. and M. S. Abdel Wahab. 2006. 'Identity Theft in Cyberspace: Issues and Solutions', *Lex Electronica*, 11 (1): 1–41. Available online at http://www.lex-electronica.org/articles/v11-1/chawki_abdel-wahab.htm

Cheney, J. S. 2005. 'Identity theft: Do definitions still matter?' Discussion Paper, Federal Reserve Bank of Philadelphia, Payment Cards Centre.

Choo, K. R. 2011. 'Transnational Organized Groups and Cybercrime', paper presented at the Asia-Pacific Regional Workshop for Fighting Cybercrime, Seoul, Republic of Korea, 21–23 September. Available online at http://www.itu.int/ITU-D/asp/CMS/ Events/2011/CyberCrime/S2_Raymond_Choo.pdf (accessed on 12 February 2012).

CIFAS. 2010. 'Digital Thieves: A Special Report on Online Fraud', October 2010, Page 4. Available online at http://www.cifas.org.uk/secure/contentPORT/uploads/ documents/CIFAS%20Reports/Digital_Thieves_October2010.pdf (accessed 12 February 2012).

Cisco. 2010. 'Cisco 2010 Annual Security Report: Highlighting Global Security Threats and Trends'. Available online at http://www.cisco.com/en/US/prod/collateral/ vpndevc/security_annual_report_2010.pdf (accessed on 12 January 2012).

Cisco. 2001. 'Cisco Security Notice: Response to BugTraq - NTP Issue – Cisco'. Available online at http://www.cisco.com/en/US/products/sw/iosswrel/ps1818/ products_security_notice09186a008026410b.html (accessed on 12 January 2012).

Cisco. 2011a. 'Annual Global Threat Report'. Available online at http://www.cisco.
     com/en/US/prod/vpndevc/annual_security_report.html (accessed on 12 January
     2012).
Cisco. 2011b. 'Annual Security Report: Highlighting Global Security Threats and
     Trends'. Available online at http://cisco.com/security/center/home.x (accessed on
     12 January 2012).
Claburn, T. 2009. 'Cyber Attack Against Georgia Blurred Civilian And Military',
     Information Week, 17 August. Available online at http://www.informationweek.
     com/government/security/cyber-attack-against-georgia-blurred-civ/219400248
Clarke, R. V. 1995. 'Situational Crime Prevention', in M. Tonry and D. P. Farrington
     (eds), *Building a Safer Society: Strategic Approaches to Crime*, pp. 91–150.
     Chicago, IL: University of Chicago Press.
CNN Tech. 2000. 'Feds find dangerous cyberstalking hard to prevent', 12 June 2000.
     Available online at http://articles.cnn.com/2000-06-12/tech/cyberstalkers.idg_1_
     cyberstalking-e-mail-messages-electronic-messages?_s=PM:TECH (accessed on
     23 February 2012).
Coleman, K. 2003. 'Cyber Terrorism', *Directions Magazine*, 10 October: 1. Available
     online at http://www.directionsmag.com/articles/cyber-terrorism/123840 (accessed
     on 18 February 2012).
Collin, B. 1997. 'The Future of Cyberterrorism', *Crime & Justice International
     Journal*, 15 (March).
Computerworld. 2007. 'Canadian Probe Finds TJX Breach Followed Wireless Hack'.
Computer Business Review. 2007. 'TJX Hack is Biggest Ever', *Computer Business
     Review*.
Constantin, L. (2012, February), 'Denial-of-Service Attacks are on the Rise, Anti-
     DDoS Vendors Report', *Computerworld.*
Csikszentmihalyi, M. 1975. *Beyond Boredom and Anxiety: The Experience of Play in
     Work and Games*. San Francisco, CA: Jossey-Bass, Inc.
Cyber insecure.com. 2008. 'Asprox Botnet Mass Attack Hits Governmental, Healthcare,
     and Top Business Websites', Section: Hacked, Malware, Mass Web Attacks, SQL
     Injections. Available online at http://cyberinsecure.com/asprox-botnet-mass-
     attack-hits-governmental-healthcare-and-top-business-websites/ (accessed on 16
     April 2012).
Data Monitor. 2009. 'Ebay,Inc. SWOT Analysis'. 1–9.
Dave, N. 2010. 'Asprox Botnet Causing Serious Concern', Posted on 24 June 2010.
     Available online at http://www.v3.co.uk/v3-uk/news/1962195/asprox-botnet-
     causing-concern (accessed on 16 April 2012).
Deci, E. L. and R. M. Ryan. 1985. *Intrinsic Motivation and Self-Determination in
     Human Behavior*. New York, NY: Plenum Press.
Dell SecureWorks. 2011. 'Anatomy of an Advanced Persistent Threat (APT)'.
     Available   online   at   http://www.secureworks.com/resources/webcasts/
     general/20120521-gen/ (accessed on March 2012).

Dempsey, P. J. 2008. 'Unprepared to Fight Worldwide Cyber Crime'. Available online at http://www.internetevolution.com/author.asp?section_id=593&doc_id=147027 (accessed on 28 January 2012).

Denning, D. E. 2000. 'Hactivism: An Emerging Threat to Diplomacy', *American Foreign Service Association.* Available online at http://www.afsa.org/fsj/sep00/denning.cfm (accessed on 12 February 2012).

Department of Homeland Security. 2010. *National Strategy for Trusted Identities in Cyberspace: Creating Options for Enhanced Online Security and Privacy.* Washington, DC: Government of United States.

Detica and Office of Cyber Security and Information Assurance. 2011. 'The Cost of Cyber Crime', February 2011. Available online at http://www.cabinetoffice.gov.uk/resource-library/cost-of-cyber-crime

Donaldson, T. 1996. 'Values in Tension: Ethics Away from Home', *Harvard Business Review*, 74 (5): 48–57.

Duggal, P. 2009. 'Important Cyber law Developments of 2009, Cyber Law Trends of 2010', IGF Dynamic Coalition on Internet and Policy. Available online at http://cyberlawindia2008.blogspot.in/2009_12_01_archive.html

EC-Council. 2009. 'What is a DDoS Attack?' *Ethical Hacking and Countermeasures: Threats and Defense Mechanisms.* EC-Council Press, Cengage Learning.

Eltringham, S. (ed.). 1995. *Prosecuting Computer Crimes*. Washington, DC: Computer Crime and Intellectual Property Section Criminal Division.

Etges, R. and E. Sutcliffe. 2008. 'An Overview of Transnational Organized Cyber Crime', *Information Security Journal: A Global Perspective*, 17 (2): 87–94.

Fertik, M. and D. Thompson. 2010. *Wild West 2.0, How to Protect and Restore Your Online Reputation on the Untamed Social Frontier.* New York: Amacon, page 44, chapter 4.0.

Fildes, J. 2010. 'Stuxnet Worm "Targeted High-value Iranian Assets"', BBC News. Available online at http://www.bbc.co.uk/news/technology-11388018 (accessed on 16 February 2012).

Finklea, K. M. 2010. 'Identity Theft: Trends and Issues', 5 January. Available online at http://www.fas.org/sgp/crs/misc/R40599.pdf (accessed on 10 February 2012).

Foreign Policy. 2005. 'Caught in the Net', *Australian Teens*, March/April, 92.

Frey, B. S. 1997. *Not Just for the Money: An Economic Theory of Personal Motivation.* Brookfield, VT: Edward Elgar Publishing Company.

Gartner. 2002. 'Cyber Security and Challenges'. Accessed on 4 July 2011.

Gercke, M. 2011a. 'An Overview of Cybercrime Offences', paper presented at the Asia-Pacific Regional Workshop on Fighting Cybercrime, Seoul, Republic of Korea, 21–23 September. Available online at http://www.itu.int/ITU-D/asp/CMS/Events/2011/CyberCrime/S2_Marco_Gercke.pdf (accessed on 10 February 2012).

Gercke, M. 2011b. 'Economic Aspects of Cybercrime', paper presented a the Asia-Pacific Regional Workshop on Fighting Cybercrime, Seoul, Republic of Korea, 21–23 September 2011. Available online at http://www.itu.int/ITU-D/asp/CMS/

Events/2011/CyberCrime/S3_Marco_Gercke_1.pdf (accessed on 9 February 2012).

Govinfosecurity. 2011. 'Obama Vows to Battle International Cybercrime'. Available online at http://www.govinfosecurity.com/articles.php?art_id=3889

Grant, R. 2007. 'Victory in Cyberspace: An Air Force Association Special Report'. Available online at http://www.afa.org/media/reports/victorycyberspace.pdf (accessed on March 2012).

Greenberg, A. 2007. 'The Top Countries for Cybercrime', *Forbes.com*, 16 July. Available online at http://www.forbes.com/2007/07/13/cybercime-world-regions-tech-cx_ag_0716cybercrime.html (accessed on 25 September 2011).

Greenberg, A. 2009. 'Cybercops Without Borders', *Forbes.com*, 1 June. Available online at http://www.forbes.com/2009/06/01/cyberbusts-security-internet-technology-security-cyberbusts.html

Grow, B. and J. Bush. 2005. 'Hacker Hunters', *Bloomberg Businessweek*, 29 May. Available online at http://www.businessweek.com/stories/2005-05-29/hacker-hunters

Hafner, K. and J. Markoff. 1991. *Cyberpunk: Outlaws and Hackers on the Computer Frontier*. New York, NY: Touchstone.

Hahn, R. W. and A. Layne-Farrar. 2006. 'The Law and Economics of Software Security', *Harvard Journal of Law and Public Policy*, 30 (1): 283–353.

Hamilton, L. 2009. 'Cyber Attack Just a Click Away'. Available online at http://www.indystar.com/article/20090824/OPINION12/908240315/Cyber-attack-just-click-away?nclick_check=1

Hamilton-Beach. 2011. 'Media Release from Hamilton-Beach Brand', 12 January. Available online at http://www.hamilton-Beach.com/ (accessed on 20 July 2011).

Harwood, M. 2008. 'Quebec Police Break Up Hacking Syndicate', *Security Management*, 22 February. Available online at http://www.securitymanagement.com/news/quebec-police-break-hacking-syndicate (accessed on March 2012).

Heathkote, P. M. and S. Langfield. 2004. *A Level Computing, Computer Crime and the law*. Oxford: Pearson Education.

Hess, P. 2008. 'Pentagon Puts Hold on USAF Cyber Effort', *Associated Press*, 13 August 2008. Available online at http://www.boston.com/news/nation/washington/articles/2008/08/13/pentagonjputs hold-on usaf cyber effort (accessed on 10 November 2011).

Hirschauer, N. and O. Musshoff. 2007. 'A Game-Theoretic Approach to Behavioral Food Risks: The Case of Grain Producers', *Food Policy*, 32 (2): 246–65.

Hirshleifer, J. 1998. 'The Bioeconomic Causes of War', *Managerial and Decision Economics*, 19 (7–8): 457–66.

Hoffman, A. J. 1999. 'Institutional Evolution and Change: Environmentalism and the US Chemical Industry', *Academy of Management Journal*, 42 (4): 351–71.

Hoffman, S. 2011a. 'WikiLeaks Suffers DoS Attack Following Cable Release, CRN', published on 31 August 2011. Available online at http://www.crn.com/news/

security/231600594/wikileaks-suffers-dos-attack-following-cable-release.htm (accessed on 4 March 2012).

Hoffman, S. 2011b. '10 Biggest Cyber Attacks of July', *CRN*, 2 August. Available online at http://www.crn.com/slide-shows/security/231003038/10-biggest-cyber-attacks-of-july.htm?pgno=6 (accessed on 19 December 2011).

Hoffman, S. 2011c. 'Washington Post Hack Compromises 1.27 Million Job Seeker Accounts', 7 July 2011, CRN. Available online on http://www.crn.com/news/security/231001179/washington-post-hack-compromises-1-27-million-job-seeker-accounts.htm (accessed on 19 December 2011).

Hoffman, S. 2011d. 'Anonymous Lulz Sec defaced the Sun Website, CRN'. 18 July 2011. Available online at http://www.crn.com/news/security/231002057/anonymous-lulzsec-deface-the-sun-web-site.htm (accessed on 19 December 2011).

Hollander, Y. 2000. 'Prevent Website Defacement', *Internet Security Advisor*, (November–December): 3–4. Available online at www.dli.gov.in/data/HACKING_INFORMATION/PRINTED%2520PAPERS/PREVENT%2520WEBSITE%2520DEFACEMENT.pdf (accessed on 11 February 2012).

Hollis, D. 2011. 'Cyberwar Case Study: Georgia 2008', *Small Wars Journal*. Small Wars Foundation. Available online at http://www.smallwarsjournal.com/blog/journal/docs-temp/639-hollis.pdf (accessed on 4 March 2012).

Horn, P. 2006. 'It's Time to Arrest Cyber Crime', *Bloomberg Businessweek*. Available online at http://www.businessweek.com/technology/content/feb2006/tc20060202_832554.htm?chan=search (accessed on 23 February 2012).

iDefense. 2006. Cyber Cyber Fraud Trends and Mitigation, An iDefense Security Report, The VeriSign iDefense Intelligence Team. Released on 19 September 2006. Available online at http://www.first.org/conference/2007/papers/thomas-ralph-paper.pdf (accessed on 12 June 2011).

iDefense. 2008. '2009 Cyber Threats and Trends: An iDefense Topical Research Report', 12 December. Accessed on 10 June 2010.

Information Warfare Monitor. 2009. 'Tracking GhostNet: Investigating a Cyber Espionage Network'. Available online at http://www.infowar-monitor.net/ghostnet (accessed on 19 July 2011).

Information Warfare Monitor and Shadowserver Foundation. 2010. 'Shadows in the Cloud: Investigating Cyber Espionage 2.0'. Available online at http://shadows-in-the-cloud.net (accessed on 12 July 2011).

Information Week. 2008.

Infoworld. 2007. 'Retailer TJX Reports Massive Data Breach'.

Internet Crime Complaint Center. 2008. 'Internet Crime Report 2008'. Available online at http://www.ic3.gov/media/annualreport/2008_ic3report.pdf (accessed on 2 July 2011).

Internet Crime Complaint Center. 2009. 'Internet Crime Report 2009'. Available online at http://www.ic3.gov/media/annualreport/2009_ic3report.pdf (accessed on July 2011).

Internet Crime Complaint Center. 2010. 'Internet Crime Report 2010'. Available online at http://www.ic3.gov/media/annualreport/2010_ic3report.pdf (accessed on 28 January 2012).

Internet Identity. 2009. 'Internet Identity—Phishing Trends Report—Second Quarter 2009', Analysis of Online Financial Fraud Threats, pp. 3–4. Available online at http://www.internetidentity.com/images/stories/docs/phishing_trends_report_q2-2009_by_internet_identity.pdf (accessed on 16 January 2012).

Internet Information Network Centre. 2010. 'Information Management and Business Review by CNNIC'. Accessed on 10 January 2012.

Ismail, I. 2008. 'Understanding Cyber Criminals', New Straits Times, Malaysia, 12.

ISMG. 2010. 'The Faces of Fraud: Fighting Back, 2010 Survey Results'. Available online at http://www.bankinfosecurity.com/surveys.php?surveyID=9 (accessed on 12 July 2011).

ITU. 2009a. 'ITU Toolkit for Cybercrime Legislation', International Telecommunication Union, April. Available online at http://www.itu.int/ITU-D/cyb/cybersecurity/docs/itu-toolkit-cybercrimelegislation.pdf (accessed on 20 January 2012).

ITU. 2009b. 'Understanding Cybercrime: A Guide for Developing Countries'. Available online at http://www.itu.int/dms_pub/itu-d/oth/01/0B/D010B0000073301PDFE.pdf (accessed on 7 February 2012).

Javelin Strategy and Research. 2010. '2010 Identity Fraud Survey Report: Consumer Version'. Available online at https://www.javelinstrategy.com/uploads/files/1004.R_2010IdentityFraudSurveyConsumer.pdf (accessed on 12 July 2011).

Javelin Strategy and Research. 2011. '2011 Identity Fraud Survey Report: Consumer Version'. Available online at http://www.identityguard.com/downloads/javelin-2011-identity-fraud-survey-report.pdf (accessed on 21 January 2012).

Kabay, M. E. 2008. A Brief History of Computer Crime.

Kaspersky, E. 2008. 'The Cybercrime Arms Race', Securelist, 25 August. Available online at http://www.securelist.com/en/analysis/204792032/The_Cybercrime_Arms_Race?print_mode=1

Katyal, N. K. 2001. 'Criminal Law in Cyberspace', University of Pennsylvania Law Review, 149 (4): 1003–114.

Kenney, M. and B. Pon. 2011. 'Structuring the Smartphone Industry: Is the Mobile Internet OS Platform the Key, The Competitive Landscape', University of California, p. 1. Available online at http://brie.berkeley.edu/publications/wp194.pdf (accessed on 16 January 2012).

Kerbsonsecurity.com. 2011. 'Where Have All the Spambots Gone?', 1 July 2011. Available online at http://krebsonsecurity.com/2011/07/where-have-all-the-spambots-gone/ (accessed on 1 September 2011).

Knowledge Globalization Institute. 2010. 'Proceedings of the Knowledge Globalization Conference, Boston, Massachusetts, 5–7 November, Vol. 2, No. 1'. Available online at http://www.kglobal.org/files/docs/2010proceedingsbos.pdf.

Koerner, B. I. 2000. 'A Lust for Profits: Pornography is a Huge and Growing Cyberspace Draw: But Will Salacious Web Sites be a Hit on Wall Street?', U.S.

News and World Report 2000. Available online at http://www.usnews.com/
usnews/biztech/articles/000327/archive_018819.htm (accessed on 12 February
2012).

KPMG International. 2011. 'Issues Monitor: Cyber Crime: A Growing Challenge for
Governments, July 2011, Volume Eight'. Available online at http://www.kpmg.
com/Global/en/IssuesAndInsights/ArticlesPublications/Documents/cyber-crime.
pdf (accessed on 14 January 2012).

Kratchman, S., J. L. Smith and M. Smith. 2008. 'Perpetration and Prevention of Cyber
Crimes', *Internal Auditing*, 23 (2, March–April): 3–12.

Krebs, B. 2008. 'Host of Internet Spam Groups Is Cut Off', *The Washington Post*.
Available   online   at   http://www.washingtonpost.com/wp-dyn/content/
article/2008/11/12/AR2008111200658_2.html?sid=ST2008111801165 (accessed
on 12 January 2012).

Kshetri, N. 2006. 'The Simple Economics of Cybercrimes', *IEEE Security and
Privacy*, 4 (1): 33–39.

Kshetri, N. 2009. 'Positive Externality, Increasing Returns, and the Rise in Cybercrimes',
Communications of the ACM, 52 (12): 141–44.

Kshetri, N. 2010. *The Global Cybercrime Industry: Economic, Institutional and
Strategic Perspectives*, p. 3. New York, NY: Springer.

Kwong, K. K., O. H. M. Yau, J. S. Y. Lee, L. Y. M. Sin and A. C. B. Tse. 2003. 'The
Effects of Attitudinal and Demographic Factors on Intention to Buy Pirated CDs:
The Case of Chinese Consumers', *Journal of Business Ethics*, 47 (3): 223–35.

Lakhani, K. R. and R. G. Wolf. 2005. 'Why Hackers Do What They Do: Understanding
Motivation and Effort in Free/Open Source Software Projects', in J. Feller,
B. Fitzgerald, S. A. Hissam and K. R. Lakhani (eds), *Perspectives on Free and
Open Source Software*, pp. 3–22. Cambridge, MA: MIT Press.

Landler, M. and J. Markoff. 2007. 'Digital Fears Emerge After Data Siege in Estonia',
New York Times, May.

Larkin, E. 2009. 'Organized Crime Moves into Data Theft', *PC World*, 27 (7): 33–34.

Lee, J. K. 2000. 'The e-citizen, social education', *Arlington*, 64 (6): 378–380.

Levi, M. 2002. 'The Organisation of Serious Crimes', in M. Maguire, R. Morgan and
R. Reiner (eds), *The Oxford Handbook of Criminology*, pp. 878–913. Oxford, UK:
Oxford University Press.

Lewis, J. 2011. 'Timeline of Major Global Cyber Incidents 2010–2011', *Govinfo
Security*, 17 March. Available online at http://www.govinfosecurity.com/time-line-
major-global-cyber-incidents-2010-2011-a-3440 (accessed on 13 January 2012).

Leyden, J. 2004. 'US Credit Card Firm Fights DDoS Attack'. Available online at http://
www.theregister.co.uk/2004/09/23/authorize_ddos_attack (accessed on 12
January 2012).

Leyden, J. 2010. 'How FBI, police busted massive botnet, Security', *The register*,
Posted on 3 March 2010. Available online at http://www.theregister.
co.uk/2010/03/03/mariposa_botnet_bust_analysis/ (accessed on 18 April 2012).

Lindenberg, S. 2001. 'Intrinsic Motivation in a New Light', *Kyklos*, 54 (2–3): 317–43.

Lipton, J. D. 2011. 'Combating Cyber-Victimization', *Berkeley Technology Law Journal*, 26: 1103–56.

Long, E. 2010a. 'CIA Gives Nod to Cybersecurity', *Nextgov*, 27 April. Available online at http://www.nextgov.com/cybersecurity/cybersecurity-report/2010/04/cia-gives-nod-to-cybersecurity/53248/ (accessed on 20 February 2012).

Long, E. 2010b. 'Cybersecurity: A Group Effort', *Nextgov*, 29 April. Available online at http://www.nextgov.com/cybersecurity/cybersecurity-report/2010/04/cybersecurity-a-group-effort/53259/ (accessed on 20 February 2012).

Lunev, S. 2001. '"Red Mafia" Operating in the U.S.—Helping Terrorists'. Available online at http://www.newsmax.com/archives/articles/2001/9/28/90942.shtml (accessed on April 2012).

Macavinta, C. 1997. 'Society's Digital Divide'. Available online at http://news.com.com/2100-1023-278007.html?legacy=cnet&tag (accessed on February 2012).

Matrosov, A., E. Rodionov, D. Harley and J. Malcho. 2011. 'Stuxnet under the Microscope'. Available online at www.eset.com, http://go.eset.com/us/resources/white-papers/Stuxnet_Under_the_Microscope.pdf (accessed on 18 March 2012).

McAfee. 2009a. 'In The Crossfire: Critical Infrastructure in the Age of Cyber War', A Global Report on the Threats Facing Key Industries. Available online at http://www.mcafee.com/us/resources/reports/rp-in-crossfire-critical-infrastructure-cyber-war.pdf (accessed on 19 June 2011).

McAfee. 2009b. 'The Carbon Footprint of Email Spam Report'. Available online at http://resources.mcafee.com/content/NACarbonFootprintSpam (accessed on 9 July 2011).

McAfee. 2009c. 'Unsecured Economies: Protecting Vital Information'. Available online at http://www.mcafee.com/us/resources/reports/rp-unsecured-economies-report.pdf

McAfee. 2009d. 'Virtual Criminology Report 2009, Virtually Here: The Age of Cyber War'. Available online at http://www.mcafee.com/us/resources/reports/rp-virtual-criminology-report-2009.pdf (accessed on 24 July 2011).

McAfee. 2010a. 'A Good Decade for Cybercrime: McAfee's Look Back at Ten Years of Cybercrime'. Available online at http://www.mcafee.com/ca/resources/reports/rp-good-decade-for-cybercrime.pdf

McAfee. 2010b. 'Web 2.0, A Complex Balancing Act: The First Global Study on Web 2.0 Usage, Risks and Best Practices'. Available online at http://www.mcafee.com/us/resources/reports/rp-first-global-study-web-2.0-usage.pdf (accessed on 27 July 2011).

McAfee Labs. 2010a. 'McAfee Threats Report: First Quarter 2010'. Available online at http://www.mcafee.com/in/resources/reports/rp-quarterly-threat-q1-2010.pdf

McAfee Labs. 2010b. 'McAfee Threats Report: Third Quarter 2010'. Available online at http://www.mcafee.com/uk/resources/reports/rp-quarterly-threat-q2-2010.pdf

McAfee Labs. 2011a. '2012 Threat Predictions'. Available online at http://www.mcafee.com/us/resources/reports/rp-threat-predictions-2012.pdf (accessed on 21 January 2012).

McAfee Labs. 2011b. 'McAfee Threats Report: Fourth Quarter 2010'. Available online at http://www.mcafee.com/us/resources/reports/rp-quarterly-threat-q4-2010.pdf (accessed on 10 January 2012).

McAfee. 2011c. 'Ten Days of Rain, Expert analysis of distributed denial-of-service attacks targeting South Korea, White Paper, MacAfee'. Available online at http://blogs.mcafee.com/wp-content/uploads/2011/07/McAfee-Labs-10-Days-of-Rain-July-2011.pdf (accessed on 17 February 2012).

Meier, J. D., A. Mackman, M. Dunner, S. Vasireddy, R. Escamilla and A. Murukan. 2003. 'Building Secure Data Access, Improving Web Application Security: Threats and Countermeasures' (Chapter 14). Available online at http://msdn.microsoft.com/en-us/library/ff648648.aspx (accessed on 18 April 2013).

Mello, J. 2007. 'Cybercrime Costs US Economy At Least \$117B Each Year', *TechNewsWorld*. Available online at http://www.technewsworld.com/story/58517.html (accessed on 20 April 2012).

Messmer, E. 2009. 'Are Security Issues Delaying Adoption of Cloud Computing?', *Network World*, 27 April. Available online at http://www.networkworld.com/news/2009/042709-burning-security-cloud-computing.html

Microsoft Corporation. 2003. 'Threats and Countermeasures, Improving Web Application Security: Threats and Countermeasures'. Available online at http://msdn.microsoft.com/en-us/library/ff648641.aspx#c02618429_006 (accessed on 6 March 2012).

Microsoft Corporation. 2010. 'Microsoft Security Intelligence Report, Volume 9, January–June 2010'. Available online at http://www.microsoft.com/security/sir/default.aspx (accessed on 21 July 2011).

Microsoft Corporation. 2011. 'Microsoft Security Intelligence Report, Volume 11, January–June 2011'. Available online at http://www.microsoft.com/security/sir/default.aspx (accessed on 2 January 2012).

Microsoft Corporation. 2012a. 'Microsoft Security Intelligence Report Volume 12, July through December, 2011'. Available online at http://download.microsoft.com/.../Microsoft_Security_Intelligence_Report_Volume_12_English.pdf (accessed on 2 June 2012).

Microsoft Corporation. 2012b. 'What is a Botnet? Microsoft Malware Protection Centre, Microsoft Security Intelligence Report', Featured Article Centre. Available online at http://www.microsoft.com/security/sir/story/default.aspx#!botnetsection, Retrieved on 12 January 2012.

Miller, N. 2008. 'Casting a Wide Net for Cyber Crims', *The Age*, Melbourne, Australia, 5 February.

Mittelman, J. H. and R. Johnston. 1999. 'The Globalization of Organized Crime, the Courtesan State, and the Corruption of Civil Society', *Global Governance*, 5 (1): 103–26.

Moisés, N. 2005. *Foreign Policy*, May/June (148): 11, 1, 6.

Moore, D., V. Paxson, S. Savage, C. Shannon, S. Staniford and N. Weaver. 2005. 'The Spread of the Sapphire/Slammer Worm'. Available online at http://www.caida.

org/outreach/papers/2003/sapphire/sapphire.html (accessed on 15 December 2011).

National Institutes of Health. 2012. 'NIH Guidance on Secure Use of Cloud Computing Technologies, National Institutes of Health', Department of Health and Human Services, USA. Available online at http://oma.od.nih.gov/ms/privacy/NIH_Cloud_Security_Guidance.docx(accessed on 14 September 2012).

NationMaster. 2012. 'Software Piracy Rate Statistics—Countries Compared'. Available online at http://www.nationmaster.com/graph/cri_sof_pir_rat-crime-software-piracy-rate (accessed on January 2012).

National Conference of State Legislatures. 2006. 'Cyber Terrorism', DENVER, NCSL. Available online at http://www.ncsl.org (accessed on 14 January 2012).

National Security Council. 2011. 'Strategy to Combat Transnational Organized Crime' *National Security Council, United States*, 25 July. Available online at http://www.whitehouse.gov/administration/eop/nsc/transnational-crime (accessed on 2 January 2012).

Natividad, K. F. 2008. 'Stepping It Up and Taking It to the Streets: Changing Civil and Criminal Copyright Enforcement Tactics', *Berkeley Technology Law Journal*, 23 (1): 469–501.

Naylor, R. T. 2005. 'The Rise and Fall of Underground Economy', *Brown Journal of World Affairs*, 11 (2): 131–43.

Neild, B. 2009. 'Downadup Worm Exposes Millions of PCs to Hijack', *CNN*, 16 January. Available online at http://edition.cnn.com/2009/TECH/ptech/01/16/virus.downadup/?iref=mpstoryview (accessed on 16 January 2009).

Ng, Kai Koon. 2011. 'Technology Solutions to Fight Cybercrime', paper presented at the Asia-Pacific Regional Workshop on Fighting Cybercrime, Seoul, Republic of Korea, 21–23 September. Available online at http://www.itu.int/ITU-D/asp/CMS/Events/2011/CyberCrime/S6_Kai_Koon_Ng.pdf (accessed on 2 February 2012).

Norton. 2011. 'Norton Cybercrime Report: The Human Impact'. Available online at http://us.norton.com/content/en/us/home_homeoffice/media/pdf/cybercrime_report/Norton_USA-Human%20Impact-A4_Aug4-2.pdf (accessed on 9 January 2012).

Null, Christopher. 2010. 'Scary "Global Hacking Offensive" Finally Outed', posted on 18 February 2010. Evolve Partners, Inc. Available online at http://www.evolvepartners.com/ABOUTnbspEVOLVE/News/tabid/62/articleType/ArticleView/articleId/75/Scary-global-hacking-offensive-finally-outed.aspx (accessed on 5 April 2012).

OECD. 2008a. 'Malicious Software (A Security Threat to the Internet Economy)', Ministerial Background Report Malware in Brief, Page-10, OECD Ministerial Meeting on the Future of Internet Economy, Seoul, 17–18 June 2008. Available online at DSTI/ICCP/REG(2007)5/FINAL, http://www.oecd.org/internet/interneteconomy/40724457.pdf (accessed 12 February 2012).

OECD. 2008b. 'OECD Report of Global Cyber Risk 2008'. Available online at http://www.oecd.org/ (accessed on 8 July 2011).

OECD. 2009. 'Chapter-3, Malware: Why Should We be concerned', in *Computer Viruses and Other Malicious Software: A threat to the Internet Economy*, p. 76. Available online at http://browse.oecdbookshop.org/oecd/pdfs/product/9309011e.pdf

OECD. 2011. 'Reducing Systemic Cybersecurity Risk', OECD/IFP Project on 'Future Global Shocks', IFP/WKP/FGS(2011)3. Available online at http://www.oecd.org/internet/46894657.pdf

Ogg, E. 2011. 'Sony: Personal Info Compromised on PSN', 26 April. Available online on http://news.cnet.com/8301-31021_3-20057577-260.html (accessed on 11 April 2012).

Oxley, J. E. and B. Yeung. 2001. 'E-Commerce Readiness: Institutional Environment and International Competitiveness', *Journal of International Business Studies*, 32 (4): 705–23.

Palmer, E. 2011. 'London Conference on CyberSpace: The Biggest Cyber Attacks of All Time', *International Business Times*, 1 November. Available online at http://www.ibtimes.co.uk/articles/241238/20111101/biggest-cyber-attacks-time-hacking-china-google.htm#ixzz1qIQ8W5at (accessed on 12 February 2011).

Parker, D. B. 1998. *Fighting Computer Crime: A New Framework for Protecting Information*. New York, NY: John Wiley & Sons, Inc.

PCWorld. 2007. 'Hackers build Private IM'.

Pethia, R. P. 1999. 'CERT, The Melissa Virus: Inoculating Our Information Technology from Emerging Threats', Testimony before the Subcommittee on Technology, Committee on Science, United States House of Representatives on 15 April 1999.

Pitman, R. J. 2009. 'Outpouring of Searches for the Late Michael Jackson', *Official Google Blog*, posted on 27 June 2009. Availble online at http://googleblog.blogspot.in/2009/06/outpouring-of-searches-for-late-michael.html (accessed on 4 March 2011).

Pollit, M. 1997. 'Cyberterrorism—Fact or Fancy?, Proceedings of the 20th National Information Systems Security Conference. Available online at http://www.cs.georgetown.edu/~denning/infosec/pollitt.html (accessed on 17 February 2012).

Poremba, S. M. 2008. 'Asprox botnet malware morphs', *SC Magazine US*, 15 May. Available online at http://www.scmagazine.com/asprox-botnet-malware-morphs/article/110169/ (accessed on 16 April 2012).

Press Information Bureau. 2012. 'Cyber Attacks', 30 November. Available online at http://pib.nic.in/newsite/erelease.aspx?relid=77958 (accessed on 6 January 2012).

PricewaterhouseCoopers. 2007. 'Economic Crime: People, Culture and Controls: The 4th Biennial Global Economic Crime Survey'. Available online at http://www.pwc.com/gx/en/economic-crime-survey/pdf/pwc_2007gecs.pdf.

PricewaterhouseCoopers. 2011. 'Cyber Security MA: Decoding Deals in the Global Cyber Security Industry'. Available online at http://www.pwc.com/en_GX/gx/aerospace-defence/pdf/cyber-security-mergers-acquisitions.pdf

Prolexic. 2011. 'Prolexic Q4 2012 Global DDoS Attack Report', *Prolexic Knowledge Centre*. Available online at http://www.prolexic.com/knowledge-center-ddos-attack-report-2012-q4.html (accessed on 16 February 2012).

Qi, M., Y. Wang and R. Xu. 2009. 'Fighting Cybercrime: Legislation in China', *International Journal of Electronic Security and Digital Forensics*, 2 (2): 219–27.

Rasch, M. D. 1996. 'Criminal Law and the Internet', in J. F. Ruh (ed.), *The Internet and Business: A Lawyer's Guide to the Emerging Legal Issues*. Computer Law Association.

Regan, K. 2006. 'FBI: Cyber Crime Causes Financial Pain for Many Businesses', *Technewsworld*. Available online at http://www.technewsworld.com/story/48417.html

Reid, T. 2007. 'China's Cyber Army is Preparing to March on America Says Pentagon'. Available online at http://technology.timesonline.co.uk/toi/news/tech_and_web/the_web article 2409865

Reilly, M. 2007. 'Beware, Botnets Have Your PC in Their Sights', *New Scientist*, 196 (2634): 22–23.

Roberds, W. and S. L. Schreft. 2009. 'Data Breaches and Identity Theft', *Journal of Monetary Economics*, 56 (7): 918–29.

Rouse, M. 2010. 'SQL Injection'. Available online at http://searchsoftwarequality.techtarget.com/definition/SQL-injection (accessed on 18 April 2013).

Rush, H. S., C. Smith, E. Kraemer-Mbula and P. Tang. 2009. 'Crime Online: Cybercrime and Illegal Innovation', *NESTA*. Available online at http://eprints.brighton.ac.uk/5800/1/Crime_Online.pdf

Ryall, J. 2011. 'A History of Major Cyber Attacks', *The Telegraph*, 20 September. Available online at http://www.telegraph.co.uk/news/worldnews/asia/japan/8775632/A-history-of-major-cyber-attacks.html (accessed on 22 January 2012).

Ryan, R. M. and E. L. Deci. 2000a. 'Intrinsic and Extrinsic Motivations: Classic Definitions and New Directions', *Contemporary Educational Psychology*, 25: 54–67, doi:10.1006/ceps.1999.1020.

Ryan, R. M. and E. L. Deci. 2000b. 'Self-Determination Theory and the Facilitation of Intrinsic Motivation, Social Development, and Well-Being', *American Psychologist*, 55 (1): 68–78.

Sai, M. 2012. 'India Has Reason to Worry', *Indian Express*. Accessed on February 2012.

Salaud, J. P. 2009. 'Grabbing the Bully by the Horns: Violence in Schools', *ABS-CBN News*, 12 September. Available online at http://www.abs-cbnnews.com/features/09/11/09/grabbing-bully-horns-violence-schools.

Sandberg, J. 1995. 'Immorality Play: Acclaiming Hackers as Heroes', 27 February, *Wall Street Journal*: B1–B8.

Schiller, Bill. 2009. 'Chinese Ridicule U of T Spy Report', *The Star.com*, 1 April. Available online at http://www.thestar.com/news/2009/04/01/chinese_ridicule_u_of_t_spy_report.html (accessed on 21 February 2012).

Schjolberg, S. and S. Ghernaouti-Helie. 2011. 'A Global Treaty on Cybersecurity and Cybercrime'. Available online at http://www.cybercrimelaw.net/documents/A_ Global_Treaty_on_Cybersecurity_and_Cybercrime,_Second_edition_2011.pdf (accessed on 9 January 2012).

Schneier, B. 1997. 'Why Cryptography is Harder than it Looks', *Information Security Bulletin*, 2 (2 March): 31–36.

Serio, J. D. and A. Gorkin. 2003. 'Changing Lenses: Striving for Sharper Focus on the Nature of the "Russian Mafia" and Its Impact on the Computer Realm', *International Review of Law, Computers & Technology*, 17 (2): 191–202.

Shackelford, S. J. 2012. 'From Nuclear war to Net war: Analogizing cyber attacks in International Law', *Berkeley Journal of International Law*, 27 (1): Article 7.

Shapira, Z. 1976. 'Expectancy Determinants of Intrinsically Motivated Behaviour', *Journal of Personality and Social Psychology*, 34 (6): 1235–44.

Shivakumar, S. 2009. 'Are You a Sitting Duck for ID Thieves?', *The Hindu Business Line*. Available online at http://www.thehindubusinessline.com/features/ investment-world/money-wise/article2907283.ece (accessed on March 2012).

Smith, K. T., M. Smith, and J. L. Smith. 2011. 'Case Studies of Cybercrime and Their Impact on Marketing Activity and Shareholder Value', *Academy of Marketing Studies Journal*, 15 (2): 67–81.

Sofia News Agency. 2003, October. 'Romania emerges as New World Nexus of Cybercrime'. Available online at http://www.novinite.com/view_news. php?id=27265 (accessed on 19 December 2011).

Sophos. 2007. 'Security Threat Report: 2007'. Available online at http://www.sophos. com/en-us/medialibrary/Gated%20Assets/white%20papers/ sophossecuritythreats2007_wsrus.pdf (accessed on 7 July 2011).

Sophos. 2009. 'Security Threat Report: 2009, Prepare for This Year's New Threats'. Available online at http://www.sophos.com/security/2008/03/1186.html (accessed on 12 July 2011).

Sophos. 2011. 'Security Threat Report: 2011'. Available online at http://www.sophos. com/security/2010/03/1186.html (accessed on 7 July 2011).

Spam laws. 'What Are Botnets and How Do They Work?' Section: How Botnet works? Available online at http://www.spamlaws.com/how-botnets-work.html (accessed on 4 February 2012).

Strang, D. and J. Meyer. 1993. 'Institutional Conditions for Diffusion', *Theory and Society*, 22 (4): 487–511.

Sullivan, B. 2007. 'Who's Behind Criminal Bot Networks?' *NBC News.com*, 10 April. Available online at http://redtape.nbcnews.com/_news/2007/04/10/6346007- whos-behind-criminal-bot-networks?lite (accessed on 10 October 2011).

Symantec. 2010. 'W32.Stuxnet—Network Information', Symantec Official Blog. Available online at http://www.symantec.com/connect/blogs/w32stuxnet- network-information (accessed on 16 February 2012).

Symantec Corporation. 2010a. 'Message Lab Intelligence Report', Symantec Intelligence Report. Available online at http://www.symanteccloud.com/globalthreats/ (accessed on 26 February 2012).

Symantec Corporation. 2010b. 'State of Enterprise Security 2010'. Available online at http://www.symantec.com/ (accessed on 8 June 2011).

Symantec Corporation. 2010c. 'State of Phishing: A Monthly Report', February. Available online at http://eval.symantec.com/mktginfo/enterprise/other_resources/b-state_of_phishing_report_01-2010.en-us.pdf (accessed on 16 January 2012).

Symantec Corporation. 2010d. 'Symantec Global Internet Security Threat Report: Trends for 2009, Volume XV'. Available online at http://eval.symantec.com/mktginfo/enterprise/white_papers/b-whitepaper_internet_security_threat_report_xv_04-2010.en-us.pdf (accessed on 9 June 2011).

Symantec Corporation. 2011a. 'Symantec Internet Security Threat Report: Trends for 2010, Volume 16'. Available online at https://www4.symantec.com/mktginfo/downloads/21182883_GA_REPORT_ISTR_Main-Report_04-11_HI-RES.pdf (accessed on 23 January 2012).

Symantec Corporation. 2011b. 'Symantec Security Intelligence Report, Quarterly April–June 2011'. Available online at http://www.symantec.com/ (accessed on 10 January 2012).

Symantec Corporation. 2011c. 'Symantec Intelligence Quarterly Report: October–December, 2010, Targeted Attacks on Critical Infrastructures', White Paper: Symantec Intelligence Q4 2010 Report, p. 5. Available online at http://www.symantec.com/content/en/us/enterprise/white_papers/b-symc_intelligence_qtrly_oct_to_dec_WP_21169903.en-us.pdf (accessed on 10 January 2012).

Taylor, R. B., B. Koons, E. Kurtz, J. Greene and D. Perkins. 1995. 'Street Blocks with More Nonresidential Land Use Have More Physical Deterioration: Evidence from Baltimore and Philadelphia', *Urban Affairs Review*, 31 (1): 120–36.

Techno Diaries. 2012. 'DOS and DDOS Attacks, Techno Diaries', 21 January. Available online at http://technodiaries.org/dos-and-ddos-attacks/#more-102 (22 February 2012).

The Chicago Syndicate. 2008. Available online at www.chicagosyndicate.com (accessed on 12 October 2011).

The Conversation. 2012. 'Anonymous Launches Largest-ever Attack in Defence of Megaupload', posted on 21 January 2012. Available online at https://theconversation.edu.au/anonymous-launches-largest-ever-attack-in-defence-of-megaupload-4989 (accessed on 17 February 2012).

The Economist. 2009. 'East Africa Gets Broadband: It May Make Life Easier and Cheaper', *The Economist*, 391 (8636): 46.

The Honeynet Project. 2004. *Know Your Enemy: Learning about Security Threats* (second edition). Boston: Addison-Wesley Professional.

Thomas, C. 2008. 'Estonian Hacker Fined for Cyber Attack', *Information Week*, January. Available online at http://www.informationweek.com/estonian-hacker-fined-for-cyber-attack/205918839

Thomas, C. 2009. 'Cyber Attack Against Georgia Blurred Civilian and Military', August 2009. Availab le online at http://www.informationweek.com/government/ security/cyber-attack-against-georgia-blurred-civ/219400248

Thornburgh, N. 2005. 'The Invasion of the Chinese Cyberspies', *Time*, 29 August. Available online at http://www.time.com/time/magazine/article/0,9171,1098961,00. html

Tikk, E., K. Kaska and L. Vihul. 2010. 'International Cyber Incidents: Legal Considerations', *Cooperative Cyber Defence Centre of Excellence (CCD COE)*, Estonia. Available at http://www.ccdcoe.org/publications/books/ legalconsiderations.pdf (accessed on 12 April 2012).

Times of India. 2008. 'Russian Mafia is Largest Cyber Crime Syndicate', 7 December, *Times of India*.

Trend Micro. 2008. 'Trend Micro Threat Roundup and Forecast—1H 2008', June 2008. Available online at http://apac.trendmicro.com/imperia/md/content/us/pdf/threats/ securitylibrary/1h_2008_threat_report_final.pdf (accessed on 17 July 2011).

Trend Micro. 2008. 'Trend Micro 2008 Annual Threat Roundup and 2009 Forecast'. Available online at http://trendmicro.com/ (accessed on 17 July 2011).

Trend Micro. 2010a. 'The Business of Cybercrime: A Complex Business Model'. Available online at http://www.trendmicro.com/cloud-content/us/pdfs/security-intelligence/reports/rpt_business-of-cybercrime.pdf (accessed on 17 July 2011).

Trend Micro. 2010b. 'Trend Micro: Trend Labs Global Threat Trends 1H 2010'. Available online at http://threatinfo.trendmicro.com/vinfo/default.asp?sect=SA (accessed on 17 July 2011).

Trend Micro. 2011. 'Security Spotlight: Top Tips for Safer and More Secure Online Experience in 2011'. Available online at http://trendmicro.com/ (accessed on 10 January 2012).

Trend Micro. 2012a. 'TrendLabs Annual Security Roundup: A Look Back at 2011, Information is Currency'. Available online at http://www.trendmicro.com/cloud-content/us/pdfs/security-intelligence/reports/rpt_a-look-back-at-2011_ information-is-currency.pdf (accessed on 12 January 2012).

Trend Micro. 2012b. 'Virtualization and Cloud Computing: Security Threats to Evolving Data Centers'. Available online at http://www.trendmicro.com/cloud-content/us/pdfs/about/rpt_security-threats-to-datacenters.pdf (accessed on 10 February 2012).

Trustwave. 2010. 'Latest M86 Security Labs Report Details New Ways Cybercriminals Are Thwarting Security', posted by M86 Press Agent on 14 July 2010. Available online at https://www.trustwave.com/trustednews/2010/07/latest-m86-security-labs-report-details-new-ways-cybercriminals-are-thwarting-security? (accessed on 16 April 2012).

Unisys. 2011. 'Unisys Disruptive Technology & Trend Point of View Whitepaper Series – CyberSecurity: Tackling CyberSecurity in the Enterprise'. Available online at http://www.unisys.com/unisys/ri/wp/detail.jsp?id=1120000970016010164 (accessed on February 2012).

United Nations Development Programme. 1999. 'UNHDR Annual Report 1999'. Available online at http://www.undp.org/ (accessed on 10 January 2012), p. 54.

United Nations Office on Drugs and Crime. 2010. 'The Globalization of Crime: A Transnational Organized Crime Threat Assessment'. Vienna: United Nations Office on Drugs and Crime. Available online at http://www.unodc.org/documents/data-and-analysis/tocta/TOCTA_Report_2010_low_res.pdf

United Press International. 2009. 'Hi-Tech Northrop Grumman Center to Fight Cybercrime'. Available online at http://www.upi.com/security/industry/2009/08/04/high-tech-northrop-grumman-center-to-fight-cybercrime/UPI-48401249417676

UPI. 2009. 'Virus Strikes 15 Million PCs', 26 January. Available online at http://www.upi.com/Top_News/2009/01/25/Virus_strikes_15_million_PCs/UPI-19421232924206 (accessed on January 2012).

UPI. 2010. 'India's Cyber Crime Challenge', report by Prakash Nanda, 9 March.

USGAO. 2007. 'Cybercrime: Public and Private Entities Face Challenges in Addressing Cyber Threats', 22 June. Report number GAO-07-705, released on 23 July.

Vallance, C. 2008. 'The Battle against the Botnet Hordes', *BBC News*, 21 February. Available online at http://news.bbc.co.uk/1/hi/technology/7256501.stm

Verizon. 2008. '2008 Data Breach Investigations Report: A Study Conducted by the Verizon Business Risk Team'. Available online at http://verizonbusiness.com/social Media (accessed on 10 October 2011).

Villeneuve, N. and D. Sancho. 2011. 'The "Lurid" Downloader: Threats Trends and Security Issues Direct from the Experts', *Trend Micro*. Available online at http://www.trendmicro.com/cloud-content/us/pdfs/security-intelligence/white-papers/wp_dissecting-lurid-apt.pdf

Voigt, K. 2009. 'Cyber Crime Poses Threat to E-Commerce'. Available online at http://www.cnn.com/2009/TECH/12/13/cybercrime.2009.review/index.html

Walden, I. 2005. 'Crime and Security in Cyberspace', *Cambridge Review of International Affairs*, 18 (1): 51–68.

Walker, C. 2004. 'Russian Mafia Extorts Gambling Websites'. Available online at http://www.americanmafia.com/feature_articles_270.html (accessed on 10 October 2010).

Wattanajantra, A. 2008. 'Ten-Fold Increase in Malware Predicted for 2008'. Available online at http://www.itpro.co.uk/186723/ten-fold-increase-in-malware-predicted-for-2008 (accessed on 10 October 2011).

Weber, T. 2009. 'Cybercrime Threat Rising Sharply', *BBC News*. Available online at http://news.bbc.co.uk/2/hi/business/davos/7862549.stm

Websense. 2010. 'Websense 2010 Threat Report: A Websense White Paper'. Available online at http://www.websense.com/content/threat-report-2010-introduction.aspx (accessed on 10 July 2011).

WEF. 2012a. 'Cyber Risk Now in the Top Five Global Risks'. Available online at http://www.weforum.org/ (accessed on 2 January 2012).

WEF. 2012b. 'WEF Insight Report: Global Risks 2012, Seventh Edition', An Initiative of the Risk Response Network. Available online at http://www3.weforum.org/docs/WEF_GlobalRisks_Report_2012.pdf

Werth, C. 2009. 'Number Crunching Made Easy', *Newsweek*, 2 May. Available online at http://www.newsweek.com/id/195734 (accessed on March 2012).

Whitman, M. E. and H. J. Mattford. 2009. *Principles and Practices of Information Security*. Cengage Learning.

Widup, S. 2010. 'The Leaking Vault: Five Years of Data Breaches', *Digital Forensics Association*. Available online at http://www.digitalforensicsassociation.org/storage/The_Leaking_Vault-Five_Years_of_Data_Breaches.pdf (accessed on October 2011).

Wikipedia. 2012. 'Zeus (Trojan Horse)'. Available online at http://en.wikipedia.org/wiki/Zeus_(Trojan_horse).

Williams, P. 2001. 'Organized Crime and Cybercrime: Synergies, Trends, and Responses', 13 August, *Office of International Information Programs, U.S. Department of State*. Available online at http://usinfo.state.gov

Willims, C. 2012. 'Anonymous Attacks FBI Website over Megaupload Raids'. *Telegraph*, 20 June. Available online at http://www.telegraph.co.uk/technology/news/9027246/Anonymous-attacks-FBI-website-over-Megaupload-raids.html (accessed on 17 February 2012).

Wilson, T. 2010. 'Researchers: Asprox Botnet Is Resurging', *DarkReading*, 14 July. Available online at http://www.darkreading.com/security/news/225800197

Wilson, W. J. 1987. *The Truly Disadvantaged: The Inner City, the Underclass, and Public Policy*. Chicago, IL: University of Chicago Press.

Wolf, J. 2000, 'Hacking of Pentagon persists', *Washington Post*, 9 August, A23.

Wolfe, D. 2008. 'Cyber Crime', *American Banker*, 173 (237): 5.

Wolfe, D. and W. Wade. 2008. 'Security Watch', *American Banker*, 173 (237): 5.

WEB RESOURCES

- http://www.spamlaws.com/slammer-worm.html
- Koobface Facebook Trojan on the March Again, http://www.webologist.co.uk/internet-security/koobface-facebook-trojan-on-the-march-again
- The Slammer Worm, http://www.spamlaws.com/slammer-worm.html
- An Overview of the Industrial Worm Called StuxNet, http://embeddedsw.net/doc/Stuxnet_white_paper.html
- http://en.wikipedia.org/wiki/Hacktivism
- http://affcoalition.org/
- http://www.us-cert.gov/cas/tips/ST06-003.html (US Computer Emergency Readiness Team)

- http://en.wikipedia.org/wiki/Antivirus_software
- http://www.veracode.com/security/botnet
- www.usccu.us
- http://www.nasuwt.org.uk/
- http://www.cyberwarzone.com/cyberwarfare
- http://cyberlawindia2008.blogspot.in/2009_12_01_archive.html
- http://www.fbi.gov/news/pressrel/press-releases/international-cooperation-disrupts-multi-country-cyber-theft.
- http://searchsecurity.techtarget.com/definition/cyberstalking
- http://www.nolo.com/legal-encyclopedia/how-does-spam-work-30013.html (Nolo.com)
- http://en.wikipedia.org/wiki/Cyber_spying
- http://www.fraw.org.uk/ehippies/index.shtml
- http://searchsecurity.techtarget.com
- http://www.sciencedirect.com/science
- http://www.scmagazine.com/uk
- http://msdn.microsoft.com/en-us/library/ms161953%28v=sql.105%29.aspx
- http://hackmageddon.com/2012/02/02/january-2012-cyber-attacks-timeline-part-2/
- http://www.dhs.gov/cybersecurity-tips
- http://wikileaks.org/About.html

SPAM STUDIES

Spamming trends and incidents are covered by Trend Micro and can be accessed at http://us.trendmicro.com. McAfee Labs is the global research team of McAfee, Inc. It is the only research organization devoted to all threat vectors—malware, web, e-mail, network and vulnerabilities. McAfee releases spam reports along with the annual threat predictions and quarterly threat reports. Securelist is another organization which is releasing monthly spam reports. These can be accessed at http://www.securelist.com/en/analysis.

MALWARE STUDIES

Malware trends and incidents are covered in the Sophos security threat reports and global threat trends reports, which are published yearly by Sophos lab. It can be accessed at http://www.sophos.com. McAfee Labs issues its annual threat predictions and quarterly Threat reports. Microsoft releases Microsoft security intelligence reports every year which can be accessed at http://www.microsoft.com/security. Symantec Corporation is also working in the area of malware. It publishes global threat reports every year along with Internet threat reports, which can be accessed at http://www.symantec.com.

PHISHING STUDIES

The Anti-Phishing Working Group (APWG) Phishing Repository is the Internet's most comprehensive archive of phishing and e-mail fraud activities. It can be accessed at www.apwg.org and publishes a global phishing survey twice a year. These studies have been conducted by the APWG since 2007.

Spam and phishing data are captured in a variety of sources, including the Symantec Probe Network, Message Labs Intelligence—a respected source of data and analysis for messaging security issues, trends and statistics; as well as other Symantec technologies. Symantec also gathers phishing information through an extensive anti-fraud community of enterprises, security vendors, and more than 50 million customers. The Symantec Internet security threat reports give enterprises and consumers the essential information needed to secure their systems effectively now and in the future. Phishing trends and incidents are also covered by Sophos security threat reports and the Trend Micro annual survey reports on a yearly basis.

IDENTITY THEFT STUDIES

Javelin Strategy and Research is a highly specialized vendor in the area of Identity theft survey. Its syndicated research, custom research and strategic consulting departments publish identity fraud survey reports (consumer version) every year, which can also be accessed at http://www.javelinstrategy.com. Symantec Corporation is also working in the area of identity theft. It releases a global threat report every year along with the Internet threat report, which can be accessed at http://www.symantec.com.

DDOS STUDIES

Symantec Corporation is working in the area of DDoS. It publishes, every year, a global threat report along with an Internet threat report, which can be accessed at http://www.symantec.com. DDoS mitigation companies Prolexic and Arbor Networks also release anti-DDoS vendors' reports since 2010, which can be accessed at www.prolexic.com/attacks

BOTNET STUDIES

Botnet trends and incidents are covered in the Trend Micro annual survey reports and global threat trend reports, published every month by Trend Micro. It can be accessed at http://us.trendmicro.com. Microsoft also announces Microsoft security intelligence reports every year along with critical security updates every quarter, which can be accessed at http://www.microsoft.com/security. Symantec Corporation is also working in the area of botnets. Every year, it releases a global threat report and an Internet threat report. These can be accessed at http://www.symantec.com.

SQL INJECTION STUDIES

SQL Injection trends and incidents are covered in the Trend Micro annual survey reports and the global threat trend reports, which are published every month by Trend Micro. They can be accessed at http://us.trendmicro.com. Symantec Corporation is also working in the area of SQL Injection. It releases a global threat report and an Internet threat report every year. These can be accessed at http://www.symantec.com. McAfee also publishes its quarterly report on threats, which it investigates, and studies about the SQL injections. These can be accessed at http://www.mcafee.com.

SOCIAL ENGINEERING STUDIES

Social engineering trends and incidents are covered in the annual Sophos security threat reports. They can be accessed at http://www.sophos.com. Social engineering trends and incidents are also covered in the Trend Micro annual survey reports and global threat trend reports, which are published every month by Trend Micro. They can be accessed at http://us.trendmicro.com.

Cisco also publishes an annual security report, which covers social engineering trends and methods in detail. It can be accessed at http://www.cisco.com. The ScienceDirect magazine also publishes a report on social engineering trends and techniques, which can be accessed at http://www.sciencedirect.com/science.

ABOUT THE AUTHOR

———•◦•———

Anjali Kaushik, PhD is an Associate Professor at Management Development Institute (MDI), Gurgaon. She has 20 years' experience in teaching, research and consulting related to IT strategy, information security, innovation and e-governance across diverse sectors. She has been the Chief Investigator for developing the 'Information Security Best Practices Framework for Government Sector in India' and associated as consultant on prestigious assignments such as the evaluation of 'National e-Governance Awards' for four consecutive years and the impact assessment of e-Governance projects as a 'Knowledge Partner' to Government of India. She is a certified ISO 27001 Lead Auditor and Lead Implementer. She has been regularly conducting work-shops and holding training programs on cyber security and e-Governance at MDI. She has authored three books, participated as speaker on cybersecurity at various forums and has more than 15 publications in various national and international journals. Her books have the following titles:

- Jaiswal, M. P. and A. Kaushik. 2002. *e-CRM: Business and System Frontiers*. New Delhi: Asian Books Private Limited.
- Kaushik, A. and M. Kumar. 2010. P*lanning for Inter-organizational Systems*. New Delhi: AK Publications.
- Kumar, L. and A. Kaushik. 2012. *Fresh Fingerprints: Cases of Innovations in Public Service Delivery*. McGraw Hill.